THE
PATHFINDER COMPANION

THE PATHFINDER COMPANION

WAR DIARIES AND EXPERIENCES OF THE RAF PATHFINDER FORCE – 1942-1945

SEAN FEAST

IN ASSOCIATION WITH THE PATHFINDER MUSEUM, RAF WYTON

GRUB STREET • LONDON

Published by
Grub Street
4 Rainham Close
London
SW11 6SS

Feast, Sean.
   The Pathfinder companion.
   1. Great Britain. Royal Air Force. Bomber Command. Group,
   No.8--History. 2. World War, 1939-1945--Aerial
   operations, British.
   I. Title
   940.5'44'941-dc23

ISBN-13: 978-1-908117-34-2

Cover design by Sarah Driver
Typeset by Sarah Driver
Edited by Sophie Campbell

Printed and bound by MPG Ltd, Bodmin, Cornwall

Grub Street Publishing only uses
FSC (Forest Stewardship Council) paper for its books.

CONTENTS

FOREWORD

To be asked to contribute a foreword to RAF Wyton Museum's book on the Pathfinder Force is an honour, tinged as it might be by the casualty factor that governed so many promotions during wartime. There are already so few of us left to fulfil that role!

As I perused the book, I was amazed by the number and the courage of so many brave airmen who had demonstrated their dedication to the defeat of Nazi Germany and under such trying circumstances. Volunteers, every one of them, they fulfilled the motto of their air force – *per ardua ad astra* – in many cases paying the price with their lives.

Despite being a long-time member of Bomber Command and PFF, I had been immersed in the daily detail of squadron and operational life; I never saw the 'big picture'. This book, an incredible collection of personal vignettes and pertinent data, has opened my eyes and given me a better understanding of the role of PFF and its courageous members.

In a few years there will be no survivors left to preserve, personally, the story of the Pathfinders: the courageous airmen who marked the targets for

Jack Watts had a most eventful flying career before joining PFF.

the main force; the skill and dedication of their leaders; and the supportive efforts of the ground crews who laboured to keep their aircraft airworthy. Perhaps this book, a most worthy book for the museum library, will serve to keep their story alive after the last Pathfinder has met his maker.

The author has worked diligently to bring to life a book which not only provides the anecdotes of many of the remarkable events which took place in the Bomber Command war in Europe, but provides those anecdotes in the words of the individuals involved, capturing and preserving those moments in history on a personal basis. There is no doubt that the veterans of PFF, myself included, will thank the author for his empathy and his diligence in researching and writing this splendid book.

I cannot close my remarks without paying respect to the leadership in PFF that was exemplified and personalised by its commander, Donald Bennett. He was a leader by qualification, by example and by performance and he ensured that the aircrew and the ground crew shared his respect for the work they were doing for PFF and for victory in Europe.

BRIGADIER GENERAL JACK WATTS
DSO, DFC AND BAR, CD

FOREWORD

When I was asked to write a foreword to this carefully-researched and thoughtfully-written book by Sean Feast I leapt at the chance because the Pathfinders mean so much to me. As a serving officer in the Royal Air Force with an avid interest in military and aviation history I knew much of their story. But it was as station commander of RAF Wyton from 2008 to 2010 that my, somewhat sterile, knowledge was transformed into a living history for both me and my young family.

Many in East Anglia, and in the Huntingdon area in particular, hold the Pathfinders very close to their hearts; the fact that the building that houses Huntingdonshire District Council is named Pathfinder House is testimony to that. For the service personnel at Wyton it is our very real privilege to hold three annual events in their memory. In spring we hold a formal station 'dining-in' night in the officers' mess to which the Pathfinders are honoured guests. These resolute and humble few are back in the bosom of their service for the evening and it is heartening to see how the young aircrew of 57 Squadron, just embarking on their flying careers at Wyton, very quickly establish a strong bond with their forebears. I can tell you that it is always a memorable evening and that it is invariably the veterans who are the 'last men standing'!

On the Saturday closest to the summer solstice hundreds of people, both service and civilian, come from as far afield as Denmark and Canada to take part in The Pathfinder March, a gruelling forty-six-mile walk around the Cambridgeshire countryside taking in the evocative place names of Oakington, Graveley, and Warboys. Although it is now an event that attracts all sorts of charitable endeavour, central to it is a commemoration of the Pathfinder Force. The march starts at Wyton in the pre-dawn silence and half light, and one's thoughts turn to the same place less than a lifetime ago, when the sky was full of aircraft returning home from the latest raid over Germany. It is an emotional moment for all who experience it.

The final and most important event is Pathfinder Sunday in August, a day when the Pathfinders and their families come to Wyton for a service in the station church, resplendent with its Pathfinder stained-glass window. They visit our museum, have lunch and tea in the officers' mess and, weather and serviceability permitting, experience a flypast from the Battle of Britain Memorial Flight's Lancaster. This is a highly emotional day when history really comes to life for those of us who were not there, and resurrects many buried memories for those who were. Watching my children sitting in the ante room utterly absorbed in the veterans' recollections has lingered long in the memory.

With *The Pathfinder Companion* Sean has, with great care and attention to detail, collated an invaluable archive and produced a fitting tribute to those brave men and women from this country, and our commonwealth and European brothers in arms, who fought for freedom. The book weaves personal anecdotes of those who were there with the facts and statistics that detail the feats of this elite force, from its inception, in adversity, in the summer of 1942, to its disbandment in September 1945.

It is nothing short of a national disgrace that Bomber Command and its personnel, of which the Pathfinder Force was part, received no recognition for the sacrifices they made on our behalf, including tens of thousands who never returned home. There has been no campaign medal, no formal thanks, and until this year, no national memorial. This work sheds rare light on the day-to-day life of real people who flew and fought through the hell that was the strategic bombing campaign of the Second World War. We are forever in their debt.

Per Ardua Ad Astra

AIR COMMODORE COLIN SMITH MA, RAF
HEADQUARTERS AIR COMMAND, RAF HIGH WYCOMBE

CHAPTER 1
A DIFFICULT BIRTH

It was a report from a civil servant, David Butt, which confirmed the need for some form of target marking to improve the accuracy of RAF bombing, and which would eventually lead to the creation of the Pathfinder Force. Unlike modern-day dossiers, however, Butt's findings needed no embellishment or 'sexing up' for their true impact to be recognised and acted upon.

In the early months of the war, the brave crews of Bomber Command, often flying already outdated aircraft, had little or no way of truly gauging the accuracy of their bombing. A study of operational record books (ORBs) of the period frequently refers to crews bombing secondary or even tertiary targets, having been unable to find their primary objective. This is not surprising, given that some navigators had little or no night-time navigation experience prior to being sent on operations 'for real', and had little more than the moon and stars to guide them if they were lucky.

The Air Ministry took action to verify the claims made by bomber crews by fitting cameras to the aircraft, with a photo taken at the point the bombs were released. Rather than relying on the honest but often wildly inaccurate assessment of the crews, the Air Ministry now had photographic evidence to confirm the veracity of each claim.

Butt was, at the time, in the War Cabinet Secretariat, an assistant to Lord Cherwell, the chief scientific advisor to Winston Churchill. It was Butt who was given the task of analysing some 650 target photographs taken during night-bombing operations on forty-eight nights between June 2 and July 25, 1941, relating to 100 separate raids on twenty-eight different targets. The results were little short of dynamite: of those aircraft recorded as attacking their target, only one in three got within five miles; for aircraft attacking the Ruhr, the proportion was one in ten. And remember, this figure relates only to those who actually attacked the target in the first place!

The moon made a big difference: in a full moon, two out of five found their target; in the new moon it was only one in fifteen. German defences similarly had an impact: an increase in the intensity of flak, perhaps not surprisingly, reduced the number of aircraft getting to within five miles of their target in the ratio of three to two.

The harsh fact of the matter was that the real damage being caused by Bomber Command fell far short of what was being reported. In some instances, bombers were missing their target by as much as seventy or eighty miles – the equivalent of a German bomber setting out to attack London and bombing Coventry instead.

There was, understandably, much hand wringing among senior commanders. Air Marshal Sir Richard Peirse, the C-in-C Bomber Command reluctantly conceded that his men could not have achieved the damage they had stated in their reports. Sir Charles Portal, the chief of air staff, was more doubtful, believing that Butt's figures might be wide of the mark. But both men agreed that the issue was not a question of bomb aiming – albeit that was difficult enough. The real issue, they concluded, was one of navigation. As the official history states:

> 'By showing the need for the development of precise aids to navigation, the scientific study of the craft, and the development of revolutionary tactics, the Butt Report had rendered a service to Bomber Command that was second to none.'

The proverbial die was cast; the scene set. The countdown to Pathfinder Force had begun and the first players in the Pathfinder drama were about to take centre stage.

The concept of target marking was by no means new. Its roots could be found in bomber operations over the Western Front in 1916. With experience of bombing 1940s style, some squadrons had already recognised that if their best navigators found the target, then all that was required was some way of attracting others to the scene.

Individuals began experimenting with flares, among them a young flying officer in 77 Squadron,

Boris Bressloff (seated left) and his skipper, Alex Thorne.

IT IS NOT 'ME' IT IS 'I'

Pathfinders came from all walks of life, from the professional career officers through to the amateur officers and NCOs in for the duration. Boris Bressloff, for example, a navigator in the crew of Flight Lieutenant Alex Thorne DSO DFC was a trainee hairdresser before the war. Others within the crew included an engineer, a policeman and a professional gymnast:

> *"Our skipper was a remarkable man. He was very self-effacing – the epitome of the English hero. He never got angry or raised his voice. There was only one thing that used to make him cross, and that was poor grammar. One night we were over Germany when flak hit the rear turret and severed the hydraulic lines, causing the turret to fill with smoke. The rear gunner, Jim Rayment, switched on his intercom:*
>
> *"My turret is on fire," he said. Given that there were two turrets, Alex replied: "Who is calling?" A voice came back: "It's me, Jim," to which Alex retorted: "it is not 'me' it is I!"*
>
> *On another occasion, we were over Walcheren, flying rather low when the German flak opened up on us. Jim says: "Can I have a go at them skip?" to which Alex replied: "Certainly, but do try not to irritate them."*

BORIS BRESSLOFF DFC
NAV TWO. 635 SQUADRON. FIFTY-THREE OPS.

James Marks, who would later emerge as one of the first of many PFF legends. For an attack on troop concentrations near Rotterdam in 1940, he proposed a group of pilots made a time and distance run from Rotterdam to the target, over which they would then drop flares such that the aircraft that followed would be assured of accurate bombing. This is sometimes quoted as being the first ever co-ordinated attempt to find a target. As it was, the venture was a failure, although that did not deter Marks, nor the squadron, from trying again.

A major improvement in Bomber Command's fortunes came with the advent of Gee, an electronic navigation aid that provided the navigator with a simultaneous 'fix' that he could plot in less than a minute. No longer would the navigators have to rely on radio bearings and dead reckoning; now they had a technology that was as reliable as it was easy to use, so much so that it was known as the 'goon box' because any 'goon' could use it. It had drawbacks, and different technologies such as H2S and Oboe were on the way, but for the time it was a revolution, and a welcome one.

The other change to Bomber Command's fortunes came with the appointment of a new commander-in-chief. Richard Peirse's reign as the head of Britain's primary (and probably only) offensive force at that time came to an unhappy end shortly after a dismal and disastrous night in November 1941. His command lost thirty-seven of its aircraft with little or nothing to show for their sacrifice. Peirse's judgment was called into question; he was perhaps tired and needed a change. Air Vice-Marshal John Baldwin assumed command on a temporary basis until on February 22, 1942, a new AOC-in-C was appointed to replace him: Air Marshal Arthur Harris.

On the day he took command, Harris had at his disposal 378 serviceable aircraft and crews, but only sixty-nine of these were heavy bombers. The position he had inherited was a far from happy one, but he immediately set about creating a new sense of purpose within the command, and planning the first of his showpiece 1,000-bomber raids.

The issue that all commanders at every level were trying to wrestle with was how to launch regular and sustained precision attacks. An obvious answer, of course, was to attack in daylight, but this proved easier said than done, especially with a force that was specifically designed, trained and intended to attack the enemy at night. Gee was an exceptional navigation aid, but it was unable to provide accurate target location. The question was then posed, therefore, not so much about whether some special target marking force was required, but rather what form such a force should take. And so the arguments began in earnest.

Chief advocate for a dedicated target-finding unit was Sydney Bufton, who had commanded 10 Squadron in the summer of 1940 and was now the deputy director of bomber operations at the Air Ministry. Bufton proposed ultimately that a separate force of six squadrons should be formed in close proximity to one another, with one third of the crews to be drawn from the best within the whole command. Bufton pushed his beliefs with great zeal, and found willing ears among certain elements within the Air Ministry, notably Sir Wilfred Freeman, the vice chief of the air staff and Henry Tizard, the RAF's chief scientific advisor.

Harris, however, was not impressed. Indeed it has been suggested that he objected strongly to being told how to run a war by such a comparatively junior officer as Bufton (he was then a temporary group captain). In his rejection of

Wing Commander Jimmy Marks as OC 35 Squadron 'Madras Presidency'. Marks was killed on the eve of being promoted group captain.

Group Captain 'Hal' Bufton – the first PFF OC of 109 Squadron whose brother was instrumental in the foundation of PFF.

Bufton's proposals, he had the complete support of his group commanders. The concept of a *corps d'elite*, as such a force would inevitably become, was an anathema to the old guard.

Harris had an alternative plan, to train and form target-marking squadrons in each group, and have what he called 'Raid Leaders'. He believed, as did his supporters, that denuding squadrons of their most successful crews would be counter-productive. It was these men, he argued, who were required as the squadron and flight commanders in their own units, and their removal 'seemed likely to lead to a great deal of trouble and might be thoroughly bad for morale' (*Bomber Offensive*, 1947).

Bufton and Harris were in truth trying to achieve much the same thing but in contrasting ways; but of course there were differences of opinion, not least their views on the effectiveness of area bombing. Harris believed that area bombing could and would win the war; Bufton saw it as temporarily expedient until a time when specific targets could be picked off with greater accuracy.

Harris was also averse to structural change but in private was as concerned as Bufton as regards the apparent lack of bombing discipline within the command. Bufton did his own analysis – a mini 'Butt Report' – and the results were still poor. He looked at eight attacks on Essen in March/April and found that as many as ninety percent of aircraft had dropped their bombs between five and 100 miles from the target!

Another report, this one by Mr Justice Singleton, perhaps proved the tipping point. His findings in *The Report on the Bombing of Germany* presented on May 20 concluded that although Gee was effective in bringing bombers within a handful of miles of the target, it was in the last few miles that the real ability of the crews was tested. The very best, with the finest equipment, stood every chance of finding the target. The creation of a specially-trained target-finding force was therefore desirable.

The final victory for Bufton was perhaps inevitable. Portal made his views clear: whether his Bomber Command chief liked it or not, he would do as he was told: an elite – and separate – corps would indeed be created. This corps, wrote Portal, would have a role 'analogous to that of the reconnaissance battalion of an army division'. It needed a name and it needed a leader. Harris would decide both.

Harris refused to refer to his new, imposed responsibility as a target-marking force. He preferred, and insisted, that the name Pathfinder Force was chosen instead. He also insisted that certain privileges be accorded his new units. He understood that an aircraft tasked with finding and marking a target visually would be obliged to stay longer over the area, and therefore be at greater risk. He believed also that those in the vanguard would receive greater attention from the enemy defences, and again that this should be recognised. Harris reasoned that the men of Pathfinder Force would be expected to work longer tours and probably miss promotion in their parent squadrons, and so he proposed that Pathfinders should gain quicker promotions and wear some sort of distinguishing badge. The former caused arguments with the Treasury on grounds of affordability; the latter created an emblem that became a major source of pride to those who earned it.

Despite his obvious antipathy, Harris also wasted no time in finding a commander for his new force. He chose an Australian officer with whom he had served previously, and although young for potential group command status, was unrivalled in his knowledge and skill as an air navigator. He also had 'current' operational experience, a rare thing in senior command, having been in charge of both 77 and 10 Squadrons. He had also recently been shot down and successfully evaded. His

DON BENNETT – PATHFINDER LEADER

Donald Bennett was the no-nonsense pre-war regular chosen by Harris to lead his new-found Pathfinder Force. A tough, single-minded Queenslander, Bennett was a perfectionist who expected the same in others.

Having joined the Royal Australian Air Force (RAAF) in 1930 and undergone pilot training at Point Cook, he arrived in the UK where he found himself, at first, flying fighters (with 29 Squadron) before volunteering for flying-boat duties. As a flight commander with 210 Squadron at Pembroke Dock he came to the attention of his squadron commander, Wing Commander Arthur Harris, who would later remark of his young protégé that: "He is very much an intellectual and had at times the young intellectual's habit of underrating experience and overrating knowledge."

Bennett's appetite for learning was virtually insatiable. During his time as an instructor at the School of Naval Co-Operation & Air Navigation (RAF Calshot), he extended his own experience and qualifications to include 'B' Pilot's, First Class Navigator's, Ground Engineer's 'A', 'C' and 'X' Licences, a Wireless Operator's Licence as well as an Instructor's Licence.

Deciding his future lay in civil aviation, he joined Imperial Airways (later BOAC) as a first officer and flew all over the world, including – famously – taking the controls of the top half of the Mercury-Maia trans-Atlantic mail plane combination as well as taking part in air-to-air refuelling experiments in 1939.

The early months of the Second World War found him undertaking VIP flights around Europe including a clandestine flight into occupied France to collect Polish military and government officials. He was then asked by the Ministry of Aircraft Production to join the team being set up to ferry aircraft to Britain from the United States, and led the first flight of seven Hudsons across the Atlantic in November 1940. With his duties completed, and a role beckoning in Training Command, he sought more meaningful employment, and after a stint helping to establish a navigation school at Eastbourne he applied for – and was given – command of an operational squadron, joining 77 Squadron at RAF Leeming as its commanding officer.

He flew on operations as often as possible and nearly always with a different crew, so that he could judge their efficiency and improve upon any weaknesses. (This was a habit he continued in PFF.) In April 1942 he took command of 10 Squadron, newly equipped with the four-engined Halifax, and was shot down later than month while on a low-level attack on the *Tirpitz*. With the help of friendly Norwegians he managed to cross the border into Sweden and eventually return to Britain resuming command of his squadron one month after baling out. He received an immediate DSO.

Having received orders that his squadron was to move to the Middle East, he was at the point of leaving when he was summoned to see his old 'boss' and offered command of Pathfinder Force.

name was Donald Bennett.

Bennett's appointment was dated July 5, 1942, and he was promoted group captain. But it was still to be another month before the PFF finally came into being as the finer details were thrashed out behind closed doors. It was on August 15, 1942, that formal instructions were received from HQ Bomber Command (HQBC) to create the Pathfinders with the following squadrons: 7, 35, 83, 109 and 156, under the command of Group Captain D.C.T. Bennett at RAF Wyton.

To carry this into effect: 35 Squadron transferred from Linton (4 Group) to Graveley; 83

HAPPY TO SEE OUT THE WAR

Squadron Leader Ian Hewitt had an eventful war. Having trained as an observer, he joined 58 Squadron at Linton in August 1941, moving to 35 Squadron the following month and settled into a routine of operations, including a number of daylights to Brest flying with a Canadian, Don MacIntyre. On one occasion they were thrown into a diving stall with a 4,000-pounder in the front bomb bay, and only just recovered. On another, they accompanied Donald Bennett for the attack on the *Tirpitz*, and were similarly shot down into the frozen fjord and rescued by a group of brave Norwegians. Hewitt managed to make it over the border into Sweden:

"In the internment camp was one Don Bennett. I would have been quite happy to see out the war in central Sweden but he was having none of that. He made such a nuisance of himself with the British Embassy, the Swedish authorities and everyone else with whom he came into contact, that after a few weeks the Swedes were glad to see the back of him. By association, Don MacIntyre and I were repatriated shortly after. Don went off east and eventually I was posted to 405, a Canadian squadron."

IAN HEWITT DFC & BAR
NAVIGATOR. 35 AND 405 SQUADRONS.

GEE

First used on an attack on Essen in March 1942, Gee was a highly effective device that enabled crews to get to the general vicinity of the target area or any point within its range of 350 miles. Three ground-based transmitters – a master station (known as an 'A' station) and two 'slave' stations ('B' and 'C') – sent sequential radio pulses to a receiver onboard the aircraft. By measuring the difference in time taken by the 'A' and 'B' signals and the 'A' and 'C' signals to reach the aircraft, the aircraft could be located on two position lines, and its ground position coincided with the point at which these two 'Gee coordinates' intersected. The data was displayed on a cathode ray tube in the navigator's compartment, and plotted on a special Gee chart. Pathfinder navigators were able to obtain a fix in less than a minute with incredible accuracy, often to within half a mile.

Squadron moved from Scampton (5 Group) to Wyton; 7 Squadron from Oakington (3 Group) was officially 'attached' having already made the move to Wyton; and 109 Squadron, also from 3 Group, was similarly moved from Stradishall to Wyton. The last squadron, 156, which was stationed at Warboys, was affiliated to 1 Group (it had previously been a 3 Group squadron).

Headquarters under HQBC was detached to Wyton with one group captain, one wing commander, four squadron leaders, two flight lieutenants, one section officer and six other ranks on its strength.

PFF was administered, in the immediate term, by 3 Group and reinforced as follows:

- 7 Squadron with Short Stirling aircraft from 3 Group – under the command of Wing Commander Boyd Sellick.
- 35 Squadron with Handley Page Halifax aircraft from 4 Group – under the command of Wing Commander Jimmy Marks.
- 83 Squadron with Avro Lancaster aircraft from 5 Group – under the command of Wing Commander Maynard Crichton-Biggie.
- 109 Squadron with Vickers Wellington and Mosquito aircraft from 2 Group – under the command of Wing Commander 'Hal' Bufton.
- 156 Squadron with Vickers Wellingtons from 1 Group – under the command of Wing Commander Reginald Cook.

7 Squadron Stirling: The first of the four-engined 'heavies' was also the first to be withdrawn from frontline service as losses mounted.

THE ROAD TO PATHFINDING

The journey to becoming a Pathfinder differed from one man to the next: some were intent on 'being the best', and trained hard to ensure they came up to the mark; others were naturally gifted or competitive, and saw Pathfinding as the next 'challenge' to overcome.

Not all were experienced aircrew necessarily, but all were volunteers. The very best from the various training units, for example, could be picked for Pathfinders without ever having first served their apprenticeship with a main force squadron. Others went to main force, and after a handful of trips the pilot or navigator might have caught the eye of the flight or squadron commanders or relevant 'trade' leaders who recommended they try their hand. Spare bods – especially gunners and wireless operators – might be posted in singularly, without even realising they were going to Pathfinder Force.

Not untypically, however, Pathfinders were 'second-tour' men who had already won their spurs and were keen to get back into the fray. In moving to Pathfinder Force, they agreed to an extended tour of forty-five operations (a main force tour was thirty; a second tour twenty), and not untypically carried on until ordered to stop. Although there were many Mosquito Pathfinders who logged more than 100 sorties, a handful of heavy pilots and crew achieved the same – a quite incredible achievement considering that the average sortie life of air crews in the command was never higher than twelve, and at one point stood at only eight sorties per crew.

Young crews would often remark upon how stripes and gongs were in such plentiful supply on Pathfinder squadrons, that they became virtually 'the norm'. Flight lieutenants and squadron leaders – exalted ranks on a main force squadron – were two a penny, helped by the fact that a 'perk' of Pathfinding was accelerated promotion.

At various stages of the war, some main force squadron commanders, reluctant to relinquish their best crews, would send troublesome units or those that were not up to the mark, and endeavour to use 8 Group as a dumping ground. Such crews, and squadron commanders, were very quickly exposed, and shown the error of their ways.

Conversely some Pathfinder COs raised the bar to such extremes that sometimes perfectly good men with admirable results were being returned to their original squadrons, either for minor misdemeanours or for failing to 'press on regardless' to the target on three engines, for example, when they might have had good grounds to abandon their operation.

The South African pilot Ted Swales was one such pilot chided for turning back when in the CO's view he should have carried on. He vowed never to turn back again, whatever the consequences, and never did, winning the Victoria Cross and paying with his life.

To many, the shortcomings of such a force were immediately apparent. The men were untried, the tactics yet to be devised, and without group status, the chain of command was somewhat convoluted. They were coming to life just at the point that the Germans, too, were getting their defences better organised, and had found a way of jamming Gee – previously the RAF's trump card.

But the more obvious difficulty was in coordinating the efforts of five disparate squadrons operating no fewer than five different makes of aircraft, with enormous variations in performance. It would be some time before the five would be rationalised to three and then ultimately two. In the immediate term, however, Bennett was obliged to play with the cards he had been dealt. And he was expected to prepare his men for operations immediately.

With the British knack of tragic inevitably that seems to surround all major events, the first use of Pathfinders on the night of August 18/19, 1942 was an unmitigated failure. The target was Flensburg on the Baltic, which although a comparatively easy target to identify, proved to be rather more elusive to find than first hoped. For the navigators, winds were not as forecast, and

although sixteen out of the thirty-one Pathfinder crews taking part claimed to have marked the target, not a single bomb was reported to have hit the town.

Flensburg was their first attack and their primary failure. The official report stated that 'a very dark night made conditions difficult'. It also led to their first casualty when a 35 Squadron Halifax

"Generally the route into Pathfinders was that you had completed a tour or part tour with main force, usually 4 Group on Halifaxes or 1 and 3 Group on Lancs. My own case was somewhat different. I had finished my flight engineer's course at St Athan and was at HCU Lindholme, waiting to be crewed up. (In converting from two to four engines, existing crews that had crewed up at OTU needed a flight engineer.) So there we were assembled and this pilot came over to me and introduced himself, and asked me whether I had any previous flying experience. As I was an ex-corporal engine fitter (I had been a 'Brat' at Halton in the Entry 40), I had a fair amount of experience in air tests on Wellingtons, Hampdens and the like and so said 'yes'. I then learned that 'my' pilot – Flying Officer Bill Neal* – had already completed a tour of operations, as had the rest of the crew, and he had just finished a period instructing on Wellingtons. I thought if I had to fly with anyone, then this was a good choice! The only thing he did say, however, was that in joining the crew I had to understand that we were going straight to Pathfinders."

(*Later Flight Lieutenant W.G. Neal DSO, DFC, MiD)

DON BRIGGS DFC
FLIGHT ENGINEER. 156 SQUADRON. SIXTY-TWO OPS.

"When the skipper, an American called Walt Reif, told us we had been selected for Pathfinders, our air bomber, Peter Uzelman, a Canadian, didn't want to go. In the end he was persuaded but perhaps we should have listened to him as when we were shot down only the mid-upper gunner and I survived."

BOB PEARCE
AIR GUNNER.
582 SQUADRON.
THIRTY-ONE OPS.

Teenager Bob Pearce (third from left) with his skipper, Walt Reif, and crew. Only Bob and his fellow gunner Jack MacLennan (second from right) would survive the war.

captained by Sergeant J.W. Smith, on his tenth operation, failed to return, having succumbed to two separate nightfighter attacks but claiming one aircraft destroyed in return. His probable victor was Feldwebel Herbert Altner of 7/NJG3, claiming his first 'kill'. He would claim twenty-two more before the war was over.

The Pathfinders were given a chance to redeem themselves a week later, but the results were only marginally better. Cloud, this time, obscured the target and most of the bombing fell in open countryside rather than on the city of Frankfurt. Of perhaps greater concern was the loss of five aircraft: two Stirlings, two Lancasters (still at the time in preciously short supply) and a Halifax. Among those killed was Wing Commander John Shewell, an auxiliary officer who was gaining operational experience prior to taking command of 7 Squadron.

TRIAL AND ERROR

"At the time the Pathfinders were formed, the aircraft had virtually no radio or electronic aids to navigation or bombing which were effective over enemy territory. This meant that finding the target depended almost entirely on map reading and dead-reckoning, using very shaky forecasts of winds. If, as frequently happens in Europe, the night was dark and the coastal features and targets well obscured by cloud, the odds were heavily against even the most determined crew pinpointing the target."

PETER CRIBB
DSO & BAR, DFC & BAR.
PILOT. 35 AND 582 SQUADRONS.
100+ OPS.

Group Captain Peter Cribb as sketched by the famous war artist, Cuthbert Orde.

It was third time lucky for the Pathfinders when on the night of August 27/28 a mixed bag of Stirlings, Lancasters and Wellingtons – some thirty-three in total – were despatched to lead a raid on Kassel. Weather conditions were more favourable, although this time they had to overcome a new phenomenon: a ground haze not unusual with large industrial centres. Despite the smog, the area was well illuminated and widespread damage was caused, especially to the Henschel aircraft factory where several large explosions and fires were reported. Three Wellingtons of 156 Squadron, however, were lost – all seventeen aircrew killed.

The crews were beginning to find form. Over Nuremberg the following night, the Pathfinders not only found the aiming point, but they were also able to mark it with the first target indicators (TIs), effectively adapted 250-pound incendiary bombs. The euphoria of a job well done, however, was tempered by the loss of another three aircraft including another 156 Squadron Wellington on a raid where no fewer than fourteen Wellingtons (more than a third of the total despatched) were missing.

In the early days of Pathfinder Force it was a question of one step forward and two to the rear. September, however, saw considerable advances in Pathfinder technique, particularly in the systems of flare laying, in navigation generally and in timing, although the weather throughout the month, especially in the latter part, prevented operations on a considerable number of nights. Attacks were made on September 1 (Saarbrücken); September 2 (Karlsruhe); September 4 (Bremen); September 6 (Duisberg); September 8 (Frankfurt); September 10 (Düsseldorf); September 13 (Bremen); September 14 (Wilhemshaven); September 16 (Essen); September 19 (Munich); and September 19 (Saarbrücken).

According to the PFF ORB, the attacks on Karlsruhe, Düsseldorf and Munich were especially successful and benign weather conditions enabled the flare-carrying aircraft to provide successful illumination for the main force. With regards the raid on Saarbrücken at the start of the month, the

Target indicators (TIs).

ORB describes how the attack 'unfortunately went astray'. The unknown author of this particular report was a master of the understatement. Although the Pathfinders marked and the main force bombed a town that they believed was Saarbrücken, it was in fact Saarlouis some thirteen miles away. Happily, Saarlouis was still a legitimate target and much damage was done, mitigating the rocket that the young PFF commander was to receive from his boss.

The attack on Bremen was also particularly noteworthy because on that night, the Pathfinders introduced a new technique: splitting their aircraft into three forces. 'Illuminators' went in first and lit up the area with white flares; they were followed by 'primary visual markers' who dropped coloured flares if they identified the aiming point visually; and then 'backers-up' who dropped their incendiary bombs on the coloured flares. This approach would form the basis of most future attacks. For the attack on Düsseldorf, the Pathfinders started employing 'Pink Pansies' – a huge target-marking device using converted 4,000-pound casings and so-called because it ignited with a distinctive pink 'flash'.

September was a dramatic month for Pathfinder Force in which the first gallantry awards for bravery of the highest order were recommended and the first of some of its finest and most experienced pilots and crews were lost.

Flying Officer John Trench of 7 Squadron received an immediate Distinguished Service Order (DSO) when on the night of September 10/11 his aircraft was hit by flak over Maastricht, losing two engines – one quite literally falling off. The aircraft struggled to maintain height, and the crew were obliged to throw overboard any unnecessary excess weight – including parachutes. Miraculously, with both luck and judgment on the part of the crew, they managed to make it to the English coast and crash land, whereupon the Stirling immediately burst into flames.

At that point their luck ran out. Trench, knocked unconscious, and the wireless operator Sergeant Ivor Edwards, were pulled clear by the navigator, Pilot Officer

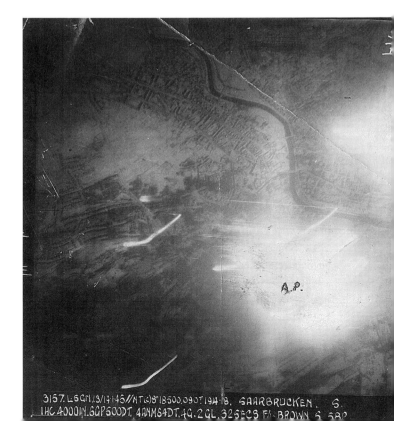

An aiming point (AP) photo from a 582 Squadron Lancaster over Saarbrücken, January 13/14, 1945. Such photos were much prized by the air bombers.

PINK PANSIES AND RED SPOT FIRES

Pathfinder Force experimented throughout the war with various target markers, the principal criteria, obviously, that they must be easy to see, and they must 'burn' for as long as possible to give the following main force sufficient time to aim their bombs. Later there was also the added problem of imitation; the Germans became adept at creating dummy markers and decoy fires to draw the bombers away from the real target and cause their bombs to fall harmlessly in the countryside.

Among the first of the rudimentary markers was the Pink Pansy. It was a 4,000-pound bomb casing filled with a mixture of benzol, rubber and phosphorus, coloured such that the initial flash was a brilliant pink. Pink Pansies were followed by Red Blob Fires which were 250-pound incendiaries filled with the same ingredients.

In August 1943, the Pathfinders used a Red Spot Fire Target Indicator, a 250-pound casing filled with cotton wool soaked in a solution of metallic perchlorate dissolved in alcohol. The advantage was that it burned on the ground as a single spot of deep red for up to twenty minutes; the disadvantage was that it could be quickly obliterated by smoke and heavy bombing. As such it tended to be used on small precision targets (as in the case of Peenemünde) or as route markers.

Much later in the war, when Bomber Command turned its hand to daylight operations, markers were developed that emitted coloured smoke.

Crofton Selman. With the rear gunner trapped, the flight engineer and bomb aimer – who had already extricated themselves from the burning Stirling – re-entered the aircraft to save him and were killed when the petrol tanks exploded. At that point the mid upper gunner made yet another attempt to save his fellow gunner, and succeeded. Trench, Selman and Edwards received the DSO, DFC and DFM respectively. The mid upper gunner, Sergeant Raoul de fontenay Jenner of the Royal Canadian Air Force, received the George Medal for his valiant action in saving his crewmate. (Trench and Selman would both be killed early the following year.)

Among the five Pathfinder crews lost on the later raid on Saarbrücken on September 19/20, two were from 35 Squadron, one flown by the commanding officer, Wing Commander James Marks DSO, DFC. With 77 Squadron he had been one of the early exponents of Pathfinding methods. As the commanding officer of one of the founding squadrons of Pathfinder Force, he had been especially proud that all but seven of his 150 aircrew had volunteered for special service.

October contained only meagre pickings for Pathfinder Force. An attack on Krefeld on October 2/3 failed and many of the bombs intended for Aachen, three nights later, fell nearly twenty miles from the target. There was better success attacking Osnabrück on October 6/7, the raid being remarkable for the Pathfinders' actions in illuminating the Dümmer See to help guide main force with their run in to the target.

A decoy fire succeeded in foxing at least half of those claiming to bomb Kiel on October 13/14 (although Pathfinder crews reported seeing fires visible 100 miles away) and on October 15/16, an

The Distinguished Flying Medal (left) for non-commissioned officers (NCOs) was less common than the DFC awarded to officers but arguably more highly respected.

attack on Cologne was again thwarted in the same way. For the rest of the month, the Pathfinders played their part in finding and marking targets in Italy, principally Genoa and Milan.

Among the aircraft lost during the month was a Halifax flown by Squadron Leader Jack Kerry

Inspecting the troops. Jimmy Marks introduces His Majesty to his men.

The brilliant Jimmy Marks – among the first to be awarded the Pathfinder 'eagle' – posthumously.

THE LOSS OF JIMMY MARKS – FIRST OF THE BEST

The attack on Saarbrücken on September 19/20 was a relatively modest raid involving 118 aircraft. The crew of Halifax W7657 coded 'L' comprised Wing Commander Marks in the pilot's seat, navigator Flight Lieutenant Alan Child DFC, wireless operator Pilot Officer Reginald Sawyer DFM, mid upper gunner Flight Lieutenant Norman Wright, and in the rear turret, Pilot Officer Richard Leith-Hay-Clark. Child and Leith-Hay-Clark were their respective section leaders, both valuable men to replace. What happened that night is recounted by the surviving flight engineer Bill Higgs:

"When we neared the target, the luck went all the Germans' way. Thick mist appeared and when the navigator thought we were near the target, the skipper descended to 2,000ft and we carried out a square search for an hour. We could not see the ground and as target markers we were not allowed to drop our special marker incendiary bombs unless we could clearly identify the target. At that time we had no 'special equipment' to help us.

"At this point I told the skipper that if we had to carry our bomb load home, we were going to have to leave soon or there wouldn't be enough fuel. The skipper immediately took the necessary action to exit the target area. As we climbed, I saw a Bf110 nightfighter flash past

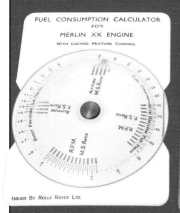

Fuel calculator issued to flight engineers. Bennett insisted on his crews achieving maximum fuel efficiency.

our starboard wing tip, nearly colliding with us. We levelled out at 11,000ft and passed out of Germany and into France. At 00.30 I was calculating our fuel consumption when there was a sudden and tremendous explosion in the port wing. I stood up and looked out to see that our number five and six fuel tanks were on fire. The flames were going back beyond the rear turret.

"The aircraft dived and I hit the roof. We then pulled out of the dive and I crashed to the floor. I could see the skipper talking into his microphone but I could hear nothing through the intercom. The aircraft began falling again and once again my head hit the roof and I thought 'this is it'. The skipper once more managed to pull the aircraft out of the dive and I moved alongside him. He pointed to where Alan (the navigator) had opened the escape hatch. I went back to my position, clipped on my parachute and moved to the hatch.

"It is amazing what strange thoughts pass through one's mind at a time like this. I looked at the opening and the small area of metal around it. I sat on the edge of the hatch and tried to drop through. Unfortunately the adjusting buckles on my parachute harness just happened to stick out above my shoulders and caught in the rim of the hatch. So there I was – half in, half out – stuck! Then I fell, and I remember the tail wheel making a dreadful noise as I flashed past it.

"My parachute opened with a sharp 'crack' as soon as I pulled the ripcord and I breathed a sigh of relief. Shortly afterwards dear old 'L' hit the ground and exploded in a great mass of flames."

The aircraft crashed at Blesme, 11km east of Vitry-le-François, with Jimmy Marks still at the controls. Alan Child and Richard Leith-Hay-Clark were killed with him. The Halifax was probably the victim of Leutnant Ferdinand Christiner of 4/NJG4 who claimed a Halifax shot down near Blesme at much the same time.

Flight Sergeant Bill Higgs. He owes his life to his skipper.

BILL HIGGS
FLIGHT ENGINEER. 35 SQUADRON.

FLYING SOLO

The raid on Saarbrücken was also remarkable for a particular incident involving Squadron Leader 'Artie' Ashworth of 156 Squadron who would later serve on the staff at HQ PFF. The flares in Ashworth's aircraft ignited in the bomb bay, and with smoke and flame entering the fuselage he naturally gave the order to abandon aircraft. Preparing to jump himself, he realised he had no parachute and so attempted to land before he was burned alive. Miraculously the fires extinguished themselves and he brought the aircraft back solo, landing at West Malling.

Ashworth's was not the only solo effort in those early days of Pathfinder operations. Another 156 Squadron pilot, Flight Lieutenant Douglas Greenup – who had claimed the honour of being the first Pathfinder to cross into enemy territory – repeated the feat on October 5, when his aircraft was struck by lightning over the French coast. Throwing the battered Wellington into a dive with only one engine working and with flak coming up in abundance, his crew thought the end was nigh and headed for the exit. Greenup somehow managed to return the aircraft to level flight and make it back to England where he crash landed at Manston.

The third and perhaps best known example of a solo flight fell to Wing Commander Basil Robinson DSO, DFC of 35 Squadron returning from a raid on Turin on November 18. His flares had hung up and over the Alps they ignited with potentially-devastating consequences. Fearing the worst, and with smoke filling the cockpit, he ordered the crew to bale out. No sooner had the order been given and the escape hatch opened, than the smoke appeared to subside, by which time, however, the rest of the crew had gone. Robinson flew his Halifax home single-handedly without further incident. He was awarded an immediate DSO.

There is more to add to the story of Robinson's solo flight, as recounted by a gunner with 83 Squadron who was good friends with Flight Sergeant Bill Potter, the rear gunner in Robinson's crew that night:

> "On the night that Basil Robinson won his immediate DSO, he took with him the regular crew of Flight Lieutenant 'Pluto' Plutte, the duty pilot that day. As they arrived at briefing, Robinson stood Plutte down and said he would be flying his aircraft. Included in the crew was Bill Potter.
>
> "When Bill was captured, because there had been no pilot onboard he was immediately arrested as a spy. He was then subjected to the most terrible beating by his Italian hosts, which only ended when the Germans arrived to escort him to a prisoner of war camp. Bill then endured months in Stalag Luft III and later IV in the cold and misery of the winter weather. So extreme was the temperature that 'Taffy' Davies, one of Bill's best friends, volunteered to break out of the camp to steal coal from the fuel store, without which they would surely die of hyperthermia. Bill tried to persuade him not to go, but in vain. Taffy made it through the wire and into the coal store. In attempting to break back into the camp, however, he was spotted by a guard and killed, despite having surrendered. Bill vowed never to forget what he had seen. After the war, the guard was found, tried, and sentenced to death for murder."

ALF HUBERMAN
AIR GUNNER. 83 SQUADRON. THIRTY-EIGHT OPS.

DFC, a flight commander of 35 Squadron, shot down over Aachen on his second tour. How Kerry was lost is still somewhat unclear, but it appears that his assailant, Oberfeldwebel Gerhard Jecke, misjudged his approach and collided with the tail of the Halifax, causing both aircraft to crash. Both Kerry and Jecke were killed.

Poor weather impaired operations throughout November, with four attacks on Genoa, four on Turin, and one each on Hamburg and Stuttgart. The ORB asserts that all of the attacks, with the exception of those on the two German targets and one on Turin, proved very successful, but were not without losses. 83 Squadron lost three aircraft out of the fifteen they sent to illuminate Genoa on

A Short Stirling takes to the air. Note the distinctive twin tail wheels, tail fin and enormous undercarriage that make this type instantly identifiable.

November 6. Pilot Officer Thomas Hackney DFC, the pilot of one of the Lancasters, was from Gwelo, Southern Rhodesia – he was one of the many thousands of commonwealth aircrew who contributed such loyal service to Bomber Command, and who made the ultimate sacrifice. 7 Squadron also lost three aircraft out of the ten Stirlings it sent to bomb Hamburg on November 9/10.

December saw a steady improvement in the methods of illumination and marking, although once again operations were affected by bad weather. Eight attacks were made, but only those on Duisberg (December 20) and the first of three attacks on Turin (December 8) were deemed in any way successful. The ORB makes special mention of the actions of Flying Officer Cyril 'Smithy' Smith (later DSO, DFC having completed not less than fifty-eight trips) whose Lancaster encountered what it took to be a Junkers Ju88 nightfighter near Frankfurt on December 2 which exploded in mid air following a long burst from the mid upper gunner, Flying Officer Ian Meikle (later DFC). This is one of the rare occasions that the author of the ORB makes mention of a specific nightfighter engagement.

The Stirlings of 7 Squadron again suffered badly, losing five aircraft in the month, three in one night. Among those lost was another ex-58 Squadron pilot, Flight Lieutenant Bill Christie DSO, DFM.

Without doubt the most significant development within Pathfinder Force that month was the arrival proper of 109 Squadron to the Pathfinder war party. For the past four months they had been training with their secret precision device, Oboe, logging a good many flying hours. But Oboe's birth had followed a difficult gestation, particularly with the transfer of the device from the Wellington Mk VI to the new, and potentially war-winning, Mosquito Mk IV.

Indeed the problems with Oboe were still not fully 'fixed' by the time it finally became operational, when on the night of December 20 'Hal' Bufton (brother of Syd), the commanding officer of 109 Squadron and his Australian navigator Flight Lieutenant Edward Ifould DFC (later DSO, DFC & Bar) dropped three bombs that fell within 200 yards of their target in Holland, the coking plant at Lutterade. It was a promising start, heralding a bright and brilliant future. Other 'nuisance' raids, as they were described, followed on the 22nd, 23rd and 24th, and a further historic event was recorded on New Year's Eve when a 109 Squadron Mosquito dropped its flares

OBOE – A MUSICAL MASTERPIECE

Oboe, an extremely accurate blind bombing device, was the brainchild of Dr F.E. Jones and A.H. Reeves who had worked out a system using two ground stations, each with a different role. One, the tracking station, sent dot-dash signals to the pilot, and was codenamed 'cat'. The second, 'mouse', was the releasing station that measured the ground speed of the aircraft, alerted the navigator of the approximate time before the bomb release, and then gave the signal.

The track to the target was along the arc of the circle of constant path range passing through the point of the bomb release (the release point – R/P) with the 'cat' at the centre. As the beam was an arc it was estimated that the average time for a pilot to settle onto it and fly it accurately was ten minutes.

A position on the arc, called point 'A', equal to ten minutes flying time, was measured back from the R/P. This was given to the crews as part of the briefing, along with the speed and the height at which the run had to be made. The navigator's role was to get the aircraft to point A ten minutes before their time on target (ToT).

Near point 'A' another beam signalled the waiting point. Oboe was switched on just before to ensure it was working and to give the crews a chance to assess the quality of the signals and their timing. Each crew was then ready to receive their own call sign transmitted from both stations. When they did so, the Oboe repeater system was switched on and they prepared for the run to the target.

Almost immediately the pilot would receive dots if he was on the side of the track nearest the station, and dashes if he was on the far side. When he settled on the beam he received an equi-signal tone that sounded like a constant note from an Oboe – hence the name. If the aircraft was some distance from the beam, both stations sent an 'X', 'Y' or 'Z' in Morse indicating it was five, ten or fifteen miles adrift. If it was further from point 'A' an 'S' was sent to show that it was short.

The 'mouse' sent 'A', 'B', 'C' and 'D' to the navigator, indicating ten, eight, six and three minutes from the R/P. Finally, the release signal – five dits and a 2.5-second dah – was given. When the navigator pressed the bomb release it automatically cut out the aircraft transmitter, and so the ground station knew the exact time of release. He then cleared the set so that the next aircraft could be called.

Used primarily at night, the 'Precision Device' – as it was often known – allowed for incredibly accurate bombing. From 30,000ft and at speeds of 300mph, it was accurate to within 300 yards of the target. Oboe-equipped Mosquitoes would mark the target enabling the rest of the main force to attack; raids using Oboe as the principal target marking system were pre-fixed with the word 'Musical'.

First used by Mosquitoes of 109 Squadron in December 1942, Bomber Command saw in Oboe an opportunity not only to bomb accurately at night, but also during the day, especially when northern France was covered in 10/10ths cloud. The drawback to Oboe was that it necessitated the aircraft to fly straight and level for a fixed time, at a set height, on a predetermined course and speed. This was essential or else the bomb aimer would lose the signal, and not be able to 'hear' the point at which the target had been reached. It left the aircraft vulnerable to predicted flak and nightfighter attack.

by navigational aids only and the supporting aircraft bombed through 10/10ths clouds in the first 'Wanganui' (i.e. marking a point in the sky rather than on the ground) raid of the war.

And so 1942 drew to a close. The Pathfinders had learned many lessons. New techniques had evolved. New technologies were coming on stream. Crews were gaining experience, evidenced by the award of a large number of PFF badges. PFF had carried out 1,089 sorties but for the loss of forty-six aircraft – sixteen Stirlings, fifteen Wellingtons, nine Lancasters and six Halifaxes – a loss rate of 4.2%.

It would not get any easier.

NO ROOM FOR ERROR

'Bill' Riley enlisted in July 1940 and trained at 2 AOS, Millon. Posted to 70 Squadron in January 1942, he flew a tour of forty operations before being rested. (His pilot, Lance Holliday, later flew with both 105 and 109 Squadrons.) Returning to operations in February 1944, he flew a further sixty-eight sorties with 105 Squadron as the navigator to Cliff Chadwick, and ended the war as a flight lieutenant with 147 Squadron Transport Command.

"To use Oboe we had to fly at a pre-determined height, speed and along a track laid down by the 'cat'. We had to fly straight and level for ten minutes, being given time checks and when to release by the 'mouse'. It was important that the markers went down bang on time and often reserves were in attendance. If they could be called in fifteen minutes before time they could be used if anything was amiss with the original aircraft or its apparatus.

"The time and distance errors were already known before we got back because a chart was produced from the Oboe information. Time and accuracy were of the essence, and if the navigator was out on how long it took or the pilot too far off the aiming point one could expect a visit to group HQ for a rocket. Under no circumstances could a release take place unauthorised."

BILL RILEY DFC & BAR
NAVIGATOR, 105 SQUADRON, 108 OPS.

BOMBING TACTICS

Although there were many variations on a theme, the Pathfinders used three principal methods of marking a target:

The most prized possession of all – the Pathfinder 'eagle' was the idea of Harris himself.

NEWHAVEN ATTACKS were essentially 'visual' raids usually in benign conditions: the target was at first illuminated using flares designed specifically for the job. Markers then dropped target indicators that were backed up in a contrasting colour as the raid progressed (the first markers could often be obliterated by the bombing). Main force bombed on the master bomber's instructions.

PARRAMATTA RAIDS varied in that the target was marked 'blindly' by crews using H2S to identify where they were. Following crews then backed up the first TIs with their own, again of a contrasting colour, having calculated the mean point of impact (MPI). Main force then bombed the centre of the secondary markers. (In a Musical Parramatta, the initial marking was carried out by Oboe Mosquitoes.)

WANGANUI ATTACKS were made when neither the target, nor the ground, could be seen. Marker crews dropped skymarkers that burst just above the clouds. Main force crews were instructed to release their bombs as soon as they had a marker in their sights, and on a designated course given at briefing. In theory their bombs would fall through the cloud and onto the target.

Visual marking using the Mk XIV bombsight was invariably the most accurate method deployed, and the results nearly always instantly apparent; not surprisingly, skymarking was usually the least accurate or satisfying.

The obscure names were derived from the home towns of Bennett, his WAAF clerk and one of his air staff officers, Squadron Leader 'Artie' Ashworth (later wing commander DSO, DFC, AFC).

CHAPTER 2
TRIAL AND ERROR

JANUARY 1943

The New Year got off to a slow start, but the Oboe-equipped Mosquitoes were kept busy with seven trips to Essen in ten days. On the last of these raids, Flight Lieutenant Campbell crashed trying to land at Wyton, writing off his Mosquito in the process. He thus earned the dubious distinction of being responsible for the loss of the very first Oboe Mosquito to be destroyed in any circumstances.

The first major raid did not take place until January 14/15, a disappointing affair to Lorient. Pathfinder marking was accurate, but not so the later bombing which was scattered at best. Things improved the following night with an attack on the same target and on January 16/17 the 'Big City' – Berlin – was notable only for being the first occasion that the Pathfinders used proper 'target indicators'. Further attacks during the month were repeated upon Berlin (January 17/18), Lorient (January 23/24) and Düsseldorf (January 27/28). This latter raid was again significant as being the first time that Oboe-equipped Mosquitoes carried out 'ground marking' – using the new TIs which exploded just above the ground. These were considerably more accurate than the parachute-type flares used previously. The TIs were then 'backed up' by the Pathfinder Lancasters. It worked, the markers were well concentrated and the attack resulted in considerable damage to a number of industrial premises.

The month ended with yet another first – the first H2S attack of the war. Hamburg was the target, an alternative to the hoped-for objective, Berlin. Eight Stirlings of 7 Squadron, six Halifaxes of 35 Squadron, and ten Lancasters from 83 and 156 Squadrons (156 had by now completed its conversion from Wellingtons to Lancasters) were detailed for the raid in a successful but extremely eventful night's work.

Red TIs were dropped by the H2S-equipped Stirlings and Halifaxes backed up by Green TIs from the Lancs, and flares were also dropped short of the target to mark the route for main force. Returning crews reported the glow of fires visible from seventy miles and most – but not all – seemed satisfied. All five of the 83 Squadron aircraft, for example, failed to make it into the air after a returning Mosquito crashed and blocked the runway at Wyton; three Stirlings and four Halifaxes returned early when their 'special equipment' failed; and a further Lancaster had to abandon due to icing. Five aircraft had to be diverted after a returning Halifax became

The Krupps steel plant at Essen. The total devastation speaks for itself.

By December 1944, there was virtually nothing left in Essen to destroy.

bogged down at Graveley and a 156 Squadron Lancaster crashed and caught fire at Warboys.

January proved relatively kind to PFF in terms of losses. Only two aircraft were missing, one each from 35 and 83 Squadrons, captained by Squadron Leader Ian Brownlie DFC and Flight Sergeant Timmons respectively. 194.6 tons of heavy and medium explosive bombs had been dropped.

H2S – 'THE MOST REVOLUTIONARY DEVICE EVER KNOWN'

The Pathfinders used two main innovations to find and identify the correct target, the first being H2S, a technology described by Dudley Saward, the first wing commander RDF at Bomber Command as being "the most revolutionary device ever known".

Developed by the Telecommunications Research Establishment (TRE), H2S – whose initials possibly derived from the phrase 'Home Sweet Home' – was, in essence, a ground-scanning radar that presented the navigator in the aircraft with an image of the terrain below.

Initially using the 10cm wavelength, the equipment was installed beneath the aircraft fuselage in a distinctive dome. It transmitted a fan-shaped beam that rotated about the vertical axis beneath the aircraft. Pulses from the beam were reflected back to the aircraft from the ground and the time the pulses took to return was in proportion to the distance the object was from the aircraft.

Referred to cryptically as 'Y' (navigators' logbooks at the time frequently refer to 'Y' runs), H2S was especially good at distinguishing between land and large bodies of water. It was not a surprise, therefore, that when a handful of Pathfinder Stirling and Halifax aircraft were chosen to fly the first H2S-equipped raid of the war on January 30, 1943, the target was Hamburg. Their success augured well for future raids.

Hamburg, Bremen, Kiel, Wilhelmshaven, Brest, Bordeaux and Lorient – all favourite targets of Bomber Command at that – time were ideally suited to prove the effectiveness of H2S; coastlines appeared "like a well-defined picture of a map".

The advantage of H2S was that it could be used in all weather and all conditions and with increasing accuracy as the skills of the set operators (re-trained air bombers who worked in tandem with the 'traditional' navigator as part of a two-man navigation 'team') improved and further innovations (including the launch of a 3cm version) strengthened the quality of the image displayed. However, since the sets transmitted a signal, the Germans could identify the aircraft as an enemy.

Also, as was feared, within a month a Stirling carrying one of the top-secret sets crashed and the Germans were able to unravel its technological secrets. They then set about developing their own countermeasures, resulting in the Naxos radar that enabled German nightfighters to home in on H2S transmissions, and for a time tip the advantage in favour of the Luftwaffe.

Pathfinders that marked a target using H2S were referred to as 'blind markers'. The set operator within a crew was referred to as a 'nav two' and was usually a retrained air bomber. He and the nav one (who managed the air plot) worked as a team.

The differences between the Stirling and Lancaster cockpits are immediately apparent, not least because the Stirling features the co-pilot's control column.

A LESSON LEARNED LATE

Squadron Leader Ian Brownlie had only recently been posted to 35 Squadron, having earned his DFC for a tour on Whitleys with 77 Squadron in the summer of 1940.

"We were briefed to bomb Berlin from the east, and get as high as we could above 20,000ft which in a Halifax would be hanging on our props. Our particular role was to drop illuminating flares. On the way in we had trouble with one of our engines that I had to feather, and that meant we could not get to the required height. I remember seeing a number of Lancasters passing above us, going at a rate of knots. Given our situation, I didn't think it wise to cross Berlin on three and decided to head for home. We then encountered another problem with our intercom that meant I effectively lost contact with some of the crew, and particularly the gunners. Looking back, this was a dreadful situation to find ourselves in, and so it proved.

"Just as we crossed Denmark, we were suddenly attacked by a Junkers Ju88 that slid in underneath us. Me, the navigator and the flight engineer made it out and survived, spending the remainder of the war as POWs. The rest of the crew was killed. The whole flight had been a chapter of accidents with many lessons to learn. Unfortunately it was too late to learn them. I had more than a 1,000 hours on Whitleys but only fifty or so on Halifaxes, and it wasn't a good aircraft. After the war I returned to the scene of the crash and met a girl whose confirmation dress had been made out of the silk from my parachute. I didn't ask for it back!"

IAN BROWNLIE DFC
PILOT. 35 SQUADRON. THIRTY-EIGHT OPS.

A remarkably clear bombing photo of Cologne – October, 1944.

But January will be remembered by Pathfinder Force for a more significant development: its elevation – with effect from January 13 – to group status, and the promotion of its leader to air commodore.

The creation of a new group meant a significant increase in administration (orders were now coming direct from HQ Bomber Command rather than 3 Group) and therefore a significant increase in staff. As his senior air staff officer (SASO) Bennett found Wing Commander Clayton Boyce to be a capable if somewhat distant colleague, and their relationship was professional rather than friendly. Boyce was, at the very least, a man of action, having flown in the Iraq campaign of 1940 and piloted a Wellington in the 1,000-bomber raid on Cologne.

Finding a senior administrative officer (SAO) proved somewhat more problematic: Wing Commander Aubrey Martin was the first and lasted only a few months before being replaced by Wing Commander William Carr. His tenure was similarly short. Indeed the only one of Bennett's SAOs to stay the distance was Group Captain Hamish White who the AOC described in his autobiography as doing 'a grand job'.

Officers who were appointed from the outset and stayed with Bennett throughout the war included: the head 'plumber' (group engineering officer) – Wing Commander Charles Sarsby – who was responsible for establishing a planned maintenance programme that ensured PFF enjoyed some of the highest serviceability rates for their aircraft in the whole command; Squadron Leader W.T.R. 'Shep' Shepherd – the group intelligence officer – responsible for gathering essential target information and debriefing returning crews; the senior medical officer – 'Doc' McGowan – who took it upon himself to fly with crews to study their responses to combat stress (and who would later earn the DFC as

'Shep' Shepherd (right), 8 Group intelligence officer, hitches a ride on a 4,000lb bomb at Graveley.

Howard Lees – the 8 Group photography officer. His many ideas and innovations included a solution to the elimination of 'fire tracks' that obscured night bombing photographs by the use of two camera shutters operating independently.

a result); Squadron Leader 'Basil' Rathbone, the group armaments officer, who Bennett described as producing 'some wonderful fireworks and bangers'; and Squadron Leader Howard Lees, the group photography officer.

A civilian, 'Tommy' Thomas took the role of senior met officer, and other staff posts were filled by recently tour-expired officers including Wing Commander Ron Hilton, Wing Commander John Slater, Squadron Leader Reginald Altman, Squadron Leader Dennis Witt, Squadron Leader Gordon Georgeson, and two of the better-known pathfinders at that time, Squadron Leaders 'Artie' Ashworth and 'Bill' Anderson. All already had a chest full of medals, and would add many more before the war was out.

One of the most important jobs, given Pathfinders' dependence on best-in-class navigation, was group navigation officer. Bennett's first choice would have been his former navigation staff officer, 'Angus' Buchan DFC, but he had been killed in August 1942. As it was, the first group navigation officer to be appointed was Squadron Leader Cliff Alabaster.

FEBRUARY

February was to prove one of the busiest months the Pathfinders had ever experienced, but it did not

A VIEW FROM 8 GROUP HEADQUARTERS

Wing Commander Cliff 'Alaby' Alabaster had joined the RAFVR in May 1939 as a u/t observer, all of the VR pilot's courses being full. He was assured that he would be transferred to pilot training as soon as a course became free. He trained in navigation at Prestwick and bombing and gunnery at Jurby before arriving at Abingdon Whitley OTU where he was commissioned. After completing his first tour with 51 Squadron, he was posted to a 'Spec.N' course in Port Albert, Ontario, eventually returning to Bomber Command in February 1942 where he stayed for three months until his posting as a group nav officer to 5 Group, Grantham. In February 1943 he was posted to the newly-formed PFF at Wyton:

"My stay at PFF HQ coincided with the delivery of the first H2S equipment, so I was concerned with training in its use. To this end, I concentrated my main attention on 97 Squadron, which had just moved down from 5 Group and were the first recipients of the equipment. Therefore I spent a lot of time at Bourn. Of course this was not my only task and I visited all the stations in turn, to see if they had any navigational problems. As much as anything these visits were to let the individual station navigation officers know that I was there to support them!"

CLIFF ALABASTER DSO & BAR, DFC & BAR
NAVIGATOR AND PILOT 97, 582, 128 AND 608 SQUADRONS. 100+ OPS.

THE ROLE OF THE NAV TWO

"I was originally trained as an air bomber in Canada. Then when my skipper wanted to join Pathfinders, I was retrained as the 'set operator' – also known as nav two. This meant that I was trained to use the H2S set. It was difficult at first, but gradually you became accustomed to it and eventually you could virtually map read from it.

"The secret was concentration, because if your mind wandered or if you became distracted, you lost where you were. It was like a noisy office job, sat behind the curtain in the nav's position. The only time I knew things were getting a little sticky was if someone left their intercom on and I could hear their breathing.

"The two navs worked as a team: the nav one managed the air plot; I worked the set. I would get a fix every three minutes and passed it to the nav one when he asked for it. He would take the fix, and factoring in wind speeds etc would mark it on the plot.

"There was only one occasion that my set went u/s, and that was down to me. The set had a modulator valve that had to be switched on below 6,000ft. One night I forgot, and the set wouldn't work. Of course it had to be one of our longest trips, to Stettin on the Baltic, and I ended up sitting there, almost as a passenger. What was interesting is that we were routed in over Sweden, and we could see the place beautifully lit up. We were absolutely on track, a great testimony to the skill of the nav one."

BORIS BRESSLOFF DFC
NAV TWO. 635 SQUADRON. FIFTY-THREE OPS.

get off to an auspicious start. Mosquito aircraft and that of 35 and 7 Squadrons, using their special equipment (Oboe and H2S respectively), dropped red TIs on Cologne on the night of February 2/3, backed up with greens. Despite their best efforts, the results were disappointing. Such misfortune was compounded further with the loss of a 7 Squadron Stirling, skippered by Squadron Leader William Smith DFC, which was shot down by a nightfighter and crashed in Holland. The Germans were therefore able to lay their hands on their first example of an H2S set on only the second occasion it had been used.

Pathfinders went back to Cologne twice more that month, and again there was disappointment. Indeed whilst the frequency of attacks in February increased, the results were at both ends of the scale. The first of four attacks on Wilhelmshaven, for example, was a stunning success for Pathfinder sky marking. Main force laid waste to an area of nearly 120 acres, after their bombs fell through the clouds and hit the naval ammunition depot at Mariensiel. There were also devastating attacks on Lorient, this time in clear visibility. But the raid on Hamburg at the start of the month did little damage, and icing obliged many of the aircraft to return early. Similarly for the attack on Nuremberg on February 25/26, the Pathfinders were uncharacteristically late, and many of the bombs fell uselessly in open countryside. (One Halifax, a 35 Squadron aircraft flown by Flying Officer Ellis Ware, had the photoflash stick in the flare 'chute which then exploded, wounding several members of the crew. The aircraft made an emergency landing at RAF Hunsdon.)

While Bomber Command and Harris satisfied the navy's appetite for area bombing of the U-boats' operational bases – and the attendant French towns – they were also obliged to maintain pressure on the Italians. The attack on La Spezia on February 4/5 is especially noteworthy since the Pathfinders trialled a new weapon – a proximity-fused 4,000-pound bomb ('cookie') that exploded a few

Photo flash.

A 4,000lb 'Cookie' being readied beneath the belly of a waiting Mosquito.

hundred feet above the ground to widen the effects of the resulting blast. Four Lancasters carried the bombs; three were dropped successfully and the fourth jettisoned in the sea.

Losses throughout February were low: five aircraft were missing in total, three from 83 Squadron and one each from 7, 35 and 156 Squadrons. Among the 83 Squadron losses was the crew of Squadron Leader Samuel Robinson DFM that included the squadron's gunnery leader, thirty-five-year-old Squadron Leader Ernest Simpson DFM. The month was also a busy one in terms of awards. Among the usual assortment of DSOs, DFCs and DFMs for deserving aircrew, there also appears the first ever Conspicuous Gallantry Medal (CGM) awarded to an airman. Although the date of the award in the ORB is February 2, it actually relates to an incident in December. The recipient, Flight Sergeant Leslie Wallace, was recognised for his role in bringing back his crippled bomber after it was subjected to no less than five nightfighter attacks. His actions included extinguishing a fire that had taken hold near the bomb bay, despite being wounded in the leg.

The CGM for NCOs was second only to the Victoria Cross for operational flying against the enemy. It was fitting that it went to an airman of Pathfinder Force.

MARCH

Weather conditions varied considerably in March, and although Pathfinder Force was busy at the beginning and at the end, the middle was punctuated by constant delays, postponements and cancellations. On ten nights, headquarters received the relevant forms authorising operations only to have those orders rescinded a few hours later. Operations could take many hours before being finally 'scrubbed', and the waiting placed tremendous strain on the crews, however experienced.

But March was to see a significant change in the direction of Bomber Command. The preference for naval targets was superseded by new orders: the Battle of the Ruhr was about to begin.

The battle started, officially, on March 5, but not before the bombers had paid their respects

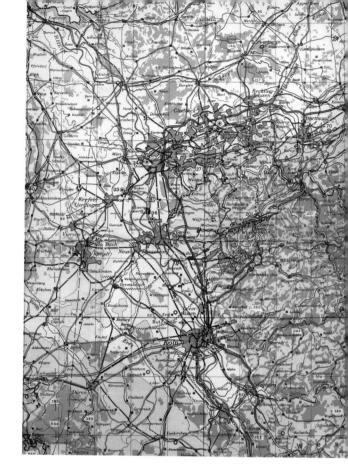

The Ruhr as represented on an observer's map.

to Berlin on the night of March 1/2 and Hamburg on 3/4. Further tactics again were evolved. For the raid on Berlin, H2S-equipped Stirlings and Halifaxes dropped yellow route markers at Bützow for main force and red flares twelve miles short of the aiming point. Red TIs were then dropped on the aiming point itself. On the return trip, special aircraft were detailed to drop four-pound incendiaries at Celle to mark the correct track home.

Although the timing of the attack was good, the concentration was poor, with the majority of bombs falling in the southwest suburbs. Ironically, some of the bombs landed on the Telefunken works where the H2S set recently recovered from the crashed 7 Squadron Stirling was being assessed. The set was completely destroyed. Any advantage to the RAF was, however, short-lived. That same night, another set was retrieved from the wreckage of a 35 Squadron Halifax, and the analysis immediately resumed. The Halifax, flown by Squadron Leader Peter Elliott, was the only PFF aircraft lost that night.

The attack on Hamburg was less successful. On this occasion, white TIs were dropped on the enemy coast to assist navigation, followed by yellow TIs, as a preliminary warning, fifteen miles short of the target and red TIs on the aiming point. Further white TIs were dropped to mark the route home, and all TIs were backed up in various shades. Theory was one thing; in practice four PFF aircraft were obliged to return early with technical failures and one Stirling bombed an aerodrome near Joldelund owing to the failure of its kit. Of those that did drop their markers, all appeared to release their TIs on the wrong bend in the river that were then erroneously backed up. Given the clear weather conditions, there could be no excuses, and Bennett's wrath could be felt the length and breadth of 8 Group stations.

It was with a sense of relief, therefore, that Pathfinder Force had an opportunity to prove its worth only a few nights later, and in spectacular fashion.

Essen was at the very heart of the Ruhr, which in turn was at the centre of Germany's industrial might and home to the giants such as Krupps – the famous steel works. Deal a hammer blow to the Ruhr, it was argued, and you would effectively cripple German industry – one that was turning out thousands of guns and tanks to fulfil Hitler's Lebensraum fantasy. Paralyse Germany's ability to wage war, and the war was won.

Pathfinders, it should be mentioned, were no strangers to the Ruhr. Perfectly within Oboe range, the Mosquitoes of 109 Squadron had carried out nuisance raids

A Caterpillar was given to anyone saved by one of Leslie Irvin's parachutes. The eyes varied in colour depending on what gemstones were available at the time.

A YOUNG MAN'S GAME?

Pathfinders attracted a diverse range of volunteers, young and old. One previously highlighted among the more veteran personnel was Aircraftman Louis Pakenham-Walsh, a Royal Flying Corps lieutenant who had the distinction of being reported 'Missing' in February 1918 but two months later was awarded the *Croix de Guerre*. Shortly after the war he received the DFC for his work as an observer spotting for enemy shipping in the Mediterranean. Although too old to fly, he volunteered and was accepted for ground duties with PFF.

Another was Stanley 'Pop' Watts AFM, a First World War baloonatic and post-war member of Alan Cobham's Flying Circus. 'Pop' was a veteran of the Royal Naval Air Service (RNAS) in 1916.

Jim Rogers was far from typical of PFF aircrew, having learned to fly in 1926 and then retrained as an air gunner in 1940.

As an experienced airman, he was seconded to the Aeroplane and Armament Experimental Establishment (A&AEE) at Boscombe Down and played a key role introducing the Handley Page Halifax into operational service and training the new generation of flight engineers required in four-engined 'heavies'. Posted to 35 Squadron, he was killed flying with Squadron Leader Peter Elliott DFC on March 1, 1943 – one of the oldest airmen to lose his life in the Second World War.

A third example is that of Pilot Officer Jim Rogers, who learned to fly in 1926. With the outbreak of war, and as a member of the RAFVR, he qualified as an air gunner, flying his first operation against the enemy with 311 (Czech) Squadron on June 24, 1940. He claimed a probable Bf109 on operations to Bremen in October, as a gunner to a Flight Lieutenant Percy Pickard (the 'star' of the wartime documentary, Target for Tonight). Another operation was flown to Mannheim with Squadron Leader Tom Kirby Green – one of the 'fifty' murdered following The Great Escape in March 1944.

Taken off operations in November, a stint at Central Gunnery School (Warmwell) saw his talents recognised with promotion to gunnery leader and a posting to 300 (Polish) Squadron.

By January 1943, Rogers had again been posted, this time to 103 Squadron, staying only two months before finally arriving at 156 Squadron, PFF. His regular skipper was Squadron Leader Brian Duigan DSO, DFC & Bar, flying primarily as rear gunner with the occasional stint in the mid upper turret. It was with Duigan when returning from operations to Dortmund that he was obliged to bale out, becoming an instant member of the Caterpillar Club, his life having been saved by a parachute. At the time he had flown not less than forty-four operations and Duigan seventy-five.

for several weeks, with major towns and cities such as Bochum, Ruhrort, Rheinhausen, Düsseldorf, Dortmund and Duisberg regularly appearing on the orders from Bomber Command HQ. Not all of the attacks were successful, of course. Frequently the ORB refers to Mosquitoes turning back or bombing secondary targets as a result of 'technical failure of their precision device'. But they were learning.

On March 5, orders came through for a combined Mosquito/heavy-bomber attack to open the new battle, with Essen as the selected target. Notwithstanding the early return of two heavies through technical failure, and three of the eight Mosquitoes, the attack was billed as 'an outstanding success'. Thin cloud and the usual haze prevented the bombers from seeing the ground detail but the markers were accurately placed and well backed up, resulting in a very heavy concentration around the aiming point, and enormous fires were reported over a large area. Post-raid reconnaissance photos would reveal the extent of the damage: more than 160 acres of destruction.

Opposition was scattered, and in the words of the ORB the defences 'appeared to be overwhelmed by the volume of the attack'. However they still took their toll. Some fourteen aircraft were lost, including two from PFF. Among the missing was Wing Commander Stanley Hookway DFC, who had, shortly before, been in temporary command of 156 Squadron while the incumbent CO, Wing Commander Tommy Rivett-Carnac (known affectionately as 'nuts and bolts') had been in hospital.

Nuremberg was next on the list, receiving the attention of more than 300 main force bombers guided to their target by a large force of forty-one Stirlings, Halifaxes and Lancasters from PFF's heavy-bomber squadrons.

Nuremberg was outside of Oboe range, and so the Pathfinders had to rely on H2S. Never as reliable as Oboe, the resultant bombing was more scattered, although PFF declared themselves satisfied with their night's work, stating that a good proportion of the attack fell on the town. They were not wrong. The M.A.N and Siemens factories were both badly damaged and more than 600 buildings destroyed.

The evening will be remembered for a bizarre incident that befell Sergeant Derek Spanton, mid upper gunner in a 7 Squadron aircraft. Returning from the raid, and low on fuel, the captain (Pilot Officer Lionel Toupin) ordered the crew to bale out over the Channel, rather than risk a ditching without power. Spanton, however, had failed to receive the instruction and found himself alone as the aircraft drifted – pilotless – over the English coast. Only then discovering his predicament – and with discretion being the better part of valour – he too baled out and landed safely. As it happens, he was the only crew member to survive. The rest were missing, presumed drowned. Among the others lost that night was Flight Lieutenant John Trench DSO.

Both the Pathfinders and main force were foxed by faulty met winds and arrived late for an attack on Munich on March 9/10. They still did considerable damage, however, notably to the BMW works that were churning out engines for Luftwaffe aircraft. Five aircraft returned home early with technical problems, and another with engine trouble opted to frighten an aerodrome near Ulm rather than bring its bombs back. One Halifax, which suffered a hang up (when a bomb failed to release) finally offloaded its cargo on a flak concentration at Saarbrücken. The following night, some Pathfinders and all of main force were again late to attack Stuttgart, therefore the raid lacked the fluency of previous operations. Decoy fires (reported for the first time by returning crews) also contributed to mixed results, with much of the bombing falling harmlessly (or comparatively so) in the fields and villages to the southwest of the city.

The Pathfinders were back to their best for the second attack on Essen on March 12/13, the combination of Oboe and H2S proving beyond any doubt that a successful formula had been found for hitting the Ruhr. Somewhat pointedly, perhaps, the author of the ORB report for this raid talks of the Mosquito bombing by means of Oboe being 'very accurate and on time'. Backing up, he writes, was also very well concentrated 'and the attack became a great success, a solid rectangle of fires were produced which could be seen from the Dutch coast'. After main force had departed, and a suitable time elapsed, two Mosquitoes arrived 'to discourage any surviving firefighters'.

Operations to Berlin and Augsburg were cancelled because of fog, and it was not until the night of 21/22 that the weather conditions improved sufficiently for Bomber Command to mount a raid on the French port of St Nazaire at the fourth time of asking. Bright moonlight and good visibility contributed to a highly successful and concentrated raid.

Weather again disrupted planned attacks on Wilhelmshaven, Kiel, and Cologne, before clearing to allow an operation against Duisberg. Mosquitoes dropped flares at the release point and at regular intervals throughout the attack after loosing warning flares five minutes and two-and-a-half minutes beforehand on track. Owing to technical failures (a now common annotation in the ORB)

Duisberg. The largest inland port in Germany and a particular favourite of the Bomber Command C-in-C throughout his tenure.

only four out of the nine Mosquitoes taking part dropped their flares, and although this proved sufficient to enable the raid to begin it meant there was a long gap without any marking and the attack soon became scattered. Indeed it was not a happy day for the Mosquito boys: one managed to drop his flare more than twenty miles *north* of Duisberg; another, flown by Flight Lieutenant Leslie Ackland DFC, with Warrant Officer Frederick Strouts DFC as his navigator, failed to return. (Ackland had won his DFC with 156 Squadron.) The pilot was last heard saying that he would have to ditch, and he is believed to have landed in the sea off Southwold. The next day, no fewer than nine PFF aircraft took part in a search for their missing comrades. Nothing was ever found.

It was a busy end to the month with two further attacks on Berlin (on 27/28 and again on 29/30) punctuated by a further raid on St Nazaire and a Mosquito-led sortie to Bochum. In sporting parlance, none of these attacks troubled the scorers with the exception perhaps of the attack on St Nazaire that left large fires. A single Mosquito of 109 Squadron flown by Flying Officer Ken Wolstenholme (later the famous world cup commentator) attacked Dortmund on the night of 29/30 in order to carry out 'a technical test'. It managed to drop its markers from 30,000ft to within thirty yards of the target. The 'test' was deemed satisfactory!

Losses for March had been high: 7 Squadron had lost six – the hardest to suffer. Among the missing was Squadron Leader Michael Thwaites DFC, a pre-war volunteer reservist who had with him that night the 'regular' crew of 'Hamish' Mahaddie – the man who perhaps more than any other typified the fighting spirit of Pathfinder Force. Between them the crew could call upon two DFMs and no fewer than six DFCs – experience that would become increasingly difficult to replace.

The six aircraft lost could so easily have been seven: Flying Officer S. Baker's Stirling was hit by flak over the target area, and on landing at Oakington the aircraft swung off the runway as the undercarriage collapsed. (Among the crew was the navigator, Flight Lieutenant Philip Coldwell DFM, who was killed in action in May 1944, by which time he had added the DSO to his list of

Wing Commander Hamish Mahaddie (seated) and his 7 Squadron crew. Tragically, the crew was lost on their first trip without their skipper.

gallantry awards.)

At Warboys, 156 Squadron also lost a number of experienced men, including the squadron navigation leader Squadron Leader William Ball DFC. Ball, a New Zealander, had been flying with Flight Lieutenant Leslie Goodley DFC when they were obliged to leave their aircraft over Munich.

But perhaps the most telling figure in the monthly summary is the number of aircraft forced to abandon their attacks owing to technical failure. Some fifty-three aircraft had returned early, no doubt much to Bennett's annoyance, especially since such early returns impacted directly on the effectiveness of PFF marking and the success of the overall attack.

APRIL

April 1943 proved to be a significant month for Pathfinder Force, although another disappointing one in terms of the weather impacting on the frequency and efficiency of operations. No operations were possible on thirteen nights and cancelled on four other occasions. Of the attacks that did take place, several were marred by high winds and clouds.

The ORB details attacks on Essen (twice), Duisberg (three times) and one raid each on Kiel, Frankfurt, Stuttgart and Mannheim. The other targets to receive PFF attention were La Spezia which was attacked twice (the second time with excellent results) and the longer haul to Pilsen and Stettin – the latter proving to be the most successful attack beyond the range of Oboe during the whole of the Battle of the Ruhr. Somewhat defensively, however, the anonymous ORB author at that time has written: 'Owing to the weather conditions only a few of these attacks could be rated as large successes, but previous to the formation of Pathfinder Force, it is doubtful they could have been attacked at all.'

To give the Pathfinders due credit, subsequent reports suggest that some of the attacks were

BENNETT'S CHIEF 'HORSE THIEF'

Hamish Mahaddie is a name synonymous with Pathfinder Force. A former Halton apprentice, he qualified as a pilot in 1935 and flew in the Middle East with 55 Squadron. On the outbreak of war he flew his first tour of operations with 77 Squadron, and after a period instructing was posted to 7 Squadron on Stirlings, winning the DSO, DFC, AFC and Czech military cross in early 1943, all within the space of thirty-two days. He rose in rank from sergeant to group captain in little more than two years.

But it is in his role as Bennett's group training inspector, his chief's 'horse thief', that Mahaddie

is perhaps best remembered. Officially he was solely responsible for the selection and training of all future Pathfinders. At a practical level this meant touring all of the main force stations and lecturing on Pathfinder techniques, and for those who suggested that Pathfinder marking was sometimes astray, his standard rejoinder was 'come and have a go if you think you can do any better'. Main force crews that constantly achieved an aiming point photograph were carefully monitored, and although there was, at first, some reluctance among squadron commanders to part with their 'star' crews, they ultimately relented.

Only once did Mahaddie famously meet his match when he thought he had secured the services of Dave Shannon, a young ace pilot, only to have his protégé stolen from under his nose by Wing Commander Guy Gibson. Gibson at the time had virtual carte blanche over the choice of crew to join his 'special' squadron then being formed. Only later would Mahaddie learn the reasons for Gibson's trump card.

A pewter tankard owned by Hamish Mahaddie, one of the most memorable Pathfinder characters, when a humble LAC at flying training school.

more successful than first thought. The first attack on Essen (April 3/4) produced some accurate bombing and the raid on the city later in the month (April 30/May 1) also resulted in 'new' damage, notably to Krupps. Thick cloud ruined the attacks on Kiel (April 4/5), Duisberg (April 8/9) and Frankfurt (April 10/11), and the raid on Stuttgart (April 14/15) is noted as being a good example of how 'creepback' (the phenomenon of bombs falling short of the target, sometimes by several miles, often as a result of bomb aimers having an 'itchy thumb' on the bomb release) could lead to the target being missed altogether.

On the day of the 15th, Pathfinder Force received news that the first of its reinforcements would soon be arriving in the shape of two new heavy bomber squadrons: 97 Squadron (5 Group) and 405 Squadron RCAF (from the newly-established 6 Group). On the same day,

Attacks on German night-fighter airfields intensified as losses to the bomber stream increased. The accuracy of PFF marking is evidenced by the two bomb explosions on the runway (centre right) at St Trond, August 15, 1944.

Oakington and Bourn were officially transferred from 3 Group administration to 8 Group, and RAF Gransden similarly became part of the PFF family.

As it happens, it was three days later, on the afternoon of April 18 that the first of fifteen Lancasters of 97 Squadron began landing at Bourn from its previous home at Woodhall Spa. At the time under the command of Wing Commander Graham Jones DFC (later DSO), this was the start of a seesaw period for 97 that would see it later snatched back by 5 Group, from whence it came, in an episode in which arguably neither Bennett nor the 5 Group Commander Sir Ralph Cochrane emerged with much dignity.

Within twenty-four hours, eighteen Halifax bombers of 405 Squadron took off from RAF Leeming for the short hop to its new home at Gransden. With the distinction of being a Canadian squadron, this raised an awkward principle for Bennett, in that he had insisted from the outset that there would be no segregation or differentiation in PFF.

When asked at one stage by the Australians if they could have an all-Australian PFF squadron, the request was steadfastly refused. Known as the Vancouver squadron, 405, however, was different, because it remained affiliated to a complete main force group. The compromise was that the crews on the squadron could not be more than fifty percent Canadian, although Bennett agreed to the squadron always being commanded by a Canadian. Here he struck lucky, since 405 Squadron arrived with a very determined officer, Wing Commander Johnny Fauquier, at the helm. He started by telling existing crews that the days of booze and cards were over, and would later achieve notoriety and respect in equal measure in PFF for his uncompromising style of leadership, rejecting more new crews sent to him than any other commander.

Meantime, the attack on the Skoda Works at Pilsen on April 16/17 proved costly, both to Bomber Command and PFF specifically. Some thirty-six out of an attacking force of 327 were lost, including five Pathfinders. One of the pilots missing, Pilot Officer 'Sammy' Milton DFM, was on his forty-fifth operation. It was a disappointing conclusion to an unsuccessful attack. Enemy nightfighters were said to have been 'very active in the bright moonlight' and although only two indecisive combats were reported by Pathfinder crews, no fewer than fifteen enemy aircraft were sighted.

Nightfighters were also in evidence over Stettin (April 20/21), with various air gunners in 7 Squadron having a busy – and successful – night, none more so than Flying Officer Baker (who had pushed his luck only a few weeks earlier). Baker was twenty miles north-west of Stettin when his mid upper gunner, Sergeant Christopher Thornhill, sighted a Bf109 heading in the opposite direction – but not for long. Soon it was engaged in battle, one which it lost when Thornhill and

Canadian Wing Commander Johnny Fauquier. The most brave and determined of types.

TYPICAL AIR FORCE

"Fauquier selected me to be his navigator. Typical air force: I had not even flown at night never mind navigated an aircraft since being knocked down in Norway over a year before, yet here I was navigating the CO in an historic moment in the squadron's history."

IAN HEWITT DFC & BAR NAVIGATOR. 35 AND 405 SQUADRONS.

IT'S GOOD TO TALK

Squadron Leader Jack Watts had just returned from 'escapees leave' having been shot down on a raid to Tobruk, swimming five miles ashore and spending four days behind enemy lines before being rescued. Reporting to RCAF Overseas HQ in London, he wangled a posting to the conversion flight at Topcliffe for a flight commander position at a new Canadian squadron in the process of being formed:

"By that time, I had learned about the existence of Pathfinder Force. Donald Bennett had been my squadron commander and I had been his navigator and bombing leader at 10 Squadron before we flew out to the Middle East. I immediately asked to be transferred to PFF, which I understood was a volunteer force. My request was refused by the senior personnel staff officer at 6 Group HQ, presumably since I was programmed to be a flight commander in the new RCAF squadron.

"Since my operational experience was out of date, I obtained permission for a liaison visit to PFF to be brought up-to-date on current tactics. At Wyton, I signed on for the navigation briefing and extended my stay by enrolling on the bomb aimer briefing as well. It was the next morning that I had a telephone call. It was Wing Commander Shepherd the group intelligence officer who had also been our intelligence officer at Leeming where we had all been serving previously. He said that Bennett had learned I was on base and had asked that I come to see him. I was surprised since we had not been that close but 'Shep' told me he was serious and that he had mellowed with the addition of the 'wide one'. 'Shep' sent a car and when I arrived at HQ I was immediately escorted to the commander's office.

"When I entered the office, Bennett rose to his feet and greeted me with a warm handshake and a cup of coffee. He was apparently aware of my escapade at Tobruk as he asked me how I was feeling and was I fit. When I said that I was fit and told him about the 6 Group refusal to assign me to PFF, he ceased the conversation, picked up the telephone and called his SPSO, Hamish Mahaddie. In terse fashion, he briefed Mahaddie on the situation and said 'Yes and call me right back!'

"We continued with our coffee and conversation for what seemed to be only a few minutes before the telephone rang. Bennett picked it up and responded with 'Right, thank you', and hung up. After a few moments, while we finished the conversation, Bennett simply said: 'Oh, Jack, by the way, you are now in PFF. 6 Group has agreed to transfer you to the RCAF Squadron, 405, here in PFF. However, now that you are in PFF, I will decide where you serve. And I have a special assignment for you on 109 Squadron on Oboe.' With that, the interview was over, and I was on my way to RAF Marham and 109 Squadron."

JACK WATTS
DSO, DFC AND BAR
NAVIGATOR. 109 SQUADRON. 100+ OPS.

the rear gunner, Flight Sergeant James Robbins DFM, conspired to shoot it down in flames. Both gunners, and the wireless operator, saw the fighter hit the ground.

That same night another PFF crew was also in the wars – and for a short time out of them – when Pilot Officer McDonald was obliged to ditch off the coast of Sweden having been badly shot about by a Ju88. The crew was interned and later returned home to resume their tour.

McDonald was lucky; a great many Pathfinder crews that month were not. A total of twenty-eight aircraft were recorded as missing in April, including eight each from 7 and 156 Squadrons. 83 Squadron also lost six, including three in one night. 405 Squadron, which with 97 Squadron had commenced PFF operations on April 26/27, also lost its first aircraft, a Halifax II, shot down

MASTER BOMBERS – THE CANADIANS

Of all the Canadian master bombers, there are perhaps three that stand out in particular: Johnny Fauquier, Reg Lane and George Grant.

Group Captain Johnny Fauquier DSO & two Bars, DFC was the first Royal Canadian Air Force officer to lead a bomber squadron on operations overseas and the only member of the RCAF to win the DSO three times. A bush pilot before the war, his experience meant he was held back as

an instructor and did not fly on operations until October 1941, becoming commanding officer of 405 Squadron the following February. His long association with the squadron included taking part in the famous Peenemünde raid as deputy master bomber, making no fewer than seventeen passes over the target. By June 1944 he was promoted air commodore, but opted to drop a rank and return to operations as commanding officer of 617 Squadron for his third tour. His reputation as a perfectionist who demanded only the very best won him supporters and detractors in equal number, but his operational record and 'press-on' determination were second to none.

Don Bennett (left) and Johnny Fauquier with the Lancaster 'Ruhr Express'. Fauquier was, at the time, officer commanding 405 Squadron RCAF.

Group Captain Reg Lane DSO, DFC & Bar similarly began operating in October 1941 with 35 Squadron, his first trip to bomb Berlin. A veteran of attacks against the German battle cruisers *Scharnhorst* and *Gneisenau*, and the battleship *Tirpitz*, he also flew in the first of the 1,000-bomber raids in May 1942, completing his first tour the following month. Returning for a second tour, he flew eighteen months of continuous bombing operations, and was awarded the DSO and the job of flying the first Canadian-built Lancaster – the Ruhr Express – from Canada to the UK to the delight of the press. Appointed to command 405 Squadron for his third tour, on one raid as master bomber he circled Berlin for up to forty minutes while directing an attack.

Group Captain George Grant, determined to join the RAF at the first opportunity, arrived from Canada in the summer of 1939 and soon after joined Coastal Command. An unremarkable early career changed dramatically when he became a founder member of 109 Squadron, taking part in some of the very first Oboe trials and operations and being awarded the DFC. A spell at 156 Squadron on Lancasters earned him the DSO as 'a leader whose fine qualities have impressed all' before he returned to 109 Squadron in May 1944 as its commanding officer.

Two other Canadian Pathfinders worthy of note include Jack Watts and Squadron Leader James Dow DSO, DFC, both remarkable for completing more than 100 bomber operations.

over Essen. The pilot, Flight Lieutenant Herbert Atkinson, was killed. Co-incidentally, Atkinson was English; his navigator who died with him, Flying Officer William Hardy, was Canadian, as were the six remaining aircrew who survived to become prisoners of war.

Among the most notable Pathfinders to lose their lives that month was Squadron Leader The Hon Brian Grimston DFC, son of the 4th Earl of Verulam. The 'Honourable Grimmy', as he was known, was described as being so tall that he could barely fit into the cockpit of the 156 Squadron Wellingtons he had flown in 1942, and was considerably more comfortable in a Lanc. His family was to have the pain of losing another son, Bruce, whilst serving with Coastal Command the following year.

Norry Gilroy (second left) and
Joe Patient (second from right).
An inseparable partnership who
survived their fair share of scrapes.

THE WEATHER MEN

"The purpose of 1409 (Met) Flight was to provide essential meteorological information for RAF Bomber Command (and the USAAF) in advance of a planned bombing operation. Our missions were codenamed 'Pampa flights (operations)' – derived from photo-reconnaissance and meteorological photography aircraft. At the time that my navigator, Norry Gilroy, and I arrived, the flight was based at Oakington before moving to Wyton in January 1944.

"All of the crews were placed on a duty roster. When you were within two of the top, you were obliged to stay on base, and when your turn came Bennett said that we needed to be in the air within twenty minutes of receiving the call. We usually managed it in thirty. On one occasion, Bennett took Norry's nav bag and said he would be flying with me. We got away in nineteen minutes, and Bennett started giving me the first course to steer while I was still taxiing! Bennett said: 'You see, you can get airborne within twenty minutes,' to which I replied: 'Yes it is possible, Sir, but not everyone is a D.C.T. Bennett!'

"Weather fronts obviously moved, so our role was to bring back information on the conditions our bomber crews could expect when they got to the target. This meant flying to where the weather was 'then', on the basis of where it would be 'later'. We reported on cloud levels, temperatures, icing conditions etc. The latter could be especially dangerous, as it meant deliberately flying into the thickest CuNimb cloud and measuring the icing index – in short, timing how long it took before ice began appearing on the wings and the windscreen, and then getting out before things became really hairy.

"Then we would get home as fast as possible to report what we had found. Norry would jump out of the aircraft and get straight on the phone to HQ. The call was scrambled, and other Groups would be listening in. There was the occasional question but that was all. We once were obliged to land at RAF Pershore, some way from home, and Norry was in a hurry to get the weather report to HQ. A senior officer (I think it was the station commander) called after Norry and said: 'I'll have you know that junior officers salute senior officers on this station', to which Norry shook the officer's hand and replied: 'Glad to hear it'.

"In Bennett's memoirs, he says that 1409 (Met) Flight flew high and fast, but the danger was extreme, and it was a nerve-racking job for the crews concerned. I agree. I consider that my time on met flight was more dangerous than my time on 139 Squadron."

JOE PATIENT DFC
139 SQUADRON AND 1409 (MET) FLIGHT. FIFTY-NINE OPS.

A similar fate befell the family of Squadron Leader Raymond McCarthy of 7 Squadron, shot down over Stuttgart. One brother Morris, a nineteen-year-old pilot with 77 Squadron, had been killed in February 1942 and another, Robert, an infantryman, had also already been lost on active service. (Raymond and Morris are buried in the same grave.) There were many other families who would share such grief before the war was out. The death of a child was, of course, an intolerable strain on any parent, but must have been especially painful for the mother and father of Sergeant Patrick Brougham Faddy. He was flight engineer to Pilot Officer Harald Andersen, shot down on the night of April 16/17. An ex-Halton apprentice (Entry 41), Brougham Faddy was only eighteen.

The Mosquito boys also suffered the loss of one of its crews – Flying Officer John Walker and Charles McKenna took off from Wyton as one of ten Mosquitoes detailed to mark Duisberg and crashed almost immediately in Hartford village.

As well as the two new squadrons arriving to join PFF, two new units were also formed that month. The first was 1499 (Bomber) Gunnery Flight at Wyton equipped with six Miles Martinets – an aircraft specifically designed for towing drogue targets for air gunners to practice air-to-air firing. The second unit was considerably more significant. 521 (Met) Squadron at Bircham Newton hived off some of its aircraft and personnel to form 1409 (Met) Flight at Oakington. Pathfinder Force would now have it own weather-reconnaissance unit whose feats would become legendary in the annals of Pathfinder history. Thenceforward, 1409 (Met) Flight could be relied upon to undertake daylight reconnaissance flights ahead of virtually every Bomber Command raid to Germany until the end of the war, as well as a large number of flights for the American Eighth Air Force. The task of commanding the new unit was given to Squadron Leader Denys Braithwaite DFC who was very shortly afterwards succeeded by Squadron Leader The Hon Philip Cunliffe-Lister.

MAY

Only seven large raids were carried out in May, all on the Ruhr: Duisberg; Bochum; Düsseldorf; Essen and Wuppertal were visited once and Dortmund twice. All of the attacks were made with Mosquito aircraft marking the target with TIs, either ground or sky markers, by means of Oboe, backed up by other Pathfinder bombers. Undoubtedly the Ruhr suffered heavily, according to the ORB records, and it would have been worse had not weather conditions caused the cancellation of attacks on eight other nights or led to the Pathfinders and Bomber Command being stood down on several other occasions. The issue was compounded by a period of full moon making the threat of nightfighter attack too risky to conduct operations.

Attacks were planned for Duisberg for May 1, 2 and 3 but all cancelled. In the event, the first successful departure was for Dortmund on May 4/5. Eight Mosquitoes were to ground mark the aiming point with green TIs; these were then to be backed up with red TIs dropped by twenty-two Lancasters and two Halifaxes. The Mossies also dropped yellow TIs on track as a preliminary marker. Six Stirlings, fifteen Halifaxes and eighteen Lancasters were then to act as 'supporters', bombing with main force to get the show under way.

There was little by way of any cloud over Dortmund and just a slight ground haze. As such, the aiming point was accurately marked and a good concentration of TIs accumulated around the target. Unfortunately some of the 'reds' dropped about three miles to the northwest attracted a certain amount of bombing and there was also some undershooting (the bombs falling short) but otherwise a very successful attack developed. Two large explosions were reported, the first one fifteen minutes after the assault began 'being one of the largest ever seen'. Fires were left burning that could be seen from the Zuiderzee on return.

But any joy felt by the returning crews was short-lived. Having flown through defences 'of the usual Ruhr standard', the greatest danger was yet to come. The weather had closed in over the UK, making wide-scale diversions necessary. The situation was then further complicated when the

THE PATHFINDER HIERARCHY

Pathfinder crews carried out a series of duties that evolved as the tactics, techniques and technologies associated with Pathfinder marking developed throughout the war.

Almost without exception, every novice crew started out as a **Supporter**. They were not, at first, trusted with markers. A supporter's principal responsibility was to arrive on time, and help the marker aircraft in ensuring there were sufficient bombers over the target to commence the attack.

Ahead of them flew the **Windowers**, crews tasked with dropping the ingenious strips of silver foil to confound the enemy radar and give the marker crews a better chance of making through to the target unmolested. (In the later stages of the war, windowing responsibility fell to the LNSF crews and served a dual purpose, making smaller raids appear as though they may have been main force attacks.)

Route Markers dropped target indicators at critical turning points to help keep the bomber 'stream' together and, if required, about twenty miles short of the target in the event that main force was obliged to execute a 'timed run'.

Blind Illuminators used H2S to navigate to the target and then drop flares to illuminate the target area so that the **Visual Markers** could mark the target by making maximum use of their MkXIV bombsight.

The most able of these crews were designated **Primary Visual Markers**, and carried with them a highly specialist air bomber. In the event that the target was covered in cloud or otherwise obscured (industrial haze often hid targets in the Ruhr), **Blind Markers** used either H2S or Oboe to drop their target indicators or Skymarkers in the event of a Wanganui attack.

Backers-up did as the name suggested, estimating the mean point of impact (MPI) of all of the primary markers and then aiming their TIs in the middle. **Recenterers** arrived over the target part way through the raid to overcome issues with creepback, dropping markers with a slight overshoot to bring main force back on target.

The raids were ultimately led by the **Master Bomber**, ably assisted by the **Deputy Master Bomber** who remained close at hand lest something should happen to his leader. The master bomber could at any stage call for the help of his various specialists in ensuring the raid progressed and was completed in good order.

In the last few months of the war, when the bombers were often hitting targets within 1,000 or so yards of their own troops, a new duty of **Long Stop** was introduced. The long stop was a grand master bomber whose role was to monitor and if necessary cancel any marking or indeed whole attacks if there was a danger to the troops on the ground. He might indicate with yellow markers a clear line beyond which his attacking force must not bomb.

Bennett's rule for all of his marker crews was consistent: if they were unclear as to their aim or their target, they were not to attack. Better to bring their target indicators and bombs home, than cause a disaster.

---

first returning aircraft to Graveley crashed, and another blocked the runway at Wyton. In total, six Pathfinder aircraft were lost to accidents: two from 35 Squadron – captains Sergeant Williams and Flight Sergeant Cobb; two from 405 Squadron – Flying Officer Weiser and Pilot Officer Harty; one each from 97 Squadron (Sergeant Reilly) and 156 Squadron (Squadron Leader Duigan). Behind the bare facts, of course, hide various tales of misfortune, misadventure and tragic bad luck.

Whereas Sergeant Williams and his crew ran out of fuel and baled out safely, Flight Sergeant Joseph Cobb crashed, killing all bar the rear gunner. Sergeant Anthony Reilly had been obliged to divert from Bourn to Waterbeach, and while coming in to land overshot the runway and collided with a parked Stirling, killing himself in the process and injuring three of his crew. This was 97 Squadron's first loss since assuming Pathfinder operations. Squadron Leader Brian Duigan, with little fuel remaining in the tanks and no sign of the airfield in poor visibility, ordered his crew to take to their 'chutes. All survived, albeit two were injured including the veteran, Gunnery Leader Rogers. Flying Officer William Weiser was lucky to survive his crash landing, having collided with a tree in heavy mist and Pilot Officer James Harty executed a highly professional crash landing having been forced to turn for home early after heavy damage caused by flak.

But as well as the aircraft and crews lost to accidents, there were also four 'planes missing due to flak and fighters. There was a remarkable escape for the pilot and flight engineer of a 156 Squadron Lancaster hit by flak over the target. With Flight Lieutenant Alastair Lang at the controls and Sergeant J.L. Clark at his side, the aircraft entered an uncontrollable dive and broke apart. They survived, but the remaining crew were killed.

There was tragedy too for 83 Squadron who lost a young sergeant pilot, John Leigh, and his crew over the target area. Flying with them was the squadron's commanding officer, Wing Commander James Gillman, who had taken over from Crichton-Biggie in February 1943. (Between March 5 and June 23, 83 Squadron lost nineteen Lancasters and crews over Europe and only twenty-five men survived.)

As for the results of the night's operations, five Stirlings, eleven Halifaxes, thirty-eight Lancasters and nine Mosquitoes attacked the target while one Halifax and one Lancaster returned early and two others jettisoned their loads because of technical trouble. One Mosquito brought its bombs back. Another of the PFF's experimental attacks was undertaken that same night on Rheine. Only five out of the eight aircraft succeeded in bombing the target.

There was bad news for 1409 (Met) Flight on the evening of May 9 when one of its aircraft was reported missing, shot down by an enemy Focke Wulf FW190 fighter at around 25,000ft over Eindhoven. It had been undertaking weather reconnaissance for a planned raid on Duisberg later that night, an operation that was subsequently cancelled on account of cloud, rain and increasingly strong winds. Both the pilot and navigator survived.

It was not until May 12/13 that Bomber Command was able to operate in strength again, with Pathfinders contributing no fewer than ninety-eight aircraft to yet another attack on Duisberg, the largest inland port in Germany. Marking was accurate and well backed up, with many fires and explosions being reported, notably one very large explosion about fifteen minutes into the attack. As the intensity of the bombing increased, the target became obscured by smoke, a not uncommon occurrence, and later results were difficult to determine.

What became clear afterwards, however, was that a large amount of destruction had been done with enormous numbers of buildings destroyed and ships sunk or damaged. Indeed so much demolition was reported that the commanders expressed themselves finally satisfied and no further attacks were mounted on this target at this time. Photographs of the attack and other intelligence suggested that more than eighty-five percent of the crews who claimed to have bombed the target were within three miles of the aiming point, and eighty percent of the TIs were plotted within two miles. Bomber Command had come a long way in the two years since Butt's devastating report.

Four Pathfinder aircraft were missing, including the 156 Squadron Lancaster of Squadron Leader Lighton Verdon-Roe DFC and the 83 Squadron Lancaster of Flight Lieutenant Leslie Rickinson DFC. Verdon-Roe was the son of the famous aircraft designer and manufacturer Alliott Verdon-Roe whose name gave rise to the 'Avro' of Avro Lancaster fame. Lighton was flying one of his father's aircraft when he died. (Lighton's older brother Eric had been killed in action in 1941 as a squadron leader with 102 Squadron.)

Leslie Rickinson's aircraft sustained attacks from a large number of fighters and the rear gunner, Horace Plant, fancied he accounted for one of them. Not surprisingly, they were soon overwhelmed, and the pilot was at the point of baling out, standing on his seat attempting to

Lancaster 'N' Nuts looks an uninviting prospect at dispersal in the cold and wet.

A STRAIN ON AIRCRAFT AND CREWS

Flight Lieutenant Eric Wilkin came to Pathfinders having completed a first tour of operations with 115 Squadron, part of 3 Group. He flew first with a Canadian, Flight Lieutenant Donald McKechnie DFC, and later with Flying Officer John 'Flash' McCollah DFC & Bar.

"Bennett was very fond of training, so much so that we used to joke that 7 Squadron was in fact 7 Squadron OTU. In the mornings we would be up at half six for practice bombing on the ranges, because there was better visibility. Then we would pick up a fighter over Ipswich for a fighter affiliation exercise and then fly up to Bradford and find it using H2S (Bradford was notoriously difficult to see on H2S). We would next fly over to Morecambe Bay to fire at a drogue and finally return home by midday. Then we'd hand the aircraft over for another crew to train that afternoon. (Bennett once grounded all gunners when he produced his own theory on gun sighting; we were all obliged to attend his lecture and take a test before being awarded our Pathfinder badge.)

"Such training had consequences, especially in relation to the serviceability of the aircraft. On main force we had our own aircraft, but not so on Pathfinders. On the day we had a brush with a nightfighter, we were flying E-Easy. A 20mm cannon shell punctured a fuel tank but fortunately did not explode. Our rear gunner, 'Tiger' Smith, could not operate his turret because the hydraulics were u/s. When I pressed my gun buttons, only one gun fired and then only one round before it too packed up. After we landed, we discovered that when the previous crew had replaced the guns, they had plastered them in grease and this had frozen. The gun that did work only fired off one shot because the switch plate was held by a matchstick – rather than a stud – so when the matchstick broke the gun jammed. Bennett was so keen to get 'at it' that I am not sure he'd really thought through the strains that it placed on the aircraft and crews."

ERIC WILKIN DFC & BAR
AIR GUNNER. 7 SQUADRON. SEVENTY-THREE OPS.

open the escape hatch, when the aircraft exploded. Miraculously, the Australian navigator, Flight Lieutenant Horace Ransome DFC survived although severely injured.

Pathfinder expertise was divided on the night of May 13/14 between two targets: forty-five aircraft were detailed to mark and support a small attack on Bochum which started well but the ultimate success of which was not immediately obvious. One 405 Squadron Halifax was missing (Flying Officer Hugh Beattie). For the second attack, forty-six aircraft were required to lead a raid on the Skoda Works at Pilsen. The weather was good with no cloud and the factory was clearly identified in the light of the flares. The TIs appeared well positioned near the aiming point but smoke from the flares 'or possibly a smokescreen' made identification difficult. It later transpired that the weight of the attack fell in open fields. One 83 Squadron Lancaster was missing (Sergeant Anthony Renshaw).

The ORB for the period May 14 to May 22 uses the same phrase with unusual monotony: 'No operations tonight'. This did not mean, however, that there was no flying. Pathfinders used this period to train, practicing everything from cross-country navigation to bombing. Even with expert crews, training played a key role in everyday Pathfinder life.

Dortmund was again the target on May 23/24 in an attack comprising 826 aircraft, the largest non-1,000-bomber raid of the war to date and the largest in the Battle of the Ruhr. The Pathfinders arrived to find good weather conditions hampered only by a slight ground haze. The Mosquitoes dropped their red TIs accurately and were well backed up by the greens of their heavier colleagues. Defences were less than usual, allowing main force a comparatively free run over the target. Two Halifaxes were missing – one from 35 Squadron (Flying Officer Alain Harvey RAAF) and one from 405 Squadron (Sergeant J. Martin) to spoil an otherwise near-perfect attack.

Harvey, a twenty-two-year-old Australian, had been in the UK since August 1942, and had flown only a handful of trips with 10 and 76 Squadrons before arriving at Graveley. He had been on 35 Squadron for exactly a month when his aircraft was reported missing. Within his crew were Sergeants Charles Shields and Stanley Groom – both ex-Halton apprentices.

Unfortunately the Pathfinders could not repeat the success two nights running, for its next attack, on Düsseldorf, was an unmitigated failure. The weather, not surprisingly, was largely to blame, and although the Mosquitoes dropped their red markers accurately, they could not be seen by the backers-up and the first green TIs did not come down until a full sixteen minutes after the reds, and as a consequence the bombs appeared to be scattered everywhere except the aiming point!

Although opposition was described as 'negligible' they were not so benign

Alain Harvey (right) and his Wimpey crew, which included two Halton apprentices, probably while still at OTU.

THE HALTON CONNECTION

Bennett demanded the very best from his Pathfinders, and not surprisingly, a good many had started out as Halton apprentices, the famous Trenchard 'Brats'. A fair number became flight engineers, their in-depth knowledge and training in engines and airframes standing them in good stead; a good many also went on to become pilots, and the very best to become squadron and even station commanders.

Names such as: 'Paddy' Menaul – 'Groupie' at no fewer than three PFF stations; John Searby – the first recognised master bomber; Hamish Mahaddie – Bennett's chief 'recruiter'; Pat Connelly – an accomplished Pathfinder and later commandant of Halton; Reg Cox – who steadied the morale of 7 Squadron after losing three COs in quick succession; and Dennis Witt, a heavy-bomber pilot awarded the DSO to add to an already impressive list of decorations after 100 trips. All have passed into Pathfinder legend.

Other heavy-bomber boys who started their RAF service at Halton include Ted Stocker, a flight engineer with an incredible 108 operations to his name, all on four-engined aircraft.

The Mosquito boys also had their fair share of impressive alumni: Joe Northrop, for example, moved from four engines to two, commanding 692 Squadron and becoming an ace LNSF pilot; Harry Scott, a 109 Squadron navigator, flew more than 100 sorties as an Oboe specialist.

Wing Commander Joe Northrop was an ace pilot on two engines and four.

Two old 'Brats' who joined the RAF together in September 1930 as fifteen-year-old apprentices were 'Johnnie' Greenleaf, whose heroism inspired all those who flew with him, and Roy Ralston, the commanding officer of (1655) Mosquito Training Unit (MTU), responsible for turning out Pathfinder crews for all Oboe and LNSF squadrons.

These men all survived; others were not so fortunate. Two men from Entry 15 – William Abercromby and Eric Porter – went on to command 83 and 156 Squadrons respectively, and lose their lives within a month of one another. Alan Cousens, from Entry 22, similarly went on to become a master bomber and command 635 Squadron before being killed in action in April 1944.

Among the other noteworthy entrants who did not survive the war were: Squadron Leaders Richard Campling DSO, DFC; Robert Bagguley DFC; Albert Collett AFC; and Samuel Robinson DFM MiD; Flight Lieutenants Robert Manvell DFC, DFM; Leslie Rickinson DFC; and Harry Steere DFC, DFM; Flying Officer George Bradley DFM; Pilot Officer Leslie King DFM; Flight Sergeant Vernon Charles Lewis DFM; and Sergeant Maurice Pepper DFM.

Wing Commander Roy Ralston, a low-level specialist who survived ninety-one sorties including twenty-one consecutive attacks on Berlin.

as to allow all of the Pathfinder aircraft to return safely, and at least six combats were reported with enemy fighters. Another Halifax of 35 Squadron and a Stirling of 7 Squadron were missing. The 7 Squadron aircraft, it later transpired, had been caught in the explosion of a 77 Squadron Halifax. The force of the blast not only knocked the pilot (Flying Officer Joseph Berthiaume) out of the sky, but also a 15 Squadron Stirling. The nightfighter had therefore accounted for three aircraft for the price of one.

Another disappointing show to Essen on May 27/28 led to further losses from 35 Squadron (Sergeant Richard Ayres), 156 Squadron (Flight Sergeant David Wallace); 405 Squadron (Sergeant Gabriel Lebihan) and a Mosquito of 109 Squadron (Flight Sergeant 'Fritz' Chrysler) – the latter recorded as having attacked the target and also being confirmed as the first Oboe-equipped Mosquito to be shot down over enemy territory. Chrysler may have been able to outpace or even outfly the enemy fighter, but

The medal ribbons of a highly-decorated Pathfinder. Top row: the DFC; DFM and 1939-45 Star. Bottom row: The Aircrew Europe Star; Italy Star; Defence Medal and War Medal.

had taken a flak hit over the target and was struggling home on one engine when the aircraft was intercepted. He was lucky to survive when the aircraft exploded, the pilot still strapped in his seat. His navigator, Ray Logan, was killed.

It was back to form, however, for the last attack in May, when a new target – Wuppertal – was added to the orders culminating in a raid described subsequently as 'the most outstanding raid of the month and probably of the whole Battle of the Ruhr'. Pathfinder Mosquitoes demonstrated 'extreme accuracy' according to the ORB, and the backers-up did not disappoint. Main force also seemed to rise to the occasion, and very soon there were large fires developing that appeared to engulf the town and could be seen from a distance of 100 miles. Some 1,000 acres of Wuppertal-Barmen was laid waste and five out of six of the town's largest factories were ruined. The number of properties wrecked and Germans killed was unusually large – due to the nature of the town and how unprepared they were for an attack of such ferocity.

But while it was a disastrous night for the citizens of Wuppertal, it was also a similarly dire night for 35 Squadron. Four aircraft failed to return, bringing the total to eight lost for the month of May. Squadron Leader Peter Johnston DFC was among those killed, as was the squadron's bombing leader, Flight Lieutenant William Tetley DFC.

In all, PFF had lost twenty-two aircraft in May, and for the first time this figure

The beautiful lines of a 105 Squadron Mosquito in flight.

DARLING – I MARRIED YOUR FATHER

The attack on Wuppertal on the night of May 29/30 was a triumph both for the Pathfinders and main force. Several Pathfinder squadrons were engaged, among them 83 and 156 Squadrons operating in H2S-equipped Lancasters for the first time.

Not every squadron was celebrating, however. 35 Squadron, out of Graveley, lost no fewer than four aircraft, all victims to nightfighters. Among them was a Halifax II (W7876) coded 'K' for

Ronald Hands, a 35 Squadron navigator, kept a remarkable diary of his two years in captivity.

King and manned by an all-sergeant crew. The pilot was a Berkshire man, the appropriately named Sergeant Sargent; his navigator (air observer) was a twenty-one-year-old volunteer reservist, Ronald Hands.

Ron's aircraft was attacked by a Messerschmitt Bf110, the twin-engined *Zerstorer* (Destroyer). The enemy's cannon shells ripped through the rear fuselage and killed the rear gunner instantly. The aircraft immediately caught fire and the skipper gave the order to bale out. Ron didn't need a second bidding, and was soon tumbling out of the escape hatch and into the night sky. He descended quickly, too rapidly as it happens, and he landed heavily in a field, injuring his leg as he did so. Locals rushed to his aid, and it would be a full twenty-four hours before he was finally captured. Ron spent more than a year in Heydekrug before the advance of the Russians led to his transfer, via cattle truck (third class must have seemed a luxury by comparison), to Thorn in Poland (Stalag 357). Then on to the neighbouring Fallingbostel some three weeks later. Both camps were already heavily overcrowded. Among many jottings and muses in his diary, is an amusing but somehow poignant list of some of the incredible but true lines written in letters officers received from home. There are more than twenty in all, but among the best are the following:

'Darling, I was so glad you were shot down before flying became dangerous.'

'I hope you behave yourself at the dances and don't drink too much'.

'Darling, I have just had a baby but don't worry. An American officer is paying all the expenses and sending you cigarettes each week.'

'Joe is in Stalag VIIIB (Lamsdorf). You should pop over and see him sometime.'

Telegram to POW from his fiancé: *'Darling I married your father. Mother.'*

A POW received a Red Cross sweater and wrote thanking the donor. Reply:
'I am sorry you have it. It was meant for a man on active service, not a coward.'

First letter from girlfriend:
'You were missing a month, dear, so I got married.'

Letter from fiancé:
'I would rather marry a '43 hero than a '39 coward.'

Left: Confirmation of Ronald Hands' membership of the Caterpillar Club.

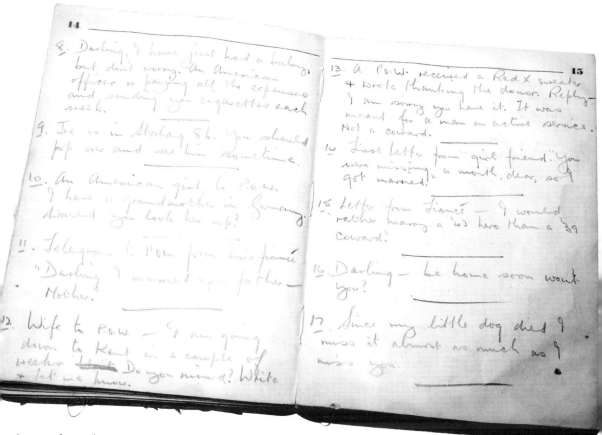

A page from the
Kriegie diary featuring apparently true extracts
from letters received by fellow prisoners.

VISITING DIGNITARIES

On May 26, RAF Wyton was honoured with an informal visit from the king and queen who stayed to lunch in the officers' mess. It was the first of many such visits that HQ PFF and the individual squadrons would receive from visiting dignitaries throughout the war, and not just from the British royal family. Kings and queens from all over came to visit, as did maharajas, princes, dukes, and all manner of diplomats, politicians and military men.

was expressed as a percentage (3.5 percent) by the ORB author. There was some comfort in the tonnage of bombs dropped however, which at a little over 2,220 tons (1,937 tons excluding those bombs jettisoned) was considered an impressive weight given the comparatively small number of raids carried out.

There was also some better news in terms of further reinforcements. Information was received that from June 1, two further squadrons would be joining Pathfinder Force – 105 and 139 Squadrons – operating from Marham. PFF Mosquito strength would be trebled overnight and its Oboe capability doubled. A dedicated Pathfinder Navigation Training Unit (NTU) was also established at Upwood, under the initial command of Squadron Leader Gilbert Elliott (soon after to be superseded by his namesake, Wing Commander Roy Elliott DSO, DFC) and through which all heavy bomber Pathfinder aircrew would in future pass. An equivalent Mosquito Training Unit (MTU) would follow in due course, commanded by Wing Commander Malcolm Sewell DFC.

Things were looking up.

CHAPTER 3
FINDING THEIR WAY

JUNE

June started as promised, with the transfer of the two Mosquito squadrons from 2 Group to PFF.

Both already had impressive track records. In a daylight raid on the German capital in January 1943, two 139 Squadron crews tried to interrupt an important speech by Dr. Goebbels, Germany's propaganda minister, in a stunning propaganda mission of their own. Although it failed to achieve its aim, this raid made news by occurring only a few hours after 105 Squadron had made the RAF's first daylight raid on Berlin and had succeeded in keeping the Luftwaffe boss Goering (also scheduled to deliver an important speech) off the air for more than an hour.

By June 1943, 105 Squadron was commanded by another one of PFF and Bomber Command's true characters, Wing Commander John Wooldridge DFC, DFM. (Wooldridge wrote a contemporary history of 105 and 139 Squadrons entitled *Low Attack*). He was succeeded within the month by Wing Commander Henry Cundall DFC, AFC. Its sister squadron, 139 (Jamaica) had Wing Commander Reginald Reynolds DSO, DFC as its commanding officer, and he was replaced in August by Wing Commander Leonard Slee DSO, DFC. Slee had won his DSO for leading the daylight attack on Le Creusot with 49 Squadron in October 1942.

The role for the two new squadrons was yet to be decided; both were equipped with Mosquito BIVs and would shortly be supplied with BIXs, fitted with 1,6880hp Merlin 72 engines and with a ceiling of more than 36,000ft. Within weeks, 105 would join 109 as the second Oboe-marking force, conducting its first operations in early July. 139 would form the nucleus of what would later be termed the Light Night Striking Force (LNSF).

In the meantime, however, there was work to be done, and the month opened badly with operations cancelled for the first nine days of June. The only exercise that could in any way be deemed a success was on June 10, when group headquarters moved from Wyton to its new home – Castle Hill House in Huntingdon – from where it would see out the war.

When a return to flying was finally forthcoming it was worth the wait. A large-scale raid was mounted on Düsseldorf, and although the timing was erratic, the Oboe markers found their target. Those that did bomb did so with great accuracy, and overall the attack caused substantial damage to the centre of the town, with all but one of the Pathfinders returning safely. That same night, twenty-two Pathfinder aircraft, all equipped with H2S, mounted an experimental raid on Münster, with a main force comprising a further thirty-nine PFF crews. This was not such a happy affair and proved expensive with five aircraft missing. Among the dead were three decorated pilots: two from 35 Squadron (Flight Lieutenant Stanley Howe DFC and Pilot Officer George Herbert DFM) and the third from 83 Squadron (Squadron Leader James Swift DFC).

But PFF was not done for the night: two further operations were also undertaken by Mosquitoes on Cologne and Duisberg. Such nuisance raids had little military value but made an enormous impact on morale. German citizens were obliged to take to their shelters as soon as the sirens sounded as they were not to know if they were to be attacked by one or 1,000 aircraft and they could not take the risk.

The Pathfinders were again up in force the following night, using sky marking via Oboe to conduct a highly satisfactory and destructive raid on Bochum that might have been more destructive still had not one of the Oboe Mosquitoes somewhat inadvertently dropped its load

THE LIGHT NIGHT STRIKING FORCE

The LNSF was very much an invention of Donald Bennett that looked to make maximum use of an aircraft he considered the finest of its time – the De Havilland Mosquito.

Aside from the two Mosquito squadrons allocated to Oboe (105 and 109 Squadrons) Bennett began by using the aircraft of 139 Squadron (the first Light Night Striking Force unit) in a supporting capacity, going in with the early markers and carrying out diversionary raids to draw the nightfighters away from the main force attack. He then evolved their role to carry out nuisance raids, an idea entirely of his own making that he then steadily 'insinuated into the operations

of the group without it being particularly noticed for some time'. When his commander-in-chief did become aware of it, however, he thoroughly approved.

As the numbers of aircraft available increased, Bennett expanded his force, creating a dedicated Mosquito training unit and running his own group maintenance unit (to complement a similar unit for the group's Lancasters) under the watchful eye of his group engineer officer, Group Captain Sarsby. With surplus crews and aircraft, Bennett applied to create new units to add to what had now been officially

The De Havilland Mosquito. Bennett was quick to realise its potentia as a war winner.

designated the Light Night Striking Force until he had nine squadrons of Mosquitoes (twenty aircraft each) in addition to the Oboe and met flight aircraft. He also increased the Mosquito Oboe squadrons from two to three flights each.

As well as nuisance raids – also referred to as 'siren raids' since the object was to keep the Germans in their shelters around the clock – from the spring of 1943 Bennett was able to send up to 120 Mosquitoes at a time to the German capital and beyond, with each aircraft carrying a 4,000-pound blockbuster. The object in these raids was not simply to damage morale, but also heap very real destruction on German industry.

The LNSF visited Berlin on no fewer than 170 occasions, sorties varying from a small handful of aircraft each night to a climax in February 1945 with a total of 122. Starting on the night of February 20/21 1945, they attacked Berlin on thirty-six consecutive nights. With their aircraft capable of flying in excess of 30,000ft, and with their high speed, losses were down to one per 2,000 sorties, a Bomber Command record. The LNSF Mosquitoes also conducted the famous raid on the Dortmund-Ems canal in August 1944, skipped bombs into railway tunnels in January 1945, and flew the last Bomber Command raid of the war.

wide of the mark – some ten miles to be precise. Another PFF crew then compounded the folly by backing the TIs up, and a number of main force completed the farce by allowing hundreds of their bombs to fall harmlessly in open country. Two PFF crews failed to return.

The two 'new' Pathfinder squadrons were detailed for a busy night (June 13/14) with six Mosquitoes allocated to Berlin, four to Düsseldorf (as if the town hadn't suffered enough) and

KEEPING THE POT BOILING

"We carried bombs until we were considered expert enough to mark. We also carried bombs rather than TIs when the weather was bad and the 'heavies' could not get off or were elsewhere.

This kept the pot boiling for the German air defences and denied them a night off.

"When we led formations of 'heavies' in daylight we also carried bombs. This was to attack the V-weapon sites which were difficult to spot visually but, using Oboe, we opened our bomb doors when appropriate (in order to slow down enough for the 'heavies' we put the undercarriage down as well). When the bomb aimers following us saw us release our bombs, they let their more substantial loads go too. Releasing four or six 500-pound bombs did not make much of a difference except the aircraft was less sluggish and called for an adjustment to trim. When we released a 4,000-pound bomb, however, the Mosquito would shoot up perhaps thirty or forty feet!"

A typical building-busting bombload in a Lancaster comprising a 4,000lb 'Cookie' and 500lb medium capacity (MC) bombs.

BILL RILEY DFC & BAR
NAVIGATOR. 105 SQUADRON. 108 OPS.

four to Cologne – all nuisance raids. On each occasion, the results were unobserved, but such attacks were to become the pattern for the coming weeks.

There was bad news for the PFF's own met flight on June 14, when one of its aircraft was reported as overdue. By evening it was clear that the aircraft would not be returning. Later still, the pilot was reported as having been captured whilst his navigator successfully evaded. The Mosquito, one of the first of the new MkIX variants, was the first of its kind to be reported missing. It was the victim of two FW190s, shot down from a height of 28,000ft. Both the pilot and his navigator survived.

However the show must go on, the operation to bomb Oberhausen that night going ahead as planned. Oboe Mosquitoes dropped red tracking flares twenty-four miles short of the release point and green flares as preliminary warnings with twelve-and-a-half miles to go followed by red with green stars and white flares at the release point. The sky marking proved accurate, and a comparatively small force (197 aircraft) contributed to a considerably large amount of damage.

Another all-H2S affair was tried on Cologne on June 16/17, but proved disappointing. Equipment failures and flak were blamed for an untidy raid with little achieved and four crews lost, three from the same unit (156 Squadron). One of the pilots to lose his life was Squadron Leader John Mackintosh who had been flying on operations almost from the start. Another was Warrant Officer Clive Busby, one of the very few holders of the Conspicuous Gallantry Medal. He had been recommended for the award less than a month earlier, having completed fifty-three operations, five with PFF. He was dead before his medal could be gazetted.

A rather over-complicated affair is how the raid on Le Creusot could best be described, and perhaps not surprisingly, it failed. The Schneider armaments factory had been the target of a famous daylight attack the previous year but had suffered little damage. It got away with it again on the night of June 19/20 when, despite PFF illuminating the target with flares, main force was unable to deliver the *coup de grâce*. All of the illuminating aircraft then flew onwards to

Montchanin to attack a transformer station, backed up and supported by a further force of PFF Lancasters. Sadly they missed.

A tragedy of truly epic proportions was to befall Pathfinder Force over Krefeld on June 21/22. The planners had much to answer for since the raid was carried out before the full-moon period was over which no doubt added to the calamity. Ironically, of course, the good visibility contributed to an almost perfect marking of the target, with initial markers well backed up, even though the timing – according to the ORB – was late. All but the first Mosquito failed to turn up at the allotted time. Defences, as reported after the event, were relatively modest, but the nightfighters were out in earnest, and making hay whilst the moon shone.

Of the 705 bombers taking part, forty-four were lost. Of these, fourteen were from Pathfinder Force, six from 35 Squadron. Two of the missing captains – Flying Officer Michael Clarke and Pilot Officer James Andrews – were killed with all of their respective crews; a third – Sergeant Donald Milne – was hit by flak and ditched thirty miles off the Norfolk coast. All survived.

But they were not the only squadron to be badly mauled that night. Debriefing at Oakington was a subdued affair as it became clear that four 7 Squadron crews were overdue and then eventually recorded as 'missing', although, unusually, of the twenty-nine aircrew aboard, a high number (twenty) survived as prisoners of war. Three out of the four pilots, however, were killed including two very highly-decorated officers: Flight Lieutenant Clarence Ince DFC & Bar and

HIT WITHOUT WARNING

Fred Maltas, a Yorkshireman, briefly followed his father's profession as a joiner and funeral director, but war came and rescued him. Joining the air force as an air mechanic and becoming a fitter at 35 MU in Sealand, Fred later trained as a flight engineer at St Athan (obliged only to take the engine course) before finally arriving at 51 Squadron in Snaith via the customary conversion unit. Selected for Pathfinders, he was flying with his regular skipper, Pilot Officer Bill Hickson RNZAF on the night of 21/22 June:

"Our gunners, 'Maxi' Brown in the rear and Joe Dowsing in the mid upper turret, were well drilled. If they saw a nightfighter attacking then they would call out the distance and direction (for example 'enemy aircraft port quarter 600 yards and closing'), and at the appropriate moment would shout for the skipper to 'corkscrew'. On the night we were shot down, however, we were hit before they could give any warnings.

"I was aware that we had been hit in the port inboard engine, and I was also conscious of Maxi saying that he was trapped. I told him I would get to him as fast as I could but first I had to feather the engine. The propeller was wind-milling in the slipstream and therefore still pumping up fuel. I couldn't just think of Maxi I had to think of all of us. I had a job to do and it took some time. Then the engine caught fire, and the glycol coolant began leaking which burned with a particular ferocity. The engines had extinguishers but they made no difference.

"The skipper told us we had had it and to abandon aircraft. I called Maxi on the intercom but there was no reply. I tried to speak to the skipper but again no-one answered. It didn't occur to me that the port inner controlled power to the intercom and it was obviously now u/s. Thinking everyone else had gone, I too made for the escape hatch and baled out, and Bill jumped immediately after. Straight after that, the burning wing fell off and the aircraft followed us down. Everyone got out except Maxi, who was stuck in his turret.

"I still feel terribly guilty about it to this day."

FRED MALTAS
FLIGHT ENGINEER. 35 SQUADRON.

Flight Lieutenant James Watt DSO, DFC. Watt had been a long-time servant of 7 Squadron, his DFC having been awarded for an action in September 1942. He was born in Cordoba and raised in Buenos Aires. Ince, whose parents lived in Barbados, had been awarded the Bar to an earlier DFC for fending off a fighter attack earlier in the year and pressing on to bomb the target despite damage to his Stirling. The surviving pilot was the OC 'A' Flight, Squadron Leader Colin Hughes DSO, DFM, a veteran bomber baron.

Of the remaining PFF losses that night, two were from 83 Squadron and one each from 156 and 405 Squadrons. (The RCAF pilot of the 405 Squadron Halifax, Flight Lieutenant Sidney Murrell DFC, was actually from Gainesville, Texas.) Unusually too, perhaps, there were no survivors from any of the aircraft, such was the lottery of life and death in Bomber Command and Pathfinder Force.

While the bulk of Pathfinder aircraft had been allocated to main force attacks on Le Creusot and Krefeld over the previous few nights, and would again be called upon to lead a wonderfully-successful attack on Mulheim on June 22/23, four Lancasters from 97 Squadron had also been busy. On the morning of the 20th, they had flown to Scampton to make up a force of sixty, 5 Group Lancasters, for an attack on the Zeppelin works at Friedrichshafen. The raid is noteworthy for several reasons: for one, it deployed a 'controller' to oversee control of the raid over w/t; and for the second, it divided the bombing into two parts. The first bombs were to be aimed at TIs dropped by 97 Squadron; and for the second part, a number of 5 Group Lancasters were to undertake a time and distance run from a point on the shores of Lake Constance to the estimated position of the factory. It is not quite clear whose technique proved the most accurate, but suffice to say one of the 97 Squadron pilots, Flight Lieutenant Joseph Sauvage, managed to drop his TIs within 200 yards of the aiming point, and photo reconnaissance after the raid showed much damage had been done.

Casualties were zero, and this was almost certainly as a result of the third noteworthy part of the plan. Rather than turning for home, the Lancasters all flew on past the target, landing at recently-secured airfields in North Africa (Maison Blanche) in one of the first 'shuttle runs' of the war. Cheekily, fifty-two of those Lancasters then attacked La Spezia on their way back, again flying on to England without loss. The force included two of the 97 Squadron Lancs, one of the others having been damaged by flak during the original raid and the fourth being used to ferry the stranded crew home via Gibraltar.

The night after the 97 Squadron crews had enjoyed their North African sojourn, a large force of Pathfinders was once again on parade with instructions to mark Elberfeld, the second 'half' of Wuppertal that had yet to be touched. The post-war British survey estimated that ninety-four percent of the Elberfeld district was destroyed in the attack, and it might have been the full ton had not main force suffered with itchy fingers and bombed early. This was a pity, given that the initial Mosquito marking had been of the highest order and the backing up similarly so. Defences had been increased since the previous attack and although described somewhat disparagingly as 'not formidable' they certainly took their toll. 97 Squadron lost the crew of Flight Lieutenant Joseph Moore DFC; 156 Squadron lost an Australian pilot, Warrant Officer Leo Brown and his crew; and Sergeant P.C. Andrews and his crew were missing from 405 Squadron, most of them later to turn up as prisoners of war. But it was an especially bad night for 7 Squadron: Flying Officer Arthur Davis and Squadron Leader John Savage, in a Stirling I and a Stirling III respectively, were both shot down and killed. (Davis' parents lived in Fiji.) The rear gunner of the Stirling III was Sergeant Derek Spanton, the sole survivor of the Stirling crash in March. His luck had finally run out.

But the biggest blow to the squadron, and Pathfinder Force, was news that Wing Commander Bob Barrell DSO, DFC & Bar and his crew, most of them decorated, were also missing in one of the squadron's first Lancasters (the squadron was at the time converting from Stirlings to Lancs). Barrell, the OC 'B' Flight, was only twenty-three, and although reports say that he made it out

MASTERS OF THE SKY

There are many different and differing opinions as to who 'invented' the master bomber role; suffice to say that it 'evolved' rather than was 'created'. 'Bill' Anderson (later Wing Commander E.W. Anderson OBE, DFC, AFC) is said to have proposed the idea formally when he was at Bomber Command HQ but his idea had been rejected; Wing Commander 'Pat' Daniels was also given permission to control an attack on Munich in early 1943, but his endeavours were thwarted by ice.

And so it is generally recognised that Wing Commander Guy Gibson of Dam Busters fame was the first to 'control' a raid and issue commentary from the air to direct the result. Over Friedrichshafen on June 20/21, a similar tactic was deployed with another small force with Wing Commander Cosme Gomm of 467 Squadron taking the lead (after the appointed 'master' – Group Captain L.C. Slee – had to withdraw with engine trouble). Gomm issued instructions 'over w/t' to change the height at which the bombers were attacking to take account of local conditions.

But the honour for the first 'true' master bomber role – that is to say the 'controller' of a full-scale main force raid – goes to Group Captain John Searby of 83 Squadron. Searby flew his first raid as 'master of ceremonies' (a phrase coined by Bennett) on the night of August 7, providing a running commentary of the raid on Turin using the new VHF air-to-air communication. He did not know at the time that this was a dress rehearsal for the main event – the attack on Peenemünde ten days later.

Although the initial marking and bombing was off target, Searby and the Pathfinders were quick to correct the error, and in the end some 560 aircraft dropped nearly 1,800 tons of bombs causing sufficient damage to put the Germans' V2 rocket programme back by at least two months. It was the work of consummate skill and bravery for which Searby received a richly-deserved (and immediate) Distinguished Service Order.

Less than a week later, Wing Commander Kenneth Burns of 97 Squadron was the appointed master bomber for a major raid on Berlin, after which the assignment of the role, and a deputy, for each raid became the norm.

'Boom' Trenchard (right) speaks to John Searby, the first master bomber (centre).

of his aircraft, his parachute somehow failed to deploy. He was on his sixtieth trip, and would have completed his second tour that night. (With Barrell gone, 7 Squadron had lost three flight commanders in as many days.)

There were further losses to PFF before the month was out. Two more crews from 35 Squadron and one from 97 Squadron were shot down over Cologne, two of them the victims of the same German nightfighter ace, Heinz-Wolfgang Schnaufer, for his fifteenth and sixteenth kills.

In the June summary, the anonymous author describes the month as 'active' in which several successful raids took place. He refers specifically to the arrival of 105 and 139 Squadrons and how they 'soon got into their stride and carried out a number of anti-morale attacks including Berlin'. Although results were difficult to observe, the author suggested that 'they undoubtedly cause[d] great trouble to the hun'.

MASTER BOMBERS – THE AUSTRALIANS

The Australians, perhaps not surprisingly given their AOC, produced a good many expert bomber captains and crews. Some of the better known among the 'heavies' include Squadron Leader Herbert Slade DSO, DFC, awarded an immediate DSO for his exploits over Hamburg, and Wing Commander Peter Swan DSO, DFC & Bar who swapped a Mosquito of the LNSF for a heavy bomber and attained master bomber status. Swan completed ninety-four operations before being grounded on the orders of Bennett himself.

Squadron Leader French Smith won the DFC in June 1944, having been credited with ten trips to Berlin, and added an immediate DSO for a master bomber raid on Calais in which he was obliged to come below 2,000ft in order to identify the target. Another heavy Australian 'baron' was Squadron Leader Richard Wiseman DFC & Bar, who won his first DFC with 50 Squadron in 1942, and by the time of his Bar had at least seventy ops to his name.

Among the Mosquito crews, there were a great many who warrant mention: Squadron Leader Bill Blessing DSO, DFC – the Oboe pioneer and Allyn Douglass DSO, DFC, another 105 Squadron veteran, who was awarded a DSO for his leadership during the battle of the Ruhr. Squadron Leader Edward Ifould DSO, DFC & Bar was an exceptional navigator and leader, who had taken part in the daylight raid on Augsburg in 1942 before moving to 109 Squadron and becoming squadron navigation officer. He was the most decorated navigator in RAAF. Flight Lieutenant James Crabb DFC & Bar and Flight Lieutenant James Falkinder DSO, DFC were both also 109 Squadron veterans, the latter completing more than 100 operations.

In all, Cologne was visited eight times, Duisberg six, Berlin six, Hamburg three times and Düsseldorf twice. The Ruhr was still far from forgotten with raids on Krefeld, Mulheim, Elberfeld and Gelsenkirchen. A total of 2,010 tons of bombs were dropped (and a further eighty-two tons jettisoned) – down on the previous month. Some thirty-eight aircraft were missing (compared to twenty-two in May) including nine from 35 Squadron and eight each from 7 and 156 Squadrons. The three Mosquito bomber squadrons were more fortunate with no casualties reported.

It was a busy month also for honours and gallantry awards, with Bennett heading the table himself with the award of a CBE to add to the DSO he had won earlier in the war. Wing Commander Reginald Reynolds, the commanding officer of 139 (Jamaica) Squadron received a further DSO to the one he had earned with 105 Squadron and a DFC awarded in 1940, and there were DSOs also for: Group Captain Oliver Donaldson DFC, Wing Commander Bob Barrell DFC (KIA) and Flight Lieutenant John Stickell DFC – all of 7 Squadron; Flight Lieutenant Oscar Rees of 35 Squadron; Flight Lieutenant Valentine Moore DFM of 83 Squadron; Squadron Leader Bill Blessing of 105 Squadron; and Flight Lieutenant Ted Sismore DFC of 139 Squadron. There was also a DSO for Flight Lieutenant Philip Cunliffe-Lister of 1409 (Met) Flight.

JULY

Even though the summer months should have meant better weather conditions, July proved a disappointment with a large number of cancellations and stand-downs. But it was notable for three heavy raids on Hamburg in the last week, all of which did enormous damage.

But before the Battle of Hamburg could begin, Bomber Command and Pathfinders first had to bring The Battle of the Ruhr to a close. June had ended with a major attack on Cologne and July started in much the same way. No cloud and good visibility made for accurate marking and sustained backing up, which in turn led to a high concentration of bombs. Three PFF aircraft were lost to defences that were described as 'intense'. Among the missing crews was that of Sergeant Donald Milne who had, only two weeks earlier, survived a ditching off the Norfolk coast. They were the victims of Hauptmann Siegfried Wandam, kommandeur of I/NJG5. They may have accounted for their nemesis, however, as Wandam was killed later that night, attempting to land on one engine. The other had been shot out during his night's work.

Minor operations were carried out by Mosquito bombers over the next four nights and it was Cologne – on the night of July 8/9 – that was again the target for the third time in a row. The attack was late in starting ('owing to technical troubles') and the red TIs could not be seen because of cloud. All aircraft bombed on the release point flares, and a successful attack ensued. One aircraft failed to return but it might so easily have been more. Wing Commander Cliff Alabaster of 97 Squadron is highlighted in the ORB as being one of those who landed away from home, on account of an attack by a fighter southwest of Aachen leaving him with an injured rear gunner.

Cologne Cathedral stands tall amongst the ruins of the city.

FIGHTER ATTACK

"The fighter attack occurred before reaching the target, not after as is suggested by the ORB. Several cannon shells hit the aircraft, wounding our rear gunner (Sergeant Hambling) and damaging the starboard motors and aileron controls.

"I was navigator and captain of the aircraft, an unusual situation that the pilot, Flight Lieutenant Alfred Eaton-Clarke, had agreed to several trips beforehand, he being new to operations and I experienced.

"One point I had made to him was that in the event of an attack, he should make a right diving turn, rather than a left. This was based on the theory that an attacking fighter would be more accustomed to making left turns, as in the circuit, racetrack, skating rink etc. It was a somewhat simplistic idea that he followed on this occasion. Whether it was successful or not we'll never know but we certainly avoided any further attack.

"As we were close to the target, we carried on, on three engines and released the TIs and bomb load, using H2S. Sergeant Hambling was conscious and able to communicate, but it was thought better to land away from Bourn to get him treatment as soon as we could. The first airfield we saw was Great Saling and Eaton-Clarke made a good landing there despite a flat tyre and on three engines. Great Saling was an American base; Hambling was taken to the base hospital and from there to Ely, where he recovered from his wounds.

"We, the rest of the crew, were driven back to Bourn by two enlisted men, who had been given permission to stay overnight in Cambridge and who kept us awake by talking loudly of their planned exploits there!"

CLIFF ALABASTER DSO & BAR, DFC & BAR
NAVIGATOR AND PILOT 97, 582, 128 AND 608 SQUADRONS. 100+ OPS.

Four other raids were mounted by Pathfinders and main force over the course of the next seven days: Gelsenkirchen which failed; Turin which was partially successful; Aachen which achieved significant damage; and Montbéliard (the Peugeot works) which missed. Four aircraft were missing, including a highly-experienced 405 Squadron crew captained by Squadron Leader Denzil Wolfe DFC (formerly of 419 Squadron RCAF).

But the month was dominated by the so-called Battle of Hamburg – a desire that had long been in the mind of the Bomber Command C-in-C to finally give Germany's second-largest city and Europe's largest port the full attention it deserved. The purpose was brutally simple: to bomb the city areas, rather than the port installations themselves, in order to hamper production of U-boats and warships by killing the people required to build them. Although out of range of Oboe, the distinctive river and coastline features made it ideal H2S territory.

The battle opened on the night of July 24/25 and the Pathfinders played their part with devastating effect. Yellow TIs were dropped as route markers, and further yellow TIs despatched to mark the target. The aiming point was then marked with red TIs backed up by greens. The weather was good with no cloud and excellent visibility. The yellow and red TIs were well placed using H2S, and superbly backed up, with the result that a highly-concentrated attack developed rapidly and a large area of fires was reported covering the whole town with smoke rising to 18,000ft.

DIRTY TACTICS

"While we were with main force, over Gelsenkirchen, we were listening out for instructions from the master bomber when we suddenly heard a banging noise and screams of 'oh my God, we're hit, we're going down' followed by shouts of 'mother, mother'. There was a moment of panic. When we got back to base, however, we all looked at one another, not really knowing what to say. We thought it had been our crew who had done all of the screaming but it wasn't. We didn't report it at the time and perhaps we should have done. After the war I was telling this story to a master bomber, Peter Swan. He told us that what we had heard was a recording, made by the Germans and transmitted on our frequency. It was a dirty trick in a sordid war."

ALF HUBERMAN
AIR GUNNER. 83 SQUADRON. THIRTY-EIGHT OPS.

Bombing photographs would later reveal that less than half of the attacking force of nearly 800 aircraft bombed within three miles of the centre of Hamburg and a creepback six miles long developed. Somehow it didn't matter. Some 1,500 civilians were killed and unusually – and with obvious satisfaction – the unknown ORB author has written: 'There were no losses in the group.'

The fact that the Pathfinders all returned home safely and only twelve aircraft were missing from main force can be explained primarily by a rather cryptic sentence included in the ORB: 'All aircraft carried a new device to defeat the enemy radio location apparatus and this appeared to work well as the defences were disorganised and the searchlights particularly ineffective.' The 'new device' to which the report refers was less electronic wizardry and more scientific cunning: 'Window' – strips of paper and aluminium exactly 27cm long and 2cm wide that effectively rendered the German radar operators 'blind'. More than ninety million of such Window strips had been dropped in bundles by the attacking aircraft, and would become a major feature of future attacks.

Harris endeavoured to press home the temporary advantage afforded by Window by mounting a large attack on Essen the following night in which 83 Squadron played host to the commander of the American VIII Bomber Command, Brigadier-General Fred Anderson. Mosquitoes marked the target well and bombs were soon falling resulting in several large explosions. As it happens,

A GRANDSTAND SEAT

In the summer of 1943, the Americans were still exploring the idea of conducting night operations, having been somewhat taken aback at the losses suffered by their crews in daylight raids. The leader of the US VIII Bomber Command, General Anderson, took it upon himself to fly with the RAF twice in July, on both occasions with Flight Lieutenant 'Ricky' Garvey DFC in R5868 'Q' Queenie – arguably the most famous Lancaster of the war.

Len Thomas kept this memento of an eventful trip in R5868 'Q' Queenie in which he was wounded.

Within Garvey's regular crew was Flight Sergeant (later Warrant Officer) Len Thomas, the bomb aimer, whose logbook lists General Anderson as a passenger for the trip to Essen (25th) and Hamburg (27th). Thomas has noted Anderson's comment on seeing the heavy explosive and incendiaries exploding over the target: 'unbelievable'.

Len Thomas was involved the following month in an eventful trip to Milan – Queenie's last with 83 Squadron. The aircraft was hit by flak and badly damaged over the target, making for an uncomfortable trip home that was made more difficult still when two Bf109s attacked them while crossing the French coast. Garvey took evasive action and escaped, but not before Thomas was wounded, a cannon shell having entered the bomb aimer's position and passing through various pipes and paraphernalia before striking Thomas in the foot. He returned to operations the following month but over Mannheim (on September 9) he passed out through lack of oxygen. On subsequent inspection it was found that his oxygen pipe had been cut, possibly – he believed – as an act of sabotage. His final trip was to Berlin on December 16 where they narrowly missed crashing into a Halifax during the bombing run and returned home to find the cloud base down to only 300ft, making for an interesting landing.

Len Thomas completed forty-nine operations; forty-seven of them were with PFF. Assessed as 'exceptional' almost from the outset, he went on to be recommended for a commission and bombing leader's course. He became a night-vision instructor and was permanently awarded his Pathfinder badge in January 1944. As for Queenie, she was later transferred from 83 Squadron to 467 Squadron RAAF as 'S' Sugar and now resides in the RAF Museum, Hendon.

Len Thomas, while training, went on to complete forty-seven PFF operations.

more damage was done in this attack than in all of the previous attacks combined, so much so that Dr Gustav Krupp of Krupps fame apparently went mad. 'Special devices' were once again carried and the defences proved ineffective – but not so benign that they did not still account for three PFF aircraft, one each from 35, 156 and 405 Squadrons (Pilot Officer Milmine, Pilot Officer John Hudson and Flying Officer Marcel Tomczak respectively. Tomczak had been a schoolmaster in peacetime).

On 27/28 it was back to Hamburg again in what was to become known as the 'night of the firestorm'. The tactics were largely a repeat on what had gone before, and when the bombers arrived over the city there was still a considerable amount of smoke and fires burning from the previous attack. A very large area of fire rapidly developed – the result of at least three separate fires merging as one to the extent that a firestorm was created, robbing the atmosphere of oxygen. Civilians who were not burned to death in the intense heat, suffocated from lack of the vital gas needed to stay alive. Post-raid reports estimate that up to 600 bombs fell into an area measuring only two miles by one mile.

Two PFF crews failed to return, both from 156 Squadron: one, Flight Sergeant G.W. Wilkins, had a particularly miraculous escape when his aircraft exploded in mid-air having been attacked by a nightfighter. Wilkins was thrown clear and survived, the rest of the crew perished – yet another example of how the pilot's 'seat'-type parachute – permanently attached – meant the difference between life and death.

Bomber Command was still not done. Harris was not yet satisfied. But for the third attack on Hamburg in five days, mistakes were made and the bombers did not have it all their own way. The attack opened well with a good concentration of markers but south of the desired aiming point, and the weight of the attack appearing to fall on the eastern half of the town. Creepback was again an issue. Enormous fires and explosions, however, were reported along with great columns of smoke.

Casualties were heavy. The Germans appeared to have recovered from their earlier confusion; searchlight activity was better coordinated and the nightfighters were up in force and busy. Seven PFF aircraft were reported missing, one – the Halifax flown by Flight Lieutenant Harold Pexton DFC, a thirty-one-year-old Yorkshireman – carried the 35 Squadron gunnery leader, Squadron Leader Charles Andrew DFC. Conversely, Flight Sergeant Malcolm Hall, skipper of a 156 Squadron Lancaster shot down that night was reported to have been on his first operational sortie.

The month closed with an attack on Remscheid in what is now recognised as the end of the Battle of the Ruhr. It was a comparatively small raid that produced a disproportionately high number of casualties, but fortunately no PFF aircraft were missing.

Whilst not exactly a turning point, and by no means representing the beginning of the end, July – to quote Churchill from another famous occasion – was perhaps the end of the beginning. Pathfinder tactics had clearly evolved, and their successes were tangible. Oboe worked, and 105 Squadron came on line as the second fully paid-up member of Bennett's Oboe force. H2S was proven to be effective when targets were beyond Oboe range. Window – which had actually been waiting in the wings for several months – had at last been deployed with promising results. Harris, Bennett and Pathfinder Force had every reason to feel confident, especially since losses in July 'showed a gratifying decrease'. Such slim advantages that Window offered, however, would prove to be short-lived. The Germans were nothing if not adaptable, and within days their own tactics had shifted to include the use of single-engine nightfighters in so-called 'Wild Boar' operations, attacking Bomber Command aircraft over the target, oblivious to their own defences.

The fast, high-flying Mosquitoes undertaking their nuisance raids were also vulnerable, as more than one Luftwaffe ace stripped their aircraft of non-essential equipment to gain the extra speed required to intercept the Mosquitoes on their own terms.

One squadron – 139 – fared the worst. Having moved from Marham to Wyton on July 4 (109 replaced them at Marham), the squadron was briefed for a nuisance raid to Berlin on the night of July 14/15. Eight aircraft took off to frighten the Berliners back into their bunkers. One returned early with technical problems and a second was missing. It was last heard sending a message that the aircraft was on fire and they were baling out. Their position was estimated to be thirty-eight miles east of Cromer. Despite an immediate search, they were never found. Flying Officer Raymond Clarke and Flight Sergeant Eric Thorne are commemorated on the Runnymede Memorial.

The second crew lost on the night of July 27/28 was more fortunate: Flying Officer Edward

A very rare photograph of HM Queen Elizabeth inspecting 156 Squadron at RAF Warboys.

Sniders and Squadron Leader Kenneth Price DFC – the group headquarters navigation staff officer – survived their ordeal to become prisoners of war. Sniders had left his regular navigator, Flying Officer George Hodder, behind, having requested to sneak in one more operation before going on leave. He was paired with Price who was himself working on ways of improving night navigation equipment. When Price went missing, his twin brother caused considerable consternation by turning up at group HQ, before explaining that he had sensed his brother had been shot down but was safe. He proved to be right on both counts.

The met flight also suffered a serious set-back when it lost its commanding officer, Squadron Leader Philip Cunliffe-Lister DSO on July 18. He had been sent out on a 'Pampas' and by the afternoon was listed as missing as no news had been received. Later it transpired that he had made a forced landing in Germany after his Mosquito ran out of fuel following a navigational error. He and his navigator, Pat Kernon, evaded capture for four days but were rounded up and sent to Dulag Luft and thence to Stalag Luft III at Sagan.

The total tonnage of bombs dropped in July stood at 2,128 (2,276 including those jettisoned) for the loss of twenty-two aircraft – six from one Squadron (156). There were no fewer than fourteen Distinguished Service Orders awarded, perhaps the most notable going to Flight Lieutenant Alec Cranswick DFC of 35 Squadron and Wing Commander Kenny Lawson DFC of 156. Both would go on to achieve their place among the immortals.

AUGUST

August was to prove a seminal month for Pathfinder Force, dominated by one major attack, and one of the most famous of the whole bomber war. But before new targets and new techniques could be explored, it first had some outstanding business to finish: Hamburg.

The attack on Hamburg at the start of August was a dismal failure. Very few of the Pathfinder aircraft managed to mark the target, or so they thought, and the majority simply brought their bombs and TIs home. Electrical storms played havoc with the attacking force and those not bothered by lightning had severe icing to contend with. The results were desultory at best: four Halifaxes, three Stirlings,

Alec Cranswick. It was to him that Bennett dedicated his autobiography, *Pathfinder*.

eleven Lancasters and one Mosquito returned early for technical reasons, an indication of the abject nature of the attack. Some thirty aircraft dropped their bombs 'on various targets in North West Germany' and four aircraft failed to return – one from 35 Squadron and three from 405. One of the 405 Squadron Halifaxes managed to limp to Sweden where all of the crew baled out successfully and were interned. The captain, Sergeant John Phillips, had only just been awarded the DFM for bringing his badly-damaged Halifax home following an attack on Cologne in which his bomb doors had been shot away by a nightfighter obliging the crew to drop the bombs manually.

Turin was the target for August 6/7, with a cryptic note in the ORB that states within the twenty-three aircraft from 7 and 156 Squadrons detailed for the attack, a single Lancaster from 83 Squadron was 'to act as commentator'. The Lancaster in question was to be flown by the 83 Squadron CO, John Searby, and as mentioned, without his knowledge, this was the dress rehearsal for a much larger and more important raid that was yet to come. As it happened, he had to wait another twenty-four hours, when a slightly larger force would accompany him to the Italian city, and Air Commodore 'Bruin' Boyce, Bennett's SASO, would go with him in his aircraft. It was a busy night for PFF: having successfully marked Turin, they then flew onwards to mark Genoa. Searby apparently 'proved very helpful' and 'probably assisted the concentration achieved' over Turin. All aircraft successfully attacked both targets, but the real significance of that night's efforts would be realised later.

Searby believed the attack, and his role as master of ceremonies, was a one-off, not to be repeated. He suggested the commentary might be used a few nights later for an attack on Nuremberg but his idea was roundly quashed. Bennett had bigger plans, and they came to fruition soon after.

At 09.40 on August 17, PFF HQ at Huntingdon received orders that ninety-seven aircraft from all squadrons were required for an attack on Peenemünde, with zero hour stated as 00.15. In addition, eight Mosquitoes of 139 Squadron were to carry out a nuisance raid to Berlin. By lunchtime the orders had been confirmed, and the bombing method passed to all groups. A great

A superb study of a 35 Squadron Halifax crew – suited, booted and ready for ops.

plan was about to come together for an historic attack.

Such was the secrecy of Peenemünde that the ORB talks of the target as being 'an RDF (radio detection and finding) station'. It was, of course, actually the main experimental site for the German 'Vengeance' weapons – the V1 (Doodlebug) and the even more deadly V2 rocket. The critical importance of the target cannot be underestimated. Pathfinder crews had become wary of briefings that suggested the success or otherwise of their attacks could shorten the war, but for once such hyperbole had merit. There was some considerable surprise, however, that the attack would comprise not just one but rather three aiming points, with a new tactic of 'shifting' the bombing as required to alter the concentration of the attack.

The weather was good, with no cloud and excellent visibility. Searby was the elected master bomber with Wing Commander Johnny Fauquier of 405 Squadron as his deputy and Wing Commander John White of 156 Squadron as third in command. The markers went down on time and were extremely accurate. The shifting of the aiming point was well carried out and a highly-concentrated attack occurred. Later observations were hampered by the clouds of smoke from the fires and the German attempt at a smoke screen, but all of the aiming points were heavily bombed. Some light and heavy flak was encountered with a few searchlights.

Such apparently 'light' defences, however, were balanced by an 'extremely active' German nightfighter force over the target, especially as the third wave of aircraft approached, and no fewer than forty aircraft were missing out of a total attacking force of nearly 600 bombers. Remarkably, only two of those aircraft were from Pathfinder Force – a 35 Squadron Halifax skippered by Pilot Officer Peter Raggett and a Halifax from 405 Squadron flown by Pilot Officer Harry McIntyre. McIntyre and his crew had strayed south of target and were believed to be that evening's first casualties.

While the majority of PFF was attacking Peenemünde, the nuisance force of eight Mosquitoes was playing its parts in diverting German defences away from the 'real' target with mixed results.

Philip Cross and Roy Crampton (standing centre) with ground crews in front of the 139 Squadron station hack, a Bristol Bisley, at RAF Marham, 1943.

Seven of the eight pinpointed Lake Müritz from which they would make a timed DR run. Heavy flak was encountered and one Mosquito was shot down and a second overshot the runway on its return, injuring the pilot (Flight Lieutenant Roy Crampton) as a result. The navigator, Flying Officer Philip Cross was also hurt, but recovered to go on to win both the DSO and DFC – a remarkable achievement made even more significant by the fact that he was a West Indian, at a time when Britain was not at its most racially tolerant.

While Peenemünde stole the limelight, it was by no means the only eventful raid in August. Both before and after the main event the Pathfinders were kept busy, initially attacking the Italians. As well as the trip to Turin and Genoa on 7/8, they targeted Turin (again) and Milan on August 12/13 (losing the crew of Squadron Leader William Butterfield DFC which included the 7 Squadron gunnery leader – Squadron Leader Cecil Myers. Both men survived). They went back to Milan on 14/15, losing another 7 Squadron crew skippered by Flight Lieutenant Sidney Matkin DFC on his forty-fourth operation, and for a third time on 15/16 without loss, although Wing Commander Cosme Gomm DSO, DFC of 467 Squadron, who had himself experimented with controlling a raid outside of Pathfinder Force, was shot down and killed on the twenty-fourth operation of his second tour.

FOR KING AND COUNTRY

There were 250 Trinidadians who flew in combat with the RAF during the war, and fifty were killed in action. Among the survivors was Philip Cross:

"I was educated at St Mary's, Port of Spain, and worked for a time for the Trinidadian government on the railways, before enlisting in 1941. A troopship took twelve days for us to reach Greenock from where I was sent to Cranwell and trained in wireless, meteorology, bomb aiming, navigation and Morse code. Commissioned as a pilot officer, I was posted to 139 'Jamaica' Squadron although, perhaps ironically, I was the only West Indian among the squadron. After completing my first thirty operations, I was given the chance of a rest, but opted instead to continue to complete a Pathfinder tour of fifty. Once I hit that, I again decided to continue, bringing my final tally to eighty before the war ended, including twenty-two trips to Berlin.

"My most harrowing mission was when one of the engines of our Mosquito was shot up over Germany and we came down to 7,000ft from 35,000ft. We struggled back to England and crash landed in a quarry. It was a narrow escape but we made it out alive."

PHILIP CROSS DSO, DFC
PILOT. 139 (JAMAICA) SQUADRON. EIGHTY OPS.

Turin received its final visit of the month and whilst the raid was a success with little opposition reported, there were still two aircraft missing (one each from 35 and 405 Squadrons – Squadron Leader Haggerty DFC and Pilot Officer Manning DFC respectively) and no fewer than fifteen aircraft had to be diverted on their return due to adverse weather. Of these, two landed at Hartford Bridge, three at Dunsfold, four at Ford, three at Horne, one at Beaulieu and two at Tangmere. Getting them back to their respective bases the following day proved quite a challenge.

German targets were by no means ignored, and two in particular are worthy of note: Nuremberg and Berlin. PFF went to Nuremberg on August 10/11 and again on 27/28. The first was described as 'useful' and may have been more useful still had not the target been obscured by thick cloud. Although the glow of the fire could be seen from some distance, the accuracy of the attack could

GOODNIGHT DARLING

"One evening whilst waiting our turn to land we were given the instruction 'L-Love (our aircraft) land left'. The pilot wasn't quite sure what this meant. Perhaps there was an obstruction on the runway and we were being instructed to land on the grass, which would have been interesting in a Lanc. Anyway, Bill Peedell (our pilot) lined up left and started his approach at which point flying control started firing off red Very flares at us so we went round again. The skipper sought clarification on our instructions at which point a voice came back and said 'Land and then turn left'. This made more sense and just after we touched down the voice came again 'Goodnight Love' at which point we all chorused 'Goodnight darling!'

DOUG REED DFM. WIRELESS OPERATOR.
156 SQUADRON. FIFTY-TWO OPS.

Doug Reed survived a parachute jump in training to go on and complete over fifty ops.

not be discerned. Again a good many aircraft landed away, and one, a 97 Squadron Lancaster, crash landed at Manston. Three aircraft failed to return, two from 97, including that of Flight Lieutenant Wallace Covington DFC who successfully evaded. The second trip to Nuremberg was similarly a case of 'what might have been' for marking was erratic both in timing and in its precision, so bombs tended to cluster around two distinct points, both some way from the actual aiming point and spread back for some considerable distance. Four Lancasters were lost: two from 97 Squadron and one each from 83 and 156 Squadrons. A further Lancaster of 83 Squadron crash landed having been hit by flak but its crew escaped unhurt.

The PFF-led main force attack on Berlin on August 23/24 employed Wing Commander Kenneth Burns DFC and Bar of 97 Squadron in the role of master of ceremonies. Despite his best efforts, the raid was only partially successful, with most of the bombs falling more than three miles from the aiming point and the weight of the attack landing in the southwest of the city. Flak, searchlights and nightfighters combined well – so successfully that they contributed to a dreadful night for Pathfinder Force with eleven aircraft missing; five Lancasters and six Halifax – four from one squadron.

There was a lucky escape by Sergeant Cliff Chatten of 97 Squadron and his crew, intercepted and badly shot up by an intruder over Norfolk, almost in sight of home. Chatten was himself seriously wounded in the stomach and leg, and his Australian mid upper gunner, Sergeant John Kraemer, killed. (Chatten recovered and was later commissioned, winning an immediate DSO while still with 97 Squadron in May, 1944.)

Sergeant H. Smith of 405 Squadron was more fortunate. Badly shot about by a Bf109, Smith was last heard at 02.32 to say that he was ditching, five miles off the Danish coast. He actually came down near Ystad, Sweden, and survived to be interned.

A Lancaster flown by Flight Sergeant Trevor Stephens of 156 Squadron also came under attack by nightfighters as well as being hit by flak, shortly after completing a successful bombing run. His rear gunner (Flight Sergeant Vincent Attree) was killed and the mid upper gunner and navigator badly injured. Stephens nursed his heavily-damaged bomber to Attlebridge where he landed safely on only two engines. Stephens, his navigator (Sergeant Arthur Clegg) and wireless operator (Sergeant Thomas Stocks) were awarded immediate DFMs.

INTRUDERS IN THE CIRCUIT

Aircrew faced danger at every stage of a bombing operation, from the moment they took off to the time they returned. Even after an arduous eight or nine-hour trip, with the runway in sight and on approach to land, an enemy fighter could still be waiting to pick them off. These so-called 'intruders' were a constant menace:

"On one particular Berlin raid I was late back having to nurse a sick engine. I arrived at the English coast at the same time as the heavies. There were obviously intruders about because I saw one heavy shot down inside the funnel of its airfield and another burning on the ground. The lights at Drem airfield were being switched off but when I arrived back at Oakington the place was a blaze of lights.

"I gave a warning to control that intruders were about and requested the lights to be extinguished except for a reduced flare path. The reply was: 'we have no knowledge of intruders – make a normal landing'. I repeated my warning but to no avail. Consequently I approached without navigation lights and kept a very careful look out.

"I had reached about 200ft in my descent with wheels and flaps down when I spotted a dark shape coming in from the starboard beam. I made a steep diving turn to port, frightened the life out of the crew in the chequered caravan at the end of the runway, and lost contact with my attacker. My next approach was extremely unorthodox to say the least. I landed in the last third of the runway and taxied in to my dispersal at considerable speed. My navigator and I quickly disembarked and were making our way to the pickup truck when there was a loud swirling noise and somebody shouted: 'down!' The intruder dived over our dispersal spraying everything in sight. In a few minutes it looked as though the whole airfield was on fire."

LES FLETCHER DFC & BAR
PILOT. 571 SQUADRON. SEVENTY-SIX OPS.

Some forty-eight men of PFF lost their lives that night; the experience and seniority of those missing was alarming. Within the crew of Pilot Officer Kenneth Fairlie of 97 Squadron was thirty-six-year-old Squadron Leader Joseph Forrest, a hugely-experienced navigator who had won the DFC in 1941 with 10 Squadron and added a DSO with 83 Squadron almost two years later to the day. At the time of his death he was group navigation officer. The 83 Squadron crew of Flight Lieutenant Brian Slade DFC, shot down and killed by a nightfighter, could claim four gallantry awards and 330 operational flights between them. Slade's aircraft was shot out of the sky at the start of his bombing run. He was on his fifty-ninth trip.

Squadron Leader Charles Lofthouse of 7 Squadron was another whose loss would be keenly felt. Lofthouse had been awarded the OBE (military) for helping to save five of his colleagues from a burning bomber that had crashed at Waterbeach. Over Berlin he suddenly found the night sky illuminated with tracer from a marauding nightfighter. He survived as did the rest of the crew which that evening had been supplemented by the station commander at Oakington, Group Captain Alfred Willetts DSO. After they had been hit, Lofthouse later described Willetts as shooting out of the escape hatch 'like a rat out of a trap!'

Willetts was not the only station commander missing that night. The mercurial Basil Robinson – at the time a group captain with four decorations – was also killed. He was flying as a 'guest' of Flight Lieutenant Harry Webster DFC. It was perhaps inevitable that Robinson's run of good fortune would finally come to an end.

PFF went back to Berlin as August became September and perhaps should not have bothered. Winds were not as forecast with the result that many crews were late and the marking suffered as a result. Bombing was scattered and the ORB notes that 'the attack must be considered a failure'.

A BAD NIGHT FOR 35

On the night that Group Captain Basil Robinson lost his life, there were three other aircraft from Graveley that were reported missing, all believed to be the victims of nightfighters. One of those was a Halifax II flown by an Australian, Pilot Officer Laurie Lahey. Lahey's crew had arrived on 35 Squadron in March 1943, having volunteered for Pathfinders after completing eight trips with 77 Squadron. They were on their thirtieth trip and detailed as a blind marker when disaster struck, as the crew's flight engineer recalls:

> "We broke cloud east of Hannover and within minutes we were faced with 20mm cannon shell from a Ju88 … as soon as the first shells hit us the skipper went into violent evasive action … when he righted the plane I could see what a mess we were in. The shells had ripped through the fuselage within an inch of my flare 'chute position, torn the starboard wings apart, set the two starboard engines on fire and the 1,000 gallons of petrol. None of the seven crew members were touched."

> WILF SUTTON
> FLIGHT ENGINEER. 35 SQUADRON. TWENTY-NINE OPS.

German defences were particularly robust: out of an attacking force of 622 aircraft, forty-seven were missing of which seventeen were Stirlings. There were some forty-two combats reported in the target area alone. Three aircraft were missing from PFF, including the Lancaster of the 97 Squadron master bomber, Kenneth Burns, shot down in a head-on attack from an FW190.

Burns survived as a prisoner of war, albeit severely injured, losing his right forearm and hand,

REFRESHER TRAINING

Flight Lieutenant Frank Leatherdale DFC (right) came to Pathfinders having completed a tour of operations with 115 Squadron, part of 3 Group. His skipper was a Canadian, Flight Lieutenant Donald McKechnie DFC. On leaving 7 Squadron having completed fifty-nine ops, Frank was posted to PFF NTU as an instructor:

> "NTU was divided into two flights: 'A' Flight was for complete crews (that is to say those that had arrived at NTU already formed) whereas 'B' Flight was made up of individual pilots, navigators etc who were then put into crews. Even experienced men needed refresher training or to be schooled in the art of Pathfinder terminology and methods. Among the experienced men that I flew with was Wing Commander Burns who had recently been repatriated from Germany. He only had one hand, and used to screw on a claw to his right stump to operate the throttles."

> FRANK LEATHERDALE DFC
> NAVIGATOR. 7 SQUADRON. FIFTY-NINE OPS.

and breaking his back on landing. Sometime later, with the Germans clearly believing his war was over, Burns was repatriated, only to resume his Pathfinder career and add the DSO to his list of decorations. The citation remarked upon his 'inflexible determination'. Rarely was a comment more justifiably written. He was appointed to PFF HQ Air Staff.

August had been a month of hard battles reflected in the casualty figures. The number of aircraft missing was forty-one, with 35 Squadron suffering the worst (ten aircraft shot down) and 405 Squadron one behind. Over Mönchengladbach on August 30/31, 7 Squadron lost three in one night: Squadron Leader Cyril Anekstein DFC and four of his crew were killed (Anekstein had won his DFC for bravery during the first 1,000-bomber raids); Pilot Officer Jack Sutherst and five of his crew were killed; but more happily Flying Officer Oliver Wells and all of his crew survived. The nuisance raids conducted by the Mosquitoes also led to the loss of five from 139 Squadron.

An attack on Berlin on 12/13 is typical of the challenges faced: eight Mosquitoes were detailed but only seven took off, the other withdrawn with technical difficulties. Five Mosquitoes attacked on the estimated position: two encountered little opposition but later aircraft reported accurate predicted heavy flak with considerable searchlight activity. One aircraft returned early with technical trouble and one failed to come back. The Mosquito of Flight Sergeant Herbert Valentine was last heard from Coltishall at 01.46.

YELLOW STREAKS AND METALLIC CLANGS

Born into the distinguished Charles Wells brewing family, Flying Officer Oliver Wells came to Pathfinders after a long period of experimental night-flying training. Posted to 7 Squadron, he found himself on operations on the night of August 30/31. Everything went well until they neared the target, when suddenly there was series of sickening flashes, yellow streaks and metallic clangs as a Bf110 nightfighter attacked:

"I realised that the port wing had caught a packet. Simultaneously the gunner called up to report the attack asking me to turn like hell to port. It was just a second or two too late. I dived the aircraft to try and blow out the flames but this was useless. I feathered the port inner engine and used the fire extinguisher. It didn't work. Flames were stretching back from the trailing edge of the wing to beyond the tail, making a noise, above that of the engines, like a giant blow-lamp.

"It didn't take me long to decide that it was all up and I told Johnny (the bomb aimer) to jettison the bombs. When this was done, I gave the order to abandon aircraft. It must be understood that although this takes some time to describe, the actual time from being hit to my order to abandon aircraft was little more than two minutes.

"Johnny was the first to go out, and the last fixed my 'chute on me whilst waiting in the queue. Then suddenly there was some sort of explosion. The nose of the aircraft dropped and she started to spiral down to port in a sort of skidding spin. The controls were useless and I decided it was high time I wasn't there.

"I left the seat and lurched towards the front escape hatch. My head and shoulders cleared it all right, but there was a tremendous sideways force of air which blew me against the side of the hatch and I stuck fast. I saw that I would be killed, and wondered what it would be like. The last thing I remember doing was releasing my parachute harness to see if I could shake it free. My next impression, however, was wondering what I was doing face downwards on the grass."

OLIVER WELLS
PILOT. 7 SQUADRON PFF. SEVEN OPS.

ESCAPE AND EVASION

Pathfinders were issued with various items of personal 'kit' to help them evade capture if shot down over enemy lines: miniature compasses were hidden in buttons; maps were printed on silk scarves or rice paper; passport-sized pictures (called 'pimpernel' photographs) were sewn into battledress tunics to be used on identity papers if they were lucky enough to find themselves part of an organised 'escape line'.

A compass was an essential part of the new aircrew escape kit.

This collar stud / compass was one of a series of escape aids issued to allied aircrew in WWII in case of being forced down in enemy territory. The glass cover of the compass was painted white to conceal the fact it was a compass. P.T.o

Certainly prior to the invasion of Europe, the vast majority of Pathfinders shot down were captured and interned. But that did not always mean that their war was over. A good number set their minds to escape. Charles Lofthouse was one. Before the war he had been a draughtsman, and these skills were deployed to good effect by the 'X' organisation in Stalag Luft III – scene of the Great Escape – as one of a team producing maps and forged documents for the escapees.

Flight Lieutenant Denis Crayford, the navigator in the Lofthouse crew, was another. He too was incarcerated at Stalag Luft III, and was employed as a 'penguin' dispersing sand from the three tunnels being built within the camp by way of sacks suspended inside his trouser legs. Allocated a space for the escape, he was inside the tunnel and a good way along it when the break out was discovered. He was perhaps fortunate that he had not made it. Of the seventy-six that did escape, fifty were executed.

A beautifully-detailed escape map of Germany, printed on silk.

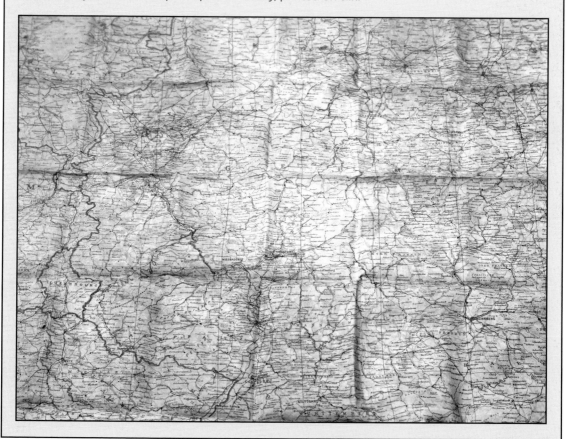

The number of sorties flown and tonnage of bombs dropped again created a record. Since its foundation, Pathfinder Force had logged some 6,210 sorties comprising more than 32,431 operational flying hours. In August it dropped 3,210 tons of bombs (including those jettisoned) for the loss of forty-one aircraft.

PFF was continuing to experiment and innovate. Red spot fires, for example, were used for the first time at Peenemünde and PFF also supported two attacks on various ammunition dumps in northwest France for aircraft from various operational training units (OTUs) – giving training crews an early taste of 'real' exercises and conditions. The Germans, too, had continued to develop new methods of attack, the most deadly being the upward-firing cannon known as *Schräge Musik*. This was similarly employed for the first time at Peenemünde and for some months to follow, bomber crews would live in fear of this new menace that plucked them from the sky without warning.

SEPTEMBER

Pathfinder Force was now one year old; although it did not pause to celebrate.

Berlin was again chosen as the target for the first main force raid in September 1943, and Pathfinders achieved a good cluster of red TIs that were well and promptly backed up by greens. Unfortunately the markers were short of the target, but the bombs that did fall started fires that could be seen from the Baltic coast. Flak and fighters, as had now become customary over the German capital, were well into their stride, accounting for seven percent of the attacking force. Four Pathfinder Lancasters were missing: three from 7 Squadron (including Flight Lieutenant Richard French DFC) and a fourth from 156. Earlier in the day (September 3), 156 Squadron had lost one of its more experienced pilots – Canadian Flying Officer Clifford Foderingham DFC – to a training accident.

A considerably more successful raid was executed on the night of September 5/6. The target area was marked with red TIs by aircraft carrying H2S which also dropped flares. The exact aiming point was then to be identified and marked visually with yellows and greens. The plan worked like a charm, and with no cloud and good visibility, an excellent raid developed and a series of large explosions reported as the ORB attests: 'Despite the usual spread back of the attack, this is thought to be the best yet made on Mannheim.' The defences were active, however, and three Pathfinders lost in return for one single-engine enemy nightfighter claimed as destroyed. The dead included an 83 Squadron crew skippered by Pilot Officer John Price and his crew who had more than 205 operations between them but not a single decoration. Such was the lottery of awards.

This was not the only successful raid on Mannheim that month; they went back to the city on

THE HAZARDS OF FLYING TRAINING

Most Pathfinder veterans have a tale to tell about the hazards of training – the lucky escape and the near death experience. Others tell of friends lost or badly injured, some before operations at OTUs or heavy conversion units (HCUs) flying aircraft that had seen better days and that, by rights, should not have been allowed in the air. Accidents, it seems, were not always the sole reserve of the novice. Even experienced flyers were at risk.

Clifford Foderingham and his crew had been on an air firing and bombing exercise when their aircraft was seen to stall at very low altitude and dive into the ground with tremendous force and explode into flames. A subsequent accident investigation stated that the pilot was guilty of negligence for disobeying orders, flying without parachutes and without a flight engineer. Although Foderingham was an experienced pilot with more than 600 hours to his name, he had only seven hours flying time on Lancasters.

A bad night for 97 Squadron recorded in the logbook of wireless op, Walter Layne.

September 23/24 to mark for a force of more than 600 bombers. The plan was to hit those areas that had escaped in the earlier attack, and again everything went according to plan. The only thing that went wrong was the diversionary raid – an all-8 Group spoof affair on Darmstadt – that fooled nobody and was in fact so close in geography to the Mannheim raid that it had little discernible effect.

Opposition that night from flak was described as negligible, but the fighters more than made up for it. Their victims included two Lancasters from 97 Squadron, one flown by Flight Lieutenant Robert Fletcher DFC, DFM. Fletcher survived to become a prisoner of war, but his navigator and both gunners were killed. The navigator, Squadron Leader Kenneth Foster DFC & Bar was the squadron navigation leader; one of the gunners, Squadron Leader Robert McKinna DFC & Bar, was the gunnery leader.

The great British weather played its part throughout the month; on ten nights various operations had to be cancelled and on one night none were possible at all. The busiest crews were in the Mosquito squadrons carrying out their nuisance raids on such targets as Duisberg, Cologne, Düsseldorf and Berlin. Not surprisingly, casualties began to rise. A senior crew in 139 Squadron was lost on an attack on the German capital on September 14/15. Eight aircraft had been detailed for the raid, and three of them managed to bomb through patchy cloud, having taken a fix on Brandenburg and various lakes to the southwest. Two others bombed targets of the last resort – Emden and Borkum Island – neither crew wanting to have gone all that way with nothing to show for it. Of the other three, one returned early because of the weather, a second with technical trouble, and the third was shot down, killing the pilot, Flight Lieutenant Maule Colledge and his navigator, Flying Officer Geoffrey Marshall.

Two nights later, another 139 crew nearly came to grief when their Mosquito was hit by flak over Berlin and their aircraft was subsequently written off; less than twenty-four hours later, yet another 139 Squadron aircraft and crew found themselves on the receiving end of a rather determined attack from German fighters who inflicted near-fatal damage, their Mosquito already down to one engine as the result of flak. Somehow the pilot, Flying Officer Joe Patient, managed to crash land at Manston and walk away unscathed, albeit somewhat shaken by his experience.

In terms of main force raids, in addition to the attack on Berlin at the start of the month and the two trips to Mannheim, Pathfinders also flew to Munich (September 6/7), Montluçon

THE CATERPILLAR CLUB

Walter Layne, the wireless operator in the Lancaster flown by Flight Lieutenant Robert Fletcher had been flying operationally since the summer of 1941. Trained as an observer and passing both his signals and air gunnery courses, he had taken part in the early attacks on the *Scharnhorst* and *Gneisenau* with 50 Squadron flying from Lindholme.

Having completed a tour of operations by March 1942, he was screened, eventually finding himself at 1661 Conversion Unit (Waddington) prior to a posting to 97 Squadron in March 1943. Here he crewed with Robert Fletcher undertaking their first night-time sortie to St Nazaire on April 2 and completing a further twenty-six operations before being shot down on the night of September 23/24.

Walter was at large for more than a week before being captured, twenty miles east of Nancy in France, and word reached his wife that he was safe before the authorities had even been officially informed of his capture.

Many months later, his wife received another letter, this time from Leslie Irvin of Irving (sic) Air Chute of Great Britain Ltd, the Hertfordshire-based parachute manufacturers. The company had established a rather fine tradition of enrolling anyone saved by one of their 'chutes into membership of The Caterpillar Club, for which they received a small gold caterpillar pin with a jewelled eye to wear on their lapel. (The caterpillar motif refers simply to the silk threads from which the original parachutes were made.)

Wartime shortages meant it was two years after being shot down that Walter Layne finally received his caterpillar.

Owing to war shortages and difficulties in supply, Mr Irvin apologised to Mrs Layne that Walter's pin might be some time in coming. Indeed Walter did not finally receive his 'award' until some months after, at the end of January 1946, by which time there were more than 34,000 members of the club.

Walter Layne (second from right).

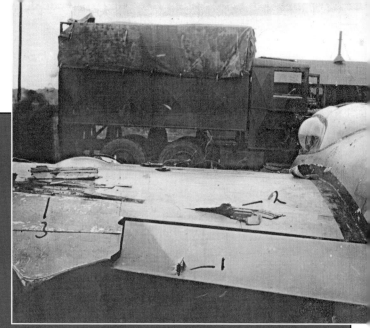

Joe Patient's Mosquito having been on the receiving end of the German defences.

FLAK, FIGHTERS AND HURDLING TYPHOONS!

Joe Patient and his navigator, Sergeant 'Norry' Gilroy, were in one of five Mosquitoes detailed to attack Berlin on September 16/17, carrying three 500-pound and one 250-pound bombs. Reaching the target early, Joe lost time in a dog-leg and started his bombing run at which point all hell broke loose:

"There were searchlights and flak everywhere, the like of which we had never seen before. Norry shouted at me to turn to port as there was flak coming up, but there was on the port also. Then we received a direct hit in the starboard engine and for some reason I feathered the port engine before realising my mistake. I restarted the port and feathered the starboard engine and asked Norry for a direct route home.

"All was well until we reached Münster, when we were again coned which forced me to dive. By now we had lost a great deal of height and were only flying on one engine. It was then that the FW190s appeared, and scored hits on the port wing and our remaining good engine, the fuel tanks, flaps, elevators and ailerons. They also hit Norry in the neck. One of the Focke Wulfs flew alongside and I could see his face quite clearly. I heeled over to ram him but he must have guessed what I was about to do and disappeared. I assume he was out of fuel, ammo or both.

"We managed to limp over the coast at 200ft and then climb to 4,000ft with the engine straining badly. Our fuel gauges were showing zero but we could just make out land. Norry fired off a flare to say that we were coming straight in, and the flare-path was lit up immediately. With no flaps and no undercarriage we landed on our belly coming to a quick stop. Unbuckling our harnesses, we were just trying to clamber out when there was a loud 'bang' as another aircraft hit ours and bounced over the top, taking off our tailplane. It was a Typhoon. We learned later that Manston control had not seen our flare, and had lit the flare-path for the Typhoon.

"I walked away from the crash like a drunkard; to survive all that was a miracle. Someone was watching down on us that day."

JOE PATIENT DFC
139 SQUADRON AND 1409 (MET) FLIGHT. FIFTY-NINE OPS.

(September 15/16), the marshalling yards at Modane (September 16/17), Hannover (September 22/23 and again on 27/28) and Bochum (September 29/30). The two attacks on Mannheim, as already noted, were deemed a success. The ORB also remarks that the raid on Montluçon was particularly prosperous, and with good reason.

Montluçon was the home of the Dunlop rubber factory, and considered important enough to warrant the use of a master of ceremonies, Wing Commander D.F.E.C. 'Dixie' Dean. Dean, the commanding officer of 35 Squadron, did his job well, bringing many of the bombers down below the cloud to bomb at between 4,000-5,000ft, with the target and factory buildings clearly

Master bomber 'Dixie' Dean was recruited by Bennett into PFF having completed a first tour with 77 Squadron. He was a group captain by the age of twenty-six.

visible. Defences were negligible, consisting of a few bursts of flak and a single searchlight. Every building in the factory was hit, and a large fire started. Despite the obvious success, this was the last occasion that Pathfinders used the master bomber technique until the spring of 1944.

Losses for the month totalled eighteen; the ORB summary does not record where these losses were allocated, but the misery was fairly evenly spread. Munich proved a bad night for 156 Squadron with three aircraft shot down or written off: captains Flying Officer Alan Lutz DFC RAAF and Flight Lieutenant Alastair MacLachlan DFC were killed; Squadron Leader Coates injured. Coates had only been with the squadron a week. They also lost Squadron Leader Peter 'Vin' Vincent DFC over Hannover on September 27/28 and Flight Sergeant Frederick Ray returning from Bochum on September 29/30. Ray and his crew, similarly, had only arrived at 156 a few days earlier.

To add to the losses suffered by 7 Squadron at the start of the month, Pilot Officer William Stenhouse went missing on the night of September 22/23 and Pilot Officer Dennis Routen DFM five nights later. Routen had joined Pathfinders from 90 Squadron and was on his thirty-sixth operation. His aircraft was believed to have been a victim of *Schräge Musik*; only the mid upper gunner, Flight Sergeant James Kanelakos DFM, survived.

There were also two aircraft lost each from 83 Squadron and 405 Squadrons. One of the 405 Squadron captains – and one of the first 405 Squadron Lancaster losses recorded – was Squadron Leader Lloyd Logan DFC who survived to become a prisoner of war. Logan, a flight commander, had a habit of surviving, having only just returned to operations following a successful evasion further to a raid on Essen in March, prior to 405 becoming a part of PFF.

Among the heavy-bomber squadrons, 35 was perhaps the most fortunate, losing only one crew in the month, that of Flying Officer Nicholas Matich DFM. One of his crew, who survived to become a POW, was Pilot Officer Frank Dolling DFM. Dolling had a lucky escape, falling more than 16,000ft to a mere 1,000ft before his parachute belatedly cracked open. He later went on to become chairman of Barclays Bank International. (Matich evaded capture and later returned to the squadron. He was awarded the DSO in May 1944.)

Along with the losses felt by 139 Squadron, 105 Squadron also lost one of its crews in September, and its first Mosquito IX. Returning from a sortie to Bochum, Lieutenant F.M. Fisher survived the crash landing that resulted; his navigator, Pilot Officer Leslie Hogan DFM did not.

OCTOBER

By the end of September, the total number of sorties flown by Pathfinder Force had risen to 7,211. A further 1,027 sorties would be recorded by the end of October for the loss of twenty-three Pathfinder aircraft, a rise on the previous month but within the realms of 'acceptable' losses. One operation more than any other is highlighted as achieving 'outstanding success' in October, the attack on Kassel on the night of 23/24.

Pathfinders in fact went to Kassel twice in October. The first, on the night of 3/4, was somewhat inconclusive. Although the attack opened well and on time, a ground haze prevented the visual markers from positively identifying the aiming point, and there was some suggestion afterwards that dummy fires and decoy markers may have been used to cause further confusion. One PFF aircraft inadvertently dropped a red TI on Paderborn that wasted a number of bombs, but some fires and two large explosions were reported, one of which was undoubtedly as a result of a chance hit on an ammunition dump at Ihringshausen. Casualties for the raid were light: only ten aircraft were missing out of an attacking force of more than 400, and only one of these – an 83 Squadron Lancaster III flown by Squadron Leader John Hayter DFC – was a Pathfinder. (Hayter had interestingly won his DFC as a pilot with 240 Squadron in the winter of 1941, at which point the squadron was engaged in Atlantic patrols having recently converted to the Consolidated Catalina.) Post-raid reports put the success down to the effectiveness of the 'spoof' target at Hannover.

For PFF's second visit to Kassel, everything went according to plan. Not only did the attack start well with flares and yellow TIs, but they were quickly followed by confirmation red TIs that were extremely well placed (eight of the nine visual markers identified the aiming point). There was 'a general impression that the concentration was well positioned' – a fact supported soon afterwards by what was described as the most devastating attack on a German city since the firestorm raid on Hamburg two months earlier. RAF PRU reports showed significant damage to the railway system and three Henschel aircraft factories that, at the time, were building the first of Hitler's weapons of revenge, the V1. Seven PFF were obliged to return early, and an eighth, a Halifax of 35 Squadron never returned at all.

No other attack during the month achieved the spectacular success of the second raid on Kassel, with the exception, perhaps, of the very first, but it was not for the want of trying, effort or indeed sacrifice on the part of Pathfinder Force. It was by no means an unproductive month. The attack on Hagen at the start of October proved that considerable damage could be done even with a relatively small number, if the target was accurately marked. A force of only 243 Lancasters and eight Mosquitoes used Oboe skymarking to perfection, destroying a number of factories including one that made vital accumulator batteries for U-boats.

A larger attack on Frankfurt also showed the Pathfinders at their best; the raid was not without casualties, however, and arguably the most significant and poignant loss was that of a young squadron leader in charge of a 156 Squadron Lancaster and on his fifty-fourth operation. Squadron Leader Syd Cook DFC, DFM RAAF was only twenty-one and one of the youngest officers of such rank to be killed in Bomber Command and Pathfinder Force during the war. Cook's name is perhaps best known for featuring in Don Charlwood's

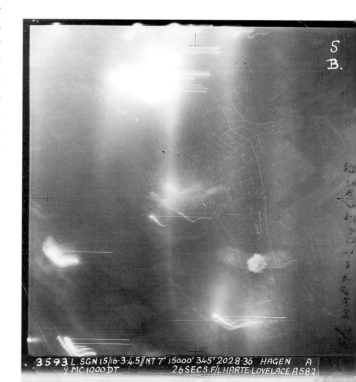

Hagen from 15,000ft. The photograph was taken by Tony Harte-Lovelace, a pre-war regular and instructor who won the DFC with 578 Squadron before moving to 582 Squadron and completing fifty operations by the close of hostilities.

haunting book, *No Moon Tonight*, in which the author sensed that the young man's luck would finally give out. And so it proved. Cook's regular navigator, Harry Wright, was not flying with him that night, having been in hospital with sinus trouble. Wright would himself go on to win both the DFC & Bar to add to an earlier DFM, and complete seventy-eight operations. He later wrote a fictionalised account of his experiences, *Pathfinder Squadron*, in which one of the principal characters was called 'Syd' and it was to Cook's memory that the title was dedicated.

An attack on Stuttgart achieved mixed results; the raid on Hannover on October 8/9 – the last to feature the Wellington in a main force attack – was more successful. The town and specific aiming point were identified visually and the bombing well concentrated in what was to be described as probably Hannover's worst attack of the war. A good many buildings were destroyed and the civilian casualty list was long. Five Pathfinder aircraft were missing and a sixth from the spoof raid on Bremen: two from 7 Squadron (Pilot Officer Philip Hartstein and Flying Officer Bruce Macpherson – whose crew included a seventeen-year-old air gunner, Sergeant Eric Brinton); Pilot Officer Graeme Nicholl RCAF from 97 Squadron (his aircraft is thought to have received a direct hit by flak that tore off the nose. Nicholl miraculously survived but the rest of his crew did not); Pilot Officer 'Johnnie' Fry of 156 Squadron (shot down by a combination of flak and fighters, Fry heroically maintained control of his aircraft long enough for some of his crew to make it out alive); and the 405 Lancaster and crew of Squadron Leader Murray Schneider RCAF. Attacking Bremen, the 35 Squadron Halifax of Flying Officer Max Muller was badly shot about by a nightfighter and ultimately crash landed in Norfolk after a long and nerve-racking trip home.

A poor run of losses for 7 Squadron followed another attack on Hannover ten days later that was by no means as successful as the first. Two crews were missing (Pilot Officer Herman Boness RCAF and Warrant Officer Alan Marshall both killed in action) and a further crew from 97 Squadron (Flight Lieutenant Duncan Moodie DFC RCAF, also killed in action). It was a heavy price to pay for an attack that achieved little.

Another poignant loss followed on the night of October 20/21, a wasted night for Bomber Command that spelled the end for six Pathfinder Lancaster crews with all but nothing to show in return. The target was Leipzig, a city at the far extreme of the bombers' range and which until

Halifax in flight.

THE PIANO MAN

In the officers' mess at RAF Wyton is an old and rather battered piano. If it could speak, it would tell of the tunes once played upon it by a gifted musician and equally talented pilot, Richard Manton.

Manton, known as John to family and close friends, was born April 12, 1913 in London into a service family – his father was a regular army officer (a sapper), his elder brother became a regular naval officer after going to Dartmouth, and his younger sister became a senior officer in the ATS.

John Manton. A gifted musician and a determined pilot.

Educated at Cheltenham College, he nursed a determined ambition to become an air pilot. In 1931 he joined Imperial Airways on the office staff, serving in a number of countries overseas, but was disappointed not to get airborne. He left in December 1936 to go to the civilian flying school in Reading, where he finally achieved his ambition and qualified as a pilot. Joining the RAF in March 1937, he was posted to the Middle East, where his flying training continued, and thence on to India where he served on the North West Frontier. By 1941 he had been transferred to the Coastal Defence Force, covering the British Army's retreat from Burma, joining 221 Group in the following year.

He was then posted back to the UK by which stage he was an acting squadron leader, and underwent retraining as a bomber officer, ultimately joining 83 Squadron at RAF Wyton in June 1943 as a flight commander to Wing Commander John Searby. On the way home from the raid on Leipzig on the night of October 20, 1943 his Lancaster was shot down over Assen, in the Netherlands, by a Bf110 night-fighter flown by German ace Oberfeldwebel Heinz Vinke for his second 'kill' of the night. (Vinke was himself shot down and killed just four months later, off Dunkirk in February 1944.)

The citizens of Assen maintain the crew's graves carefully, and have erected a memorial stone and a Lancaster propeller. Every year they commemorate the crash on its anniversary, and local schoolchildren are encouraged to participate.

John was an outgoing young man, an able sportsman with modern tastes in music (jazz) and cars (a very early SS Jaguar), but his musical abilities included fine piano-playing, his 'party piece' being the show-off classical 'Rustle of Spring'. He never married, but a succession of good-looking girlfriends deeply impressed his young brother!

---

then had largely escaped the planners' attention, more out of practicalities rather than desire. The bombers were not only hindered by the range, but also poor weather resulting in heavy icing. Of the seventy-three Pathfinder Lancasters detailed, fifty-three attacked the prime target, ten returned early, four attacked last resorts (among them the airfield at Texel, Mücheln and Magdeburg) and six were missing.

The missing included the crews of Flying Officer James Leitch DFC RAAF and Flight Sergeant Donald Watson of 7 Squadron; Pilot Officer Kenneth Painter of 97 Squadron; a 405 Squadron Lancaster III flown by Pilot Officer Kemble Wood RAAF; and two Lancs from 83 Squadron. Warrant Officer Stanley Hall and his crew were lost without trace; Squadron Leader Richard Manton was shot down by a nightfighter and crashed near Assen in Holland.

Two Mosquitoes were also missing from that night's operations, engaged in a variety of minor operations. Both were from 139 Squadron. The Mosquito IV of Flight Lieutenant Archie Mellor suffered a major instrument failure a short while into its flight home from Berlin, followed soon after by a serious glycol leak from one of its engines. Although Mellor successfully shut down the failing engine, the aircraft struggled to maintain height and with the port engine spluttering he decided to bale out. Mellor successfully evaded capture but his navigator was not so fortunate and spent the rest of the war 'in the bag'.

(This was not the first time that Archie Mellor had experienced a close call with death. A few months earlier he had been operating over Düsseldorf with George Cash, his regular navigator with whom he had crewed up at 1655 MTU [Mosquito training unit], at his side, when their aircraft was hit by flak, setting the port engine ablaze. Mellor managed to quell the fire but had to shut the engine down. At this point the starboard engine started to play up, and the navigator worked out a course for home taking the shortest possible route, even if that meant flying over known areas of searchlights and flak. Mellor used every ounce of skill honed over many hundreds of hours as an instructor to adjust the throttle settings sufficiently to keep the aircraft above stalling speed, but even his skill could not prevent them from losing height at a rate of almost 200ft per minute. With expert flying and a bit of luck in navigation they found themselves over base with just enough height to go straight in. The following morning they found that, as well as the dud engine, there were huge lumps of shrapnel in the starboard engine such that it was only capable of seventy-five percent of its total power. Mellor was so shaken by the experience that he was told to rest; George Cash, without a pilot, was posted to 1409 Met Flight that had need of a spare navigator.)

No-one knew what became of the second crew lost that night, but their squadron colleagues Flight Sergeant Thomas Forsyth RAAF and Sergeant Leonard James are remembered on the Runnymede Memorial.

October was a bad month for the Mosquito boys, although the list of targets was impressive: Aachen (which included the first operational, if unsuccessful, trial for the G-H blind bombing

equipment – a device that worked like Oboe in reverse), Berlin, Brauweiler, Cologne, Dortmund, Duisberg, Düsseldorf, Emden, Hamborn, and the Ruhr. All were described as having 'no doubt a considerable effect on the morale of the people in the target area' as well as achieving 'a certain amount of damage'.

A 109 Squadron Mosquito disintegrated during a training flight on October 22, killing the pilot Flying Officer Frederick Jackson. Jackson, an Australian, had won an immediate DFM flying with 460 Squadron almost exactly a year earlier. The very next day, on an operation to attack the

John Jackson was an exceptional gunner who spent much of the war instructing. After a handful of trips with 149 Squadron he joined 156 as gunnery leader, usually flying with the flight and squadron commanders. Over Paris on July 7 he fought off six separate attacks from a Ju88. By the war's end he had completed fifty-five ops and been awarded the DFC.

A GUNNER'S ROUTINE

"We were trained to run away and live to fight another day. The German fighters, if you saw them, were faster and their cannons had a considerably longer range than our machine guns. I saw quite a few fighters in my time – that was quite difficult in the dark – but only once did I open up, on the last flight of my first tour. It helped to keep yourself fit. PT and exercise helped to keep you alert, and on a long flight you could not afford to lose your concentration or daydream, not even for a minute. You could never relax. I always used to take my 'wakey wakey' tablets just to make doubly sure."

ALF HUBERMAN
AIR GUNNER. 83 SQUADRON. THIRTY-EIGHT OPS.

"Standard procedure if we saw a night-fighter was to call for a corkscrew starboard or port, depending on where the aircraft was, and engage it if we could. Discretion was always the key, however. He had a much better chance of picking you off than you had of shooting him down."

PERCY CANNINGS DFM
MID UPPER GUNNER.
97 SQUADRON.
FORTY-SEVEN OPS.

Knapsack power station near Cologne – described as 'a training flight for Mosquitoes fitted with special equipment' – Flight Lieutenant Gordon Sweeney DFC and his navigator of 105 Squadron were lost without trace, becoming the first crew to be reported missing since the squadron had joined Pathfinder Force. The month ended in another tragedy for 139 Squadron, when Warrant Officer Bernard Wright and his fellow Warrant Officer Frederick Spencer failed to return from an operation to Cologne.

November had to get better. Sadly no-one had reckoned with Harris' master plan, and an all-out attack on Berlin that would prove the graveyard for even some of Pathfinder's most experienced crews.

CHAPTER 4
BERLIN OR BUST

NOVEMBER

By the middle of November 1943, the C-in-C Bomber Command at last had the weapons – and more than 700 four-engined bombers – at his disposal to launch his main assault on the German capital. An improved version of H2S was being fitted into Pathfinder aircraft and would now be tested, but perhaps the real test was for the crews, rather than the equipment. The advantage of attacking Berlin in the winter was the longer nights that he hoped would help cloak the bombers from the probing eyes of the German defences; the disadvantage would be the inevitable bad weather.

But before the first of the raids was mounted, the command had a number of other tasks to perform. A heavy raid on Düsseldorf appeared inconclusive, although returning Pathfinder crews reported a good number of fires taking hold within the area of the TIs followed by a series of explosions. No aircraft were lost, but a 35 Squadron Halifax was damaged in a crash landing upon its return and the next day a 405 Squadron Lancaster dived into the ground on a training flight, killing the pilot, Flying Officer Bertram Pringle.

Due to the weather only a number of minor operations were conducted over the next few days, keeping the Mosquito squadrons and their crews busy. Multiple attacks were mounted on Aachen, Bochum, Cologne, Dortmund, Duisberg, Düsseldorf, Essen, Hamburg, Hannover and Leverkusen – the latter proving a success and crews reporting fires burning in other cities on their return. The number of technical difficulties during this period appears unusually high, and the anonymous ORB author chooses to separate out 'last resort' attacks from the main summary.

The entry for the night of November 4/5, for example, shows that five Mosquitoes suffered 'technical failures' meaning that all bombed on a DR run using their last Gee 'fix'. The following night, up to 150 searchlights greeted an attacking force of ten Mosquitoes sent to bomb Bochum with better results. All but one managed to attack the primary, although a 105 Squadron aircraft was lost that night on its way back to Marham. The Mosquito crashed into a field near Norwich, killing the pilot Flight Lieutenant John Gordon and his navigator, Flying Officer Ralph Hayes. Both men had been awarded the DFC for their part in a long-range attack on Berlin in January 1943 – a raid for which no fewer than ten medals for gallantry were awarded.

There was some satisfaction on the night of November 11/12 when a force of a little over 300 aircraft attacked the railway yards at Modane in good weather conditions with no cloud and excellent visibility. Visual markers had no difficulty in identifying both the railway track and the aiming point, and consequently a concentrated number of TIs and then bombs fell on the target.

Another French target, Cannes, was on the target list the following night as the planners looked to further disrupt rail activity between France and Italy. Cannes, as well as being the playground for the rich and famous, was also the hub of a supply route, via Italy and Hungary, transporting food to enemy troops in Russia. It was another clear night and whilst the Pathfinders' visual markers were confident that they had done their job effectively, the subsequent results proved disappointing. In a bad night for 35 Squadron, three of their aircraft were missing: Flight Lieutenant William Dallin and all of his crew, with the exception of one of the air gunners, survived as prisoners of war; Pilot Officer Ron Daniel RAAF, on his twentieth trip with the squadron, was the only survivor from his crew, and managed to evade capture. (Ron was sheltered by the resistance, ultimately being picked up off the coast of Brittany by motor torpedo boat along with twenty-six other downed aircrew,

DITCHING OFF THE COAST OF SARDINIA

"*Before arriving at the target, we lost an inboard engine but succeeded in placing markers and flares. When turning over the sea to check our accuracy in marking, the second inboard engine also failed. There was no chance of returning to base now, but the wireless operator managed to get a message through (at 2,000ft) whilst we set course for Sardinia with the remaining two engines running on 'five minutes emergency power'. Reaching red heat, they lasted fifty minutes before one more failed and there was just enough time for the crew to get into position before we ditched.*

"*The crew escaped from the roof hatch, but the hatch over my head jammed; in shoving it open with my shoulders, my foot was trapped in the trimmer controls. Suddenly, as the years of my short life flashed through my brain, I was out, with no flying boot! Now [it was] very much 'get yourself together' time.*

The business end of an emergency axe, recovered from the crash site of Lancaster ND 906.

"*I went back inside to recover it and also grabbed my parachute with its small dinghy attached. The empty Halifax was now deep in the water and the large crew dinghy had not emerged from the wing. The immersion switch did not operate. Taffy, my engineer, was chopping with the axe at the cover of another release, but it was difficult to locate in the dark and under the water. Backhouse, the second navigator, went back into the fuselage to collect the crew's one-man dinghies but was soon rendered unconscious by petrol fumes from a fuel tank ruptured when we hit the water.*

"*I went back inside again to find Backhouse who was floating on his back in total darkness, and with great difficulty he was pushed out through a small escape hatch. By this time the large dinghy had appeared from the wing, and we all scrambled quickly into it, with Backhouse still unconscious. He recovered fairly quickly, once in the open air. Shortly afterwards the aircraft sank, leaving us floating safely under the beautiful moonlit sky.*"

JOE PETRIE ANDREWS DFC, DFM
PILOT. 35 SQUADRON, SIXTY-EIGHT OPS.

Flying Officer Joe Petrie Andrews (in peaked cap). Joe lied about his age and commenced training at the age of sixteen.

Second navigator Backhouse (left) was lucky to survive a ditching by his skipper off the coast of Sardinia.

reaching England in March 1944.)

As for the third, the pilot, Flying Officer Joe Petrie Andrews DFC, DFM flew on from the target towards Sardinia, and ditched his aircraft in the sea.

With the weather closing in once again it was left to the Mosquitoes to keep up their pattern of nuisance raids. The met flight lost one of its crews on November 14, undertaking a weather-reconnaissance flight and coming to grief over Merville. Pilot Officer Frank Clayton DFM and Flying Officer William John DFC were both killed.

On November 15/16, Pilot Officer Charles Guest from 139 Squadron was killed carrying out an attack on Bonn – a rather useless affair in which the only other aircraft on the raid was obliged to jettison its bombload owing to engine trouble. This was the first Mosquito IX reported missing from the Squadron. Guest's navigator, Pilot Officer George Sleeman, was taken prisoner.

Mannheim featured as the final target before the main assault, with the IG Farben chemical plant as the aiming point. It was an unusual all-8 Group affair – presumably an experiment – in which there was no marking and all aircraft bombed with the aid of H2S. The target was chosen because of its proximity to a bend in the river that the radar men believed should show up well on the cathode screens. Many fighter flares were reported and the 405 Squadron Lancaster of Flight Sergeant Richard Larson and his crew went missing. They were all killed, the victim of a

Joe Petrie Andrews (centre) early in his flying career. Joe flew with 102 and 158 Squadrons prior to joining PFF.

nightfighter – the only success claimed by the Nachtjager that night.

The Battle of Berlin offensive began in earnest – and officially in the general post-war consensus – on the night of November 18/19 – the first of four raids that month to kick off Harris's belief that he could wreck Berlin from end to end (assuming the Americans would do their own bit in the plan). The first raid was by no means an all-out attack, but then Harris decided to split his forces into two almost equal parts: one half – a Lancaster-only force – would attack Berlin; the second, comprising mostly Halifaxes with just over 100 Stirlings thrown in for good measure, would raid Mannheim. The bulk of the Lancaster Pathfinder aircraft – sixty-four of them – along with six Mosquitoes went to Berlin, leaving twenty-three Lancasters to accompany twenty-one Halifaxes to Mannheim.

Crews arrived over Berlin to find a good deal of heavy flak and 10/10ths cloud, making the successful blind marking and subsequent bombing of the target doubtful. Mannheim was little better: haze obscured the target making visual identification impossible. Marking achieved a fair concentration, however, and many fires were observed along with several large explosions.

Four PFF aircraft were missing, two each from each raid. Flight Lieutenant Andrew Harding DFC and his crew from 7 Squadron were lost over Mannheim, as was the 35 Squadron crew of Flight Lieutenant Ernest Baker. There was not a single survivor from either aircraft, a fact made more tragic with the knowledge that had Harding returned from operations, he and his entire crew would have been screened.

Kiwi Flight Sergeant Albert Johnson DFM of 97 Squadron was hit by flak over Aachen, but managed to keep the aircraft in the air long enough for the rest of the crew to bale out and survive, either as prisoners of war or by evading capture altogether. Sadly Johnson was killed. But arguably the greatest loss that evening was the death of Wing Commander John White DFC. He was on his forty-third trip with 156 Squadron, and had been a flight commander since May 1943. He had previously played a key role in the success of the Peenemünde raid in support of the master bomber. Every member of his crew was decorated with either the DFC or DFM and between them they could claim close to 300 operations. Pathfinders could ill-afford to lose such experience at such a critical time.

A much larger raid was mounted on Berlin on November 22/23 involving a huge effort from PFF – ninety-one Lancasters, twenty-one Halifaxes and twelve Mosquitoes. Weather conditions were favourable for the attackers and five of the PFF aircraft were equipped with the very latest (Mk III) H2S sets on 3cm, giving better definition and – hopefully – greater reliability. Unfortunately it didn't prove to be the case. Three out of the five aircraft with their special equipment suffered technical failures and bombed Texel as a last resort. Whether by luck or judgment, and perhaps a little of both, the two remaining aircraft had more success, and a Mosquito over the target shortly after reported that there appeared to be two well-defined areas of fires approximately seven to ten miles apart reflected in cloud.

(Actually this proved to be the most devastating raid on Germany of the war: huge amounts of damage were done with at least 3,000 houses and twenty-three industrial premises destroyed and 175,000 civilians bombed out.)

That night the bomber stream opted for a 'straight in, straight out' approach to the target, putting a huge concentration of bombers over the target area in as short a time as possible. They adopted a similar tactic the following night, adding to the devastation of the previous evening, with many of the main force crews appearing to aim their bombs at the fires that were still burning more that twenty-four hours on.

The price paid by the four-engined bombers across these two raids was heavy: forty-six Lancasters, Halifaxes and Stirlings were lost; seventeen of these were from Pathfinder Force. This was a deeply worrying statistic. In the first attack, the Pathfinders lost seven out of 111 aircraft that took off, a loss rate of 6.3 percent. In the second, they lost ten aircraft out of ninety, a loss rate of a little over eleven percent. The average loss rate, therefore, was more than eight percent, and it doesn't take much working out to appreciate that if such losses were sustained, the Pathfinders would fast become ineffective and in due course, would cease to exist altogether.

What was perhaps of most concern, once again, was the loss of some very senior crews – for it was those with the most experience that were trusted with the important task of accurately marking the target, and putting Harris's destructive theory into practice. Over the two nights, 7 Squadron lost four of its captains of aircraft: Warrant Officer Stanley Dorrell; Squadron Leader Eric Nesbit (having flown at least thirty-seven trips); Flight Sergeant George Tindle RNZAF; and Flight Sergeant Frank Page. There were no survivors from any of the crews, including at least one – Flight Lieutenant Leslie Allum DFM – who was on his second tour. A fifth captain, Flying Officer Peter Williams, was obliged to abandon his aircraft with his crew near home, badly hit by flak but all lived to tell the tale.

From Warboys, 156 Squadron also lost four captains: Flight Sergeant Trevor Stephens DFM (who had displayed such courage in bringing his crippled bomber and injured crew home from Berlin in August); Squadron Leader Douglas Anset DFC; Pilot Officer Walter Rose DFC; and Warrant Officer Gordon Fordyce. Fordyce nearly made it home but crashed killing himself and two of his crew. Of the other three crews, there were no survivors.

From Bourn, 97 Squadron listed three captains missing, two of whom were killed: Flight Lieutenant James Munro DFC and Pilot Officer Eugene McEgan RAAF.

The Canadians also suffered the loss of two aircraft captained by Flight Lieutenant Henry Lefroy DFC and Flying Officer Clarence Clark. Out of fourteen men there was only one survivor, and he had the distressing duty of identifying the bodies of his fellow crewmen.

From these four squadrons alone they lost more than eighty men, including two squadron leaders and fifteen flight lieutenants. A quarter of the men had been decorated. Another decorated captain, Pilot Officer Ralph Henderson DFM was killed in action with a crew which included his

THE DANGERS OF BOMBING UP

Perhaps not enough is made of the perils on the ground as well as in the air. Bombing up, for example, was always a dangerous exercise, a fact never lost on the ground crews. Although accidents were few, they were not so uncommon as to be ignored, and great care was taken when handling high explosive, incendiaries, target indicators and flares, especially at the point of winching the munitions into the bomb bay.

Before the attack on Berlin on November 26, Flying Officer Horace Hyde and the crew of his 83 Squadron Lancaster JA686 were with their aircraft in the late afternoon, running through a series of pre-flight checks and talking through various snags with the ground crew. The aircraft already had her payload – in this case one 4,000lb 'cookie' and six 1,000lb TIs – as well as approximately 1,600 gallons of fuel onboard. Without warning, an electrical fault caused the photoflash to explode, which in turn acted like a detonator that blew the whole aircraft apart.

No trace was ever found of one of the crew, the navigator, who had been sitting in the aircraft at the time. Nor were there any mortal remains of Warrant Officer Maurice Murphy of the ground crew. In all, three of the aircrew were killed and the rest injured. Five of the ground crew died including Corporal Marion McDowell.

This was by no means the only such incident. In September 1944, the CO of 156 Squadron (Wing Commander Bingham-Hall) returned from an unsuccessful trip to Le Havre with his bombs still onboard. As the ground crews loaded them on to a trailer, they suddenly exploded.

The noise of the explosion could be heard for many miles around but the damage nearer to home was catastrophic. Seven airmen were killed, four of whom literally disappeared and were listed as 'missing, believed killed'. The flight engineer in the CO's crew, Norman Piercy, had his leg blown off and not a single aircraft in 'B' Flight emerged without some degree of damage.

thirty-four-year-old navigator, Sergeant Henry Dulieu whose parents lived in St Lucia. Henderson had only just returned to 83 Squadron from Spain having been shot down on an earlier sortie.

But there was an even greater loss to 83 Squadron, and indeed to Pathfinder Force, in the second of the two raids when Wing Commander Ray Hilton DSO, DFC & Bar was reported missing with all of his crew, which included Squadron Leader Alexander Chisholm DFC, a navigation expert. Both Hilton and Chisholm had served with Bennett on the staff at Pathfinder headquarters, and the loss of their chief was keenly felt. Bennett described Hilton as 'one of the early Pathfinders' whom he much admired. He had completed his first tour and won his first DFC with 214 Squadron towards the end of 1941 and taken part in the very first Pathfinder operation to Flensburg.

Many of his trips were as the regular pilot of the famous R5868 'Q' Queenie. He was held in similarly high regard by his crews at 83 Squadron, for having been once a flight commander he later returned to command the squadron. At the time of his death he had flown not less than sixty-four operations, something of a record at that time. His place as commanding officer was taken, albeit temporarily, by Wing Commander William Abercromby DFC.

Ray Hilton, a much-admired early Pathfinder, who had served on Bennett's staff.

Frankfurt provided a temporary distraction on November 25/26, a raid of little consequence save for the two crews missing: Pilot Officer Desmond Lander and five of his seven crew from their 35 Squadron Halifax survived as prisoners of war; Flight Lieutenant Carlos Brown CdG, an American serving in the RCAF, was not so lucky. He and all of his 97 Squadron crew were killed. Both aircraft were shot down by Luftwaffe 'experten' – Major Wilhelm Herget and Oberleutnant Eckart-Wilhelm von Bonin. Both men would add to their scores in the coming weeks.

It was then back to Berlin for the final operation of the month, an attack involving 443 Lancasters and seven Mosquitoes. This time the tactics were different, with the bombers approaching from the south, and a large diversionary raid on Stuttgart to split the German defences. The marking started well and on time, and numerous fires appeared and spread rapidly. Three Pathfinders were lost: two each from 7 and 83 Squadrons including another wing commander – the third of such senior rank to be killed in just ten days. Wing Commander Frederick Hilton AFC (no relation) was also a friend of Bennett's who had only just joined Pathfinder Force. His aircraft was set on fire by a nightfighter and despite attempts to extinguish the flames the order was given to bale out and the crew spent the rest of the war in a prison camp. There had been a tragedy too, before the raid, when an 83 Squadron Lancaster exploded at dispersal, killing eight air and ground crew and injuring twelve others.

While the heavy boys and some of the Mosquitoes were occupied with Berlin, the balance of the Light Night Striking Force – now augmented by 627 Squadron under the command of Wing Commander Roy Elliott (posted from PFF NTU) – continued its series of spoofs and nuisance raids, and took casualties as a result. The accidents, however, were surprisingly light given that they visited the Ruhr on twenty-one occasions. Pilot Officer Eric Wade BEM and his navigator Flying Officer Alfred Fleet were killed when their aircraft failed to return from an operation to Knapsack – by now a familiar target. It crashed almost in sight of home.

Roy Elliott, officer commanding 627 Squadron, was described as 'friendly, considerate and ultra efficient'. He was also incredibly brave, sometimes marking the target at only fifty feet.

Operational flying time for the month amounted to 5,632 hours, with the number of individual sorties totalling 1,143. An interesting figure is the number of sorties that were aborted – seventy-seven – and the number of aircraft missing – thirty-one. There were thirteen DSOs. In the words of the ORB: 'The month as a whole could be considered quite memorable.'

It was a month that many would have preferred to forget.

DECEMBER

December turned out to be similarly memorable for all of the wrong reasons. It began where November had left off, with the continued assault on the German capital and further heavy losses.

The first attack, on the night of December 2/3, was thwarted mainly by poor weather, with the markers scattered over a wide area. The bombs tended to fall to the south and southeast of the city, although a good many fires were started. Nine PFF Lancasters, four Halifaxes and three Mosquitoes (i.e. more than fourteen percent of the total Pathfinder effort) were unable to fulfil their duties: four aircraft attacked a last resort; four returned early; one jettisoned; and the remainder were missing. German defences were notably stronger, with heavy flak being thrown up in a thick barrage, and considerable light flak experienced by those who flew too low into their range. Fighter flares became more numerous as the attack developed and a good many nightfighter combats took place. German nightfighter forces claimed forty-five 'kills' – by comparison, more than twice the number they had claimed for the previous attack on Berlin/Stuttgart and three times the number lost on November 23/24.

Sadly, 156 Squadron bore the brunt, losing three Lancaster crews and twenty men: Flight Lieutenant Brian Staniland and his crew (all killed); Flight Sergeant James Redfern and his crew (all killed); and Warrant Officer Reginald Wicks RAAF and his crew, from which there was only one survivor. The fourth Lancaster crew missing on operations was a 97 Squadron aircraft flown by Squadron Leader John Garlick DFC & Bar, the commander of 'B' Flight. He had been an army officer prior to transferring to the RAF.

Two crews were missing from 35 Squadron: Flight Sergeant Harley Stinson and his crew were all killed in action; 1st Lieutenant Gunnar Høverstad of the Royal Norwegian Air Force was also killed but the rest of his crew survived as POWs. Høverstad had come to 35 via 76 Squadron which had an impressive Norwegian contingent.

The new boys, 627 Squadron, also suffered their first loss since becoming Pathfinders. Flight Sergeant Simpson's Mosquito IV lost an engine at 32,000ft, having been hit by flak. Making for home they got as far as Caen in northern France before being forced to abandon their aircraft. Both Simpson and his navigator evaded capture. The crew of a second Mosquito lost that evening also managed to avoid being put in the bag. While the heavy jobs went to Berlin, a small force of six Mosquitoes executed a nuisance raid on Bochum, although only one of them was actually able to attack the primary target. A 109 Squadron Mosquito IX, flown by Flying Officer Leonard Bickley, came down in Holland but both crew members survived.

Bomber Command departed slightly from the script for its next main force attack, choosing Leipzig in the east of Germany as the target. The routing of the main force was intended to make it look like Berlin was the target, and with nine Mosquitoes dropping target indicators as a 'spoof' over the city, the sleight of hand worked to perfection. The German controllers directed all of their fighters to Berlin, leaving the skies of Leipzig virtually clear, at least in the early stages.

The Pathfinders did well, in fact they did very well, and the two aircraft carrying the Mk III H2S equipment helped ensure a good concentration of TIs that was well backed-up. A large area of housing and a good portion of industrial premises were destroyed in what was actually the most damaging attack on Leipzig of the war. The German defences, of course, eventually rallied, and four Lancasters were lost. They included Pilot Officer Alan Coleman RAAF of 97 Squadron who was killed with his entire crew; and Flying Officer Norman Bowring of 405 Squadron who was also killed. Bowring, like Squadron Leader Garlick, had been an army officer before opting to fly.

The losses over the last two raids were grievous but almost pale into insignificance compared to the disaster that befell Bomber Command and Pathfinder Force mid-way through the month in a night that has become infamous as 'Black Thursday'. The 8 Group ORB sums it up most succinctly: 'Weather at bases on return proved disastrous for the heavies'. This, however, tells only half the story.

In fairness to the Pathfinders, they executed their part of the raid splendidly. Despite the city being covered by cloud, the skymarking was reasonably accurate, and a fairly good concentration was achieved. Although they became 'ragged' later, the bombs still inflicted considerable damage, and the sustained bombing over the previous few weeks had rendered more than a quarter of Berlin's housing as uninhabitable.

But whereas the German defences had been fooled over Leipzig, they were not so easily duped on this occasion, and the bombers' course was plotted with great accuracy resulting in a good number of successful intercepts on the way in and over the target. The diarist at Oakington would later record 7 Squadron's worst losses ever sustained in a single night since converting to Lancasters, and unusually, perhaps, all of the pilots fell victim to nightfighters.

One, Warrant Officer Wallace Watson RAAF, had the great misfortune of coming across Germany's greatest nightfighter ace, Oberleutnant Heinz-Wolfgang Schnaufer, and was system-atically despatched. (By the end of the war, Schnaufer had accounted for 121 kills, of which at least ten were Pathfinders.) The other three captains missing were two more Australians, Pilot Officer Geoffrey Tyler and Flying Officer Francis Rush (a Tasmanian), and a New Zealander, Flight Lieutenant John Petrie DFC. Of the four aircraft, there were only three survivors out of the twenty-eight men posted as missing.

The reason for noting these four losses as being unusual, along with a 156 Squadron Lancaster that disappeared without trace (and with it the pilot Flight Lieutenant Charles Aubert DFM, RAAF and his highly-experienced crew), is that nearly all of the thirteen other PFF aircraft lost that night were victims of the weather. The biggest calamity befell a single outfit – 97 Squadron – which lost eight aircraft and thirty-six men, including two highly-decorated squadron leaders. One of them, Squadron Leader Ernest Deverill DFC and Bar, AFC, DFM had won his first award for gallantry as far back as July 1940. Deverill, who had only recently returned to operations after a period instructing, was making for Graveley – equipped with a fog-busting system known as FIDO – but crashed on the airfield itself. Squadron Leader Donald MacKenzie DFC, a quiet young Scot, flew his aircraft into the ground within a few hundred yards of the runway at Bourn, killing himself, the flight engineer and the bomb aimer instantly. The station sick quarters at Bourn was later described, grimly, as 'overflowing with bodies'.

(In one of the 405 Squadron aircraft which crashed, and indeed its only survivor, was Warrant Officer Sinclair Nutting DFM on his forty-fifth trip. It was a hell of a way to complete a tour.)

Combined with the losses suffered by the other squadrons, in one raid Pathfinders were stripped of more than ninety men. Whether they should have been sent on such an operation is a moot point. Weather conditions were poor at the time of departure and by the time they returned, visibility at some airfields was no greater than 300 yards. Landing a heavy bomber almost totally blind was a dangerous occupation at the best of times, and so it proved, taking the lives of pilots with hundreds if not thousands of flying hours to their names.

After the debacle, the bombers went back to Berlin twice more before the year was out, but on both occasions the casualty rate was mercifully low, 156 Squadron lost one (Flying Officer Norman Warfield DFM) and one also shot down from 35 Squadron (Flying Officer Ronald Williams DFC). The spoofs laid on by 8 Group were again praised for keeping the German controllers on their toes, and certainly on the second raid (December 29/30), wrong-footing them.

Before these two final scenes, Bomber Command also put up a main force attack on Frankfurt where the Germans had better luck, or benefited from better guesswork, and the diversionary raid failed to divert their attention from the real target. Pathfinders did not have one of their more successful nights, with their efforts hampered by the weather and decoy fires and target indicators. Creepback was also an issue, but in this case helped cause more damage than might otherwise have occurred. A 7 Squadron Lancaster nearly came to grief after being badly shot up over the target, but the pilot (Flying Officer Dennis Field) managed to bring the bomber back to friendly territory where the order was given to bale out. In doing so, the rear gunner Warrant Officer Richard Smith DFC smashed his head on the tail assembly as he made his exit, and was killed.

The poor run of luck at 156 Squadron continued, with two aircraft overdue. One, piloted by Flying Officer Peter Watts crashed near Hanau, killing all onboard. The second was brought down near Hannover, killing the pilot – Flight Lieutenant Michael Sullivan DFC, RNZAF – and all of the crew. They included five Australians and an Englishman (Flight Sergeant George Mason DFM), all of whom had been decorated.

The Halifaxes of 35 Squadron also suffered. One, piloted by Flight Lieutenant James Wright DFC RNZAF, came down in Belgium but four of the crew survived. A second, flown by Squadron Leader Julian Sale, crashed in spectacular fashion at Graveley where all but the rear gunner emerged unscathed but even he survived to recount his experiences to anyone who would listen.

And so 1943 drew to a close. A conference held towards the end of the month saw all of the senior officers and tacticians assembled to discuss Pathfinder techniques and where they could improve. The weather, it was agreed, was the great variable in planning for a successful operation and so in future it was decided that conditions would always be assumed to be 'unknown'. As such two methods would be considered: Wanganui and Newhaven, or Wanganui and Parramatta, using separate aircraft. It was further decided to use green TIs in preference to yellows by blind markers in Parramatta attacks.

Casualties for the month were down on November, but high in proportion to the number of raids undertaken. The heavies suffered worst, but the Mosquito squadrons did not escape the grim reaper. A 105 Squadron aircraft crewed by Flying Officer Benjamin Reynolds and John Phillips crashed in Holland during an operation to Essen and both were killed. The more unfortunate,

Gordon Carter's personal details filed by the authorities within Oflag Luft 3.

A NIGHT TO REMEMBER

Squadron Leader Julian Sale DSO, DFC was no stranger to excitement. In May 1943, on his way to bomb Duisberg, his aircraft had been intercepted by a nightfighter and crashed on the Dutch/German border. Two of his crew were killed and four more taken prisoner. Sale, however, not only managed to evade capture, but also made it home. In December 1943, and with a new crew, he was returning from operations to Frankfurt when a TI caught fire. The navigator Squadron Leader Gordon Carter, had himself evaded capture in February 1943 returning from a raid on Lorient.

"I had, by now, forty-five ops under my belt, a normal tour of duty in the Pathfinder Force. Keen types, however, sought to press on to sixty. The trip to Frankfurt on December 20 was therefore my extended service.

"Visibility was poor, so we decided against releasing our target indicators, having already made four unsuccessful runs at 5,000ft over the city and finally losing our three 1,000-pounders over what looked like a small factory. We returned uneventfully until Julian (the pilot) let down to 1,200ft on the approach. Then all hell broke loose. The safety cover for the TI fuse had detached itself in flight, setting off the TI in the bomb bay when descending below its normal detonating height. Things happened mighty fast. The plane filled with smoke and flames and Julian gave the order to bale out which I did post haste, going out first. I remember seeing a tree upside down and instantly hitting the ground in a ploughed field which turned out to be just beyond the perimeter track.

Gordon Carter (second left standing) next to his skipper Julian Sale. Carter was shot down, evaded, and returned home only to be shot down again. Sale failed to return from his fiftieth trip.

"Just as he was about to jump himself, Julian sensed the mid upper gunner, Flight Lieutenant Roger 'Sheep' Lamb's presence beside him, pointing out desperately that his 'chute pack had been damaged by fire, as his turret was above the bomb bay. Julian, who could not see his instrument panel, stuck his head out of the side of the window and brought the aircraft round to face the runway, the remainder of the crew had already jumped. He landed her, taxied her onto the grass whereupon he and Sheep leapt out and ran for their lives. Almost at once the 'plane blew up.

"Julian was awarded a Bar to an earlier DSO. His citation reminds us that 'in circumstances of great danger, Squadron Leader Sale displayed his great determination setting an example of the highest order'. The Times newspaper, shortly after, reported the incident under the heading 'Landed blazing bomber to save comrade'. As was customary we were rushed back into the air the very same day to avoid a mental blockage setting in, but oddly enough I see no mention of it in my logbook. I have before me a voucher which certifies that my Irvin jacket, goggles, helmet, silk gloves and flying gauntlets were destroyed in Halifax III HX328-J when it caught fire and crashed on the night of December 20, 1943."

Gauntlets and goggles belonging to Thomas Godfrey, a veteran of sixty-one trips.

GORDON CARTER DFC & BAR
NAVIGATOR. 35 SQUADRON. FORTY-FIVE PLUS OPS.

however, were the weather men – 1409 Met Flight – who lost Flight Sergeant Harold Addis and his navigator Sergeant John Sharpe on December 3 when their aircraft crashed in the proximity of Exeter airfield. Both were killed. Two days later and they lost another crew, also in a crash. The pilot, Flying Officer Harry Taylor had been awarded both the DFC and the Conspicuous Gallantry Medal.

Four DSOs were awarded during the month, including one to the outgoing officer commanding 35 Squadron, Wing Commander 'Dixie' Dean (his place had been taken in November by Wing Commander Pat Daniels DSO, DFC). There was also a Bar to the DFC for another squadron commander – Wing Commander William Abercromby. He would not live long to enjoy it.

The ORB includes a detailed summary of all of the changes in command within the group up to and including December 31. Of the station commanders, Oakington had lost Group Captain Willetts, and Group Captain Robinson was missing from Graveley. At a squadron level, 83 had lost two COs, Wing Commander Gillman and Wing Commander Hilton.

Bennett opines in his auto-biography the dreadful price paid by his men in the winter of 1943/1944. Crews could be replaced in number or enthusiasm, but their skill was a commodity in increasingly short supply. Many good men had already died; many more would soon do so. It would get worse before it got any better.

ORDER OF BATTLE

DECEMBER 1943

HEADQUARTERS 8 GROUP – HUNTINGDON

Graveley	35 Squadron	Halifax
Oakington	7 Squadron	Lancaster
	627 Squadron	Mosquito
Wyton	83 Squadron	Lancaster
	139 Squadron	Mosquito
Bourn	97 Squadron	Lancaster
Warboys	156 Squadron	Lancaster
Gransden Lodge	405 (RCAF) Squadron	Lancaster
Marham	105 Squadron	Mosquito
	109 Squadron	Mosquito

JANUARY 1944

The opening lines of the ORB for January 1944 tell the reader virtually all they need to know about the first raid on Berlin for the New Year: '86 Lancasters detailed. Five withdrawn. Three returned early. Two jettisoned. Ten missing. 10/10ths cloud over the target.' It would be the pattern for raids to come.

The targets had been selected in the early morning. A heavy raid on Berlin was planned alongside a host of smaller ancillary attacks on precision targets to keep the Mosquitoes busy and the Germans guessing. The steel works at Ruhrstahl AG and August Thyssen AG are mentioned by name as well as a feint involving fifteen aircraft to Hamburg but the main event was still the German capital and the defenders were not deceived.

The attacking force of some 421 Lancasters (the Stirlings had now been withdrawn from main force raids and various Halifax units would soon follow suit) were intercepted early, and the German controller was at the top of his game. Despite the size of the stream, and the successful guesswork, the fighters were not as successful as they should have been. By the end of the evening the nightfighters and flak had accounted for twenty-eight machines. That in itself was a high percentage loss; what was worse, was that ten of these – as the ORB attests – were Pathfinders.

The argument had always been made that Pathfinders faced the greatest peril; that being at the front of the attack, and being obliged to remain over the target area in case further illumination, marking or backing up was required, carried enormous risk. This was why they received an automatic step-up in rank, and wore a coveted badge. With a loss rate that night of more than twelve percent (assuming that eighty-one aircraft took off), some may have felt it wasn't worth it, especially when it was revealed later that many of the bombs had fallen fruitlessly into wooded countryside.

The German controllers were similarly in charge for the next attack, when their defences hacked down another twenty-seven Lancasters and, more pointedly, another ten from Pathfinder Force.

On January 5/6, Harris decided against Berlin for the bomber crews. And would instead choose a supposedly 'easy' target just over the Channel, or a relatively short trip to the Ruhr – not that the Ruhr could ever be considered plain sailing. This time he chose the Baltic Sea port of Stettin, at the far extreme of the bombers' endurance, a return flight of nine hours or more.

Whereas the two previous attacks on Berlin had achieved little or nothing, the raid on Stettin was rather more promising. For once, the Mosquito diversion to Berlin worked, leaving the Pathfinders comparatively free to do their work. The attack opened early and with the aiming point identified visually, a good concentration of bombing was achieved. Gradually the bombing began to drift, but not before a substantial amount of damage was done and fires were started. Five Pathfinder aircraft were missing, a considerable improvement on previous weeks.

With the winter weather doing its worst, Harris had to wait more than a week to launch his next main force raid, though the Mosquitoes were active throughout, and three of their kind were lost – two following an attack on Frankfurt and one over Essen. Again, however, it was not Berlin but rather Brunswick that was on the hit list in what was to prove the most disastrous night for Pathfinders up to this point in the war. Indeed it is worth pausing, momentarily, to reflect upon the casualties inflicted on PFF on the four major attacks since the New Year with thirty-eight aircraft lost to enemy action in only one month.

One squadron in particular suffered more than any other in those first three weeks of 1944: 156 lost four crews in the first attack on Berlin; five in the second; and five more failed to return from Brunswick. A staggering fourteen aircraft were lost and eighty-nine men left dead, with only nine survivors languishing in a prison camp. Warboys began to gain a reputation as a dangerous place to be.

Only perhaps by detailing some of the experience within these crews can a better understanding of their loss – both to the squadron and to Pathfinder Force – be realised. Squadron Leader Rowland Fawcett DFC, for example, lost on the first trip to Berlin was on his third tour and had flown no less than sixty-nine bomber operations. He had been in the wars since being shot down in 1941 near Tobruk. Squadron Leader Ronald Stewart DFC, also lost that night, had flown around forty-nine operational sorties and had recently been promoted. While Pilot Officer Gerald Bond had, only days before, been awarded the DFC (and his rear gunner the DFM) for their spirited defence against a determined nightfighter attack.

From the second attack on Berlin, Flying Officer Charles Cairns DFM who had won his decoration in 1942 with 150 Squadron and had forty-six operations to his credit, and Flight Lieutenant James Ralph DFM, RNZAF who could claim a similar track record, were both lost.

At the age of thirty-seven, Flying Officer William Raper (an Australian flight engineer in the crew of Flying Officer Thomas Docherty) was considered comparatively old for a member of a Bomber Command crew, and had been a regular within the Royal Australian Air Force; at the other end of the scale, Sergeant Ronald Hillman, the wireless op to Sergeant Alan Barnes was young enough to be his son.

The most senior officer to be killed was the captain of one of the five aircraft lost during the attack on Brunswick. Wing Commander Nelson Mansfield DFC was a New Zealand-born RAF regular who had been with the squadron for seven months and whose sorties had reached fifty-three. The navigator onboard, Squadron Leader Edward Alexander DFC, DFM, a Canadian, was also well into his second tour. He completed his first with 419 Squadron where he had won his DFM for helping to bring back a crippled bomber from Kiel, despite being wounded.

New crews and new faces were swiftly drafted in to replace those that had 'gone west' and a sense of gloom descended over the station. They were, of course, not the only squadron to suffer losses – and would not claim to be in any way special – but the scale of the casualties was extraordinary in every sense of the word.

Further experience was lost from other stations. From 7 Squadron, seven crews were missing and forty men dead. Among them was Squadron Leader Albert Taylor (navigator in Squadron Leader Harold Jaggard's crew) who had won the DFM as far back as July 1940 at the start of the Battle of Britain. Flight Lieutenant Ian Pearson DFC, lost on the night of January 2/3, had flown not less than forty-eight operations and another flight lieutenant, David Thomas DFC shot down over Brunswick had flown forty-four. Within the Thomas crew was Warrant Officer Ronald Haywood CGM.

At Bourn, 97 Squadron had also suffered, losing three crews and there were five crews missing from Gransden Lodge (405 Squadron) and two from Graveley. Squadron Leader Thomas Hutton (later DFC) of 35 Squadron could consider himself very lucky to have survived with three others in his crew when his aircraft was attacked by a nightfighter, set on fire and then exploded.

The most senior 405 Squadron crew to go missing was led by Flight Lieutenant William Cloutier DFC who was only five trips short of completing his Pathfinder tour and whose DFC was gazetted after his loss.

At RAF Wyton, 83 Squadron lost four in one night (January 2/3) but its biggest loss came the night before when their interim commanding officer, Wing Commander William Abercromby DFC & Bar failed to return. Abercromby, an ex-Halton apprentice (Entry 15), aroused mixed passions among his crews at 83 Squadron, though this might have had more to do with him being an 'unknown quantity' and following in the footsteps of a CO they all adored.

His supposed order that his crews flew straight and level over the target area, and not weave, was not especially well received, and ignored by a good many. Whatever their likes and dislikes, there was nobody who could doubt his commitment to the cause. With 50 Squadron he had taken part in the famous daylight raid against Le Creusot, and another daylight to Milan in October 1942 when he released his incendiaries onto the target at only 100ft. He won the DFC for this effort and added a Bar when in command of 619 Squadron at Woodhall Spa. His place was taken by Wing Commander Laurence Deane DSO, DFC, a veteran flight commander of 156 Squadron PFF with six trips to Berlin to his name.

So many killed. So many irreplaceable crews that would never return. And Pathfinders were only half way through the month.

Respite came not in the form of any benevolence from Bennett (who in January was granted the war substantive rank of group captain) or his commander-in-chief but rather the weather. The winter – for so many the enemy – for a brief period became their friend, at least for a day or two when a series of planned attacks were ultimately cancelled. Indeed not even the Mosquitoes were allowed out to play as fog effectively shut down airfields across the country. Given the carnage of the recent operations, it was a blessed relief, allowing new crews to be posted and squadrons brought back up to operational strength.

In periods of bad weather, Pathfinders were never idle. Although there could be no flying, there was still plenty to learn in the classroom, honing navigation or bomb-aiming skills and reminding crews of the latest tactics and techniques being practiced.

Bennett was also busy during this period of (relative) inactivity, with various delegations and deputations keen to secure an hour or two of the AOC's time, some through insistence, some by invitation and others by appointment. Meetings with the AOC 100 Group (Air Commodore 'Eddie' Addison CBE) and the AOC 4 Group (Air Vice-Marshal Roddy Carr CB, CBE, DFC) and his SASO were punctuated by a visit from Sir Fred Handley Page whose Halifax aircraft had served

PFF so admirably well. They would soon, however, all be phased out in favour of the Lancaster, thus simplifying future training, supply and maintenance. A gunnery leaders' conference was held at HQ PFF on January 19 – no doubt given greater urgency by the recent upsurge in enemy nightfighter activity and performance.

Losses to German nightfighters were noticeably on the rise. The brief advantage provided to Bomber Command by Window had now largely subsided, and new radar was being delivered to the Nachtjager that was allowing German crews to improve their interception rates, and with them the number of aircraft shot down. Ironically, H2S – the 'special equipment' increasingly called into action to aid accurate navigation and target identification – was also the bombers' Achilles heel. By taking bearings from H2S emissions, German controllers were getting better – and perhaps luckier – at guessing where the main force was headed, with Pathfinders in the lead. The radar-assisted 'Tame Boar' fighters and their freelancing 'Wild Boar' comrades were taking their toll, pouncing on aircraft damaged by flak or caught in the deadly beam of the myriad of searchlights that were now appearing in increasing numbers.

Arguably the greatest bomber of the war – the Avro Lancaster. Bennett standardised all of his heavy-bomber squadrons on the type.

Spoof attacks and diversionary raids did not always succeed in drawing the fighters away from the bomber stream. During the attack on Berlin on the night of January 20/21, for example, multiple Mosquito raids on three separate Rheinmetall-Borsig AG factories in Düsseldorf, and further raids on Hannover and Kiel failed to prevent the main stream from being infiltrated early, and the Luftwaffe experten scored steadily throughout the night.

The time from the first aircraft falling to German guns to the last was more than two hours. A nightfighter certainly accounted for the loss of the 7 Squadron Lancaster flown by Squadron Leader Maurice Baird-Smith DFC, shot down from a height of 19,000ft. It was ironic given that he had won his DFC for a spectacular attack at very low level in the Greek campaign of 1941. On that occasion he got away with it; this time he was not so lucky. His forty-year-old mid upper gunner, Flight Lieutenant Raymond Ridley and his colleague in the rear turret, Warrant Officer William Brown, probably never saw their assailant and were both killed, along with three others. Baird-Smith was reported a POW eight weeks later.

Four other PFF heavies were missing, three from 83 Squadron. In the rear turret of one of those aircraft, piloted by Canadian Pilot Officer Glen Ransom, was Flight Sergeant Alfred Millard. Millard had won the DFM before joining Pathfinders for his part in the destruction of two enemy fighters during the same operation. His excellent gunnery skills, however, were of no defence against accurate flak, for it was more likely a burst of flak and not a nightfighter that finally accounted for this gallant airman. It was definitely flak that claimed the lives of six of the crew of Flight Lieutenant Roland King DFC, including his air bomber Flight Lieutenant William Ross DFC, DFM. King survived but was seriously wounded – so much so that he was repatriated before the war was over.

The diversions and feints were marginally more successful for the return to Berlin a week later (January 27/28), possibly because they involved a new tactic. The whole of the PFF Halifax force was despatched to Heligoland to bomb the harbour, and to lure the fighters away from Berlin. Meanwhile, seventy-five PFF Lancasters and fourteen Mosquitoes successfully attacked the capital, and although the weather hampered matters, the crews were confident that they had achieved a good concentration of Wanganui flares that were regularly maintained, and the fact that the glow from the fires could be seen from a distance of 100 miles on the homeward route caused a similar glimmer of satisfaction for a job well done. Mosquitoes flying over the target shortly after confirmed what the ORB describes as 'a very considerable area of conflagration'. Only one PFF aircraft was missing: Flight Lieutenant Selwyn Alcock DFC and his crew became Hauptmann Wilhelm Herget's sixty-second kill.

Another new tactic was adopted for the raid on Berlin the following night – the planners took full advantage of the hours of darkness. For the spoofs and diversions, sixty-three Stirlings led by four PFF Halifax aircraft carried out mine-laying operations in Kiel – the first occasion PFF had been used in such a role – and four Mosquitoes visited Hannover. For the attack on Berlin, in the first phase, six Mosquitoes were detailed to bomb the city using a combination of Gee and DR. (Three completed the operation successfully.) Four hours later, the main force arrived, just at the point that the people of Berlin were emerging from their shelters in the false belief that they had nothing else to fear from the night.

The plan worked up to a point, and the losses could have been far worse had it not been for a further party of Mosquitoes sent to bomb various airfields (among them Gilze-Rijen, Leeuwarden, Deelen, and Neule) to disrupt the nightfighters' response. Notwithstanding these efforts, Pathfinders still lost six of their number – two each from 7, 83 and 97 Squadrons. Most noteworthy among them was Wing Commander Ralph Young DSO, DFC, a former royal engineer who had come to Bomber Command and Pathfinders after a spell in fighters. Most unfortunate, perhaps, was Flight Lieutenant Horace Hyde, the pilot who as a flying officer had seen members of his crew and ground crew blown up in front of his very eyes only eight weeks earlier, and had now himself paid the ultimate price. Most experienced, probably, was 97 Squadron's Flying Officer Frank Allison DFM who had at least forty-eight operations to his name. From the six crews, thirty-three men were dead.

But neither the losses, nor Harris's fixation with Berlin ended there. A further eight crews were lost on the final attack on the city at the end of the month, which was undertaken once again in thick cloud. Numerous fighter flares signalled an active nightfighter force, with 405 Squadron suffering the worst, with three of its aircraft failing to make it home to Gransden.

The ORB bemoans the unfavourable weather as the cause for having to cancel some ten attacks, but it kept the casualty rate lower than it might have been had further raids been made on 'The Big City'. Ironically it was not Berlin, but rather an attack on Magdeburg, that proved the most distressing for PFF in a raid that achieved little because of stronger than forecast winds. Pathfinders were rewarded for their efforts with the loss of ten of their number, four Halifaxes from 35 Squadron (including Squadron Leader John Jagger DFC), two from 83, and one each from 7, 97, 156 and 405.

The Germans, however, did not have things all their own way. That night they lost one of their top scoring aces at the time – and indeed of the whole war – when Heinrich Prinz zu Sayn-Wittgenstein was shot down and killed. His aircraft was possibly hit by return fire from the rear gunner of his final victim for the night, a 156 Squadron aircraft skippered by Flight Lieutenant Leslie Kilvington DFC. It was small return for the loss of more than sixty men killed or prisoners of war.

The statistics for January make interesting reading: the number of sorties carried out totalled 1,383 comprising some 7,136 operational flying hours. Some eighty-six sorties were aborted, a reflection both of technical issues and adverse weather conditions, but most alarming of all was the number of aircraft missing: sixty-nine.

The details were certified correct and signed by a certain Squadron Leader A.P. Cranswick, to whom Bennett would later dedicate his autobiography.

THE ORIGINAL MULTI-TASKERS

Donald Bennett was the primary multi-tasker, and not surprisingly expected the same of his crews. As such, every individual in a Pathfinder crew was trained to do at least two jobs and sometimes three. A flight engineer, for example, as well as his specific duties was invariably trained to drop the bombs. The original air bomber in the crew had been retrained as the set operator (the nav two) at Pathfinder NTU. The flight engineer (or the navigator, as many had set out to be pilots and remustered after elementary flying training) might also be entrusted to fly the aircraft in the event of an emergency.

The idea was that if the pilot was wounded, or even killed, there was somebody capable of getting the rest of the crew home. Many a flight engineer or navigator would spend his spare time in the Link Trainer (a basic flight simulator) or be given a go at the real thing when the occasion allowed. While many pilots believed their protégés capable of keeping an aircraft in the air, landing was another matter. At least one told his flight engineer that if it ever came to it, he was to keep the wheels up, get as close to the ground as possible and then cut everything!

FEBRUARY

The number of sorties and operational flying hours fell dramatically in February. So too mercifully did the casualty rate, although the number of operations that had to be aborted remained comparatively high.

After the mauling of the previous month, the heavy squadrons were left to 'make and mend' during the first two weeks of February – a phrase that hides the arduous task faced by ground crews in repairing damaged aircraft and for the medical and support staff to repair broken men. Depleted ranks were filled with new crews and new faces in the mess.

There was no pause, however, for the Mosquito squadrons who carried out a series of sorties to Aachen, Berlin, Cologne, Dortmund, Frankfurt, Elberfeld, Hamborn, Hannover, Krefeld, Mannheim and Rheinhausen, often in miserable flying conditions as befits the continent at that time of year. In every raid at least one of the Mosquitoes was abortive, and in one case – an attack on Elberfeld on the night of February 4/5 – seven out of the eight returned home with their duty not carried out (DNCO).

Losses were comparatively light: 627 Squadron lost the crew of Pilot Officer Anthony Willmott and Flying Officer John Hughes at the start of the month, their aircraft coming down near Hannover; a 109 Squadron Mosquito with an all-New Zealand crew (Flying Officer Robert Leigh and Flight Lieutenant Mervyn Breed DFC) was lost over Krefeld, the pilot killed and the navigator becoming a POW. And just to prove the point that the danger was not always on operations, Flight Lieutenant John Slatter and his navigator Flying Officer Peter Hedges were both killed on a training flight when their Mosquito collided with a B17 Flying Fortress, sending both men to their deaths. The Fortress landed safely.

A signal honour was bestowed upon Pathfinder Force on February 10 with a visit from His Majesty King George VI and Her Majesty Queen Elizabeth. The ORB reports that: 'The king and queen visited three stations in the group. Their majesties were received at Warboys by the AOC and after chatting to aircrews and ground staff, took luncheon in the officers' mess. In the afternoon the party moved on to Graveley and later to Gransden Lodge, where their majesties had tea with the station commander.'

On the following day, His Royal Highness the Duke of Gloucester visited Marham, similarly taking luncheon, 'examining the aircraft and chatting to personnel'. Such visits were good for morale, and a pleasant distraction from the brutalities of war, although some aircrew admitted to being so nervous they couldn't eat!

With the Mosquitoes fully engaged, Harris gave thought to how his heavy-bomber squadrons

THE OPTIMISM OF YOUTH

On February 2, Flying Officer Tony Hiscock and his crew were posted to 156 Squadron to fill the ranks left by recent losses:

> "We joined 156 Squadron in February 1944, just after the tragic losses of the New Year Berlin raids. We had flown a handful of trips with 103 Squadron at Elsham Wolds before volunteering for Pathfinders.
>
> "The navigator was twenty-nine – considerably older than the rest of the crew, but by comparison the flight engineer at thirty-five was positively ancient. He was almost twice the age of our Canadian rear gunner who was only nineteen at the time.
>
> "The main reason we volunteered for Pathfinders was that after thirty trips we could stay on and do another twenty, rather than being sent off for a period of instructing and then joining a new squadron and having to form a new crew. This way we could keep together. And we did. I was twenty at the time (I celebrated my twenty-first birthday with the squadron) and we were confident that we would complete our tour. The optimism of youth I suppose. As it was we did the fifty together and later, when my first rear gunner was tour-expired and decided to leave, I picked up a new rear gunner, Rupert Noye, for another eighteen. By the war's end I had flown sixty-eight ops, and Rupert seventy-two.
>
> "We were known as primary blind marker illuminators. In short, we used H2S to identify the target area, and then would drop flares to illuminate the scene so that the specialist bomb aimers that followed could identify the precise aiming point. H2S could be temperamental and the picture a little difficult to interpret at times, but our bomb aimer (nav two) became quite expert."

Tony Hiscock.

TONY HISCOCK DFC & BAR
PILOT. 156 SQUADRON. SIXTY-EIGHT OPS.

could be better deployed, or more precisely, the tactics he could employ to reduce the attrition rates and further improve the damage inflicted on the enemy. Harris, in keeping with his contemporary commanding officers, would not wilfully sacrifice his men for a lost cause. The criminal waste of human life in the trenches in the First World War was still a sharp and painful memory to many, and morale was a constant concern. A new crew arriving on a squadron to see their flight or squadron commander soon after lost in action could be forgiven for thinking how long they might themselves survive.

Certain tactics were already being tried: the mining of German and Baltic ports, for example, and the use of aircraft from training units flying Bullseyes (leaflet raids) along the same routes used if the main force were heading for Berlin. Both could fox the German controller into sending his nightfighters on a fool's errand. Harris also considered how technology was being employed, and began restricting the use of H2S and other devices on his bombers that now made those aircraft visible on German radar screens.

His favourite new tactic was the use of a staggered attack, where he divided his force into two and allowed a gap of around two hours before the second force attacked. Designed to keep the German defences on their toes and catch the emergency and rescue services out in the open, it was perhaps a beastly tactic in a wholly horrid war, but devilishly effective.

But before he would see whether his new-found thinking would work or not, the planners couldn't help themselves but return to Berlin for what transpired to be a record-breaker on several counts: it was the largest force ever sent to Berlin; the largest non-1,000-bomber force sent to any target; and the first time that more than 500 Lancasters and 300 Halifaxes had combined in a single attack. It was also the end of the 'true' Battle of Berlin. A diversionary raid to Frankfurt failed to lure the fighters away and the bombers suffered heavy losses, both before and after reaching the target. The Pathfinders fared particularly badly losing seven of their number. And it might have been more.

Flight Sergeant Ken Doyle, a relatively new arrival at 156 Squadron who would later go on to become a master bomber, was approaching the target when he received a warning from one of the gunners, an Australian named Geoff Smith, that a fighter was closing in fast. Smith already had at least one enemy aircraft to his name and no doubt fancied another. And he got it. But soon after they were attacked by another fighter and this one struck home, wounding both gunners and causing considerable damage.

Smith was himself wounded in the leg, but with the mid upper out of action, he refused to leave his turret, despite being in severe pain. Forced to abandon their attack, the flight home was not without further incident, including a fire at the back of the aircraft, but eventually the pilot made an excellent landing at Woodbridge, saving the crew from any further harm. Smith was immediately taken to Ely hospital where his right leg was amputated. For his gallantry in staying at his post, Geoff Smith was awarded the Conspicuous Gallantry Medal.

As mentioned earlier, the most difficult targets warranted the attentions of the most experienced crews, but the price paid was sometimes arguably unacceptably high. Of the thirty Pathfinders killed or captured that night, between them they held some twenty-two awards for gallantry.

At Oakington, for example, four crews were missing from 7 Squadron. They included Flight Lieutenant Roy Barnes DFC and his crew, all killed; Flight Lieutenant Peter Williams DFC and his crew, with only two survivors, one of whom was the pilot (this was the second time that Williams had been obliged to take to his 'chute and get away with it); and the vastly-experienced Squadron Leader Richard Campling DSO, DFC and his crew, all killed, including a rear gunner (Warrant Officer Charles Quinn) with the DFC and DFM from an earlier tour. They also lost a forty-year-old New Zealander with a DSO, DFC combination, Squadron Leader John Hegman, who had apparently lied about his age in order not to be refused enlistment. Within his crew to gain operational experience was Wing Commander James Tattnall OBE; if Tattnall had survived, he would have taken command of the squadron soon after.

It was a quiet night in the officers' mess and the mood did not improve when a few nights later two more of their number were lost over Leipzig in what was the most disastrous raid of the war up until that point. It was a large raid involving more than 800 aircraft, including more than 100 Lancasters and Halifaxes from Pathfinder Force, and a considerable number of Mosquitoes detailed to attack the city. There was also a host of other targets as spoofs and diversions from the main event. The German controller did just about everything right that night, and the bomber stream was under attack all the way to the target. The issues were compounded by strong winds that meant many reached the target early, and were forced to orbit, waiting for the Pathfinders to arrive and open the show. When they did, heavy cloud meant that Wanganui marking had to be employed, although the crews were confident that a good concentration was achieved.

Defences were summarised thus: slight to moderate heavy flak, with considerable fighter activity en route. This 'considerable fighter activity' could be interpreted as a highly-successful night's work for the Luftwaffe. They claimed seventy-seven aircraft destroyed, and although this number is slightly exaggerated, Bomber Command did indeed lose a total of seventy-eight aircraft that night, some 9.5 percent of the attacking force. So calamitous was the raid for the Halifax squadrons, that immediately afterwards all Halifax II and Vs were permanently withdrawn from future operations to Germany.

Pathfinders also had a disastrous raid, losing ten 'heavies' and one Mosquito on the Berlin spoof. (The Mossie was crewed by Flight Lieutenant Walter Thomas DFC and Flying Officer Joseph Munby DFC. Both were killed, becoming 692 Squadron's first casualties.)

Again the quality of the crews missing and their bravery was second-to-none. Two crews were missing from 83 Squadron and 156 Squadron, including Squadron Leader Anthony Saunders DFC with at least forty-eight operations under his belt.

Squadron Leader Kenneth Davis of 7 Squadron, whose gunners had accounted for a Junkers 88 over Berlin, lost his life crash landing his Lancaster in an attempt to save his wounded wireless operator. From the same unit, Squadron Leader Francis Curtis DFC, who had himself beaten off no less than three attacks from separate nightfighters over the capital a fortnight earlier, survived along with his flight engineer when his aircraft exploded in mid air. The rest of the crew was killed, including Squadron Leader Thomas Nixon DFC, DFM, who had many years previously been one of only a handful of NCO observers, proud of their 'Flying Arsehole' brevet.

At Graveley, the home of 35 Squadron, the ground crews waited patiently for news of 'their' aircraft but for four of those loyal teams, no further news would be heard until many weeks later. Among those missing and later reported killed was Flight Sergeant Gerald Carrel, rear gunner in Flying Officer Randall-Jones's crew. Carrel had won an immediate DFM for shooting down a German nightfighter and driving off a second.

At the dispersal of Halifax III HX325, the ground crew could have been forgiven for not being unduly concerned when their aircraft was overdue. The pilot, Squadron Leader Julian Sale DSO & Bar, DFC, seemed indestructible. He had shown it time and time again. Now, however, he would not be coming home. It was his fiftieth trip. Outbound and at 22,000ft, his aircraft was on the receiving end of a determined nightfighter attack, which set fire to the rear overload tank.

Sale stayed at the controls, giving five of the crew – including the squadron navigation leader and, similarly indestructible, Gordon Carter – time to get out safely. No-one knows exactly what happened next; Sale was certainly wounded, and his rear gunner already dead. The aircraft crash landed and Sale got out, despite his injuries. A month later, on March 20, Sale succumbed to his wounds, though it has been suggested he took his own life by jumping out of a hospital window.

If Harris were in any way hesitating before trying out his new tactics, the loss of more than 130 frontline aircraft and crews in two raids would have convinced him that change was needed. And change came. For the attack on Stuttgart on February 20/21, a sweep over the North Sea by aircraft from various training units and a diversionary raid on Munich succeeded in fooling the Germans, to the extent that only nine bombers were lost out of an attacking force of nearly 600 (a loss rate of 1.5 percent compared to the 9.5 percent over Leipzig!), and good fires were reported visible from 130 miles. Three out of those nine, however, were PFF aircraft – another graphic illustration of the disproportionate risks such crews faced.

One of the aircraft, a Lancaster from 97 Squadron piloted by Flight Lieutenant Derick Emerson, crashed just short of the runway attempting to land. The aircraft had been involved in a collision over the target area, one that no doubt contributed to its ultimate demise. All seven aircrew were killed. Six out of seven were also killed in the 156 Squadron Lancaster listed as missing, skippered by Flight Lieutenant Donald MacKay DFC, a Canadian. Most of them were on their second tour, including the squadron gunnery leader, Squadron Leader Andrew Muir DFC who was occupying the rear turret. MacKay, who had thousands of flying hours to his name from his time as an instructor, had survived a nightfighter attack only three weeks before when both of his regular gunners had been wounded.

The burned-out remains of Julian Sale's Halifax at Graveley. Sale stayed with the aircraft to save one of his gunners. Both walked away from the crash moments before the aircraft exploded.

There was an interesting change in targets from Harris for the next two raids, supporting the US Air Force in their daylight attacks on German industry and specifically its aircraft manufacturing capability. There was also yet another adjustment in tactics.

For the raid on Schweinfurt, home to Germany's main ball-bearing factories, the planners opted for the combination of a two-phase attack with yet another diversionary sweep, this time involving almost 180 training aircraft. They added to the mix further mine-laying operations and multiple raids on German nightfighter bases.

Although the bombing suffered from undershooting, and subsequent reports suggest only 'nominal damage' inflicted, the crews expressed themselves more than satisfied with 'an excellent concentration of markers' (ORB) that were well maintained within the built-up area. As the Pathfinders left, their rear gunners had a grandstand view of extensive fires, as well as some fifty searchlights dancing in the skies. The casualty rate was reassuringly low, at 4.5 percent, well within the realms of 'acceptable' attrition.

The number of Pathfinder aircraft lost, however, was high: 97 Squadron lost one; 405 Squadron lost two, both to nightfighters; and 156 Squadron lost three, including one of its senior officers, Wing Commander Eric Porter, a pre-war regular determined to 'get some in'. Porter, who had been posted to 156 from 83 Squadron four months earlier, had flown at least sixteen operations, including five to Berlin.

A similarly sophisticated plan was devised for a raid on Augsburg on February 25/26 and losses were lower still. For once, the Pathfinders were not hampered by bad weather. Indeed the skies over the city were clear, and the raid was an outstanding success. In the first wave, marking was good and well backed-up, and bomb bursts and incendiaries were clear to see, with many fires started.

By the time the second wave arrived, with more than fifty Pathfinders in the vanguard, they needed little help in navigating their way to the target for the glow of the fire could be seen from 100 miles distance. The only difficulty now was in discerning the target indicators through the smoke, as the centre of the town appeared well alight, with fires spreading to the marshalling yards. An hour after the heavies had departed, a handful of Mosquitoes arrived to add to the misery. Compared to what the Pathfinders had been used to, defences over Augsburg were poor and only one of their aircraft was lost.

The ORB entry for February closes with rather more positive news than the previous month. The number of aircraft missing had fallen from sixty-nine to 'only' twenty-nine, although this has to be seen in the context of far fewer operations (1,086 sorties) and operational flying hours (4,952).

March would be busier.

CHAPTER 5
LEADING FROM THE FRONT

Operations were planned for every night of the month of March, though the inclement weather led to cancellations. Nine heavy-bomber operations were delayed, and on three nights, not even the Mosquitoes were allowed to take to the skies.

PFF made the best of those nights when operations were 'on', however, with Stuttgart and Frankfurt, in particular, being singled out for special attention. Stuttgart was raided at the beginning of the month and on the night of 15/16. On the first, the attack opened promptly with TIs and flares, but the TIs were bursting beneath heavy cloud and disappearing immediately. Despite the difficulties, and gaps in both the marking and the subsequent bombing, a good number of fires and explosions were reported and returning crews fancied that they may have done a good job, albeit the bombing was scattered. The cloud that threatened to disrupt the accuracy also worked in the bombers' favour, however, since it hid them from the German defences. Only four aircraft were reported missing including one 156 Squadron Lancaster that the nightfighters did manage to find. Flight Sergeant Robert Baker RAAF and his crew were all killed.

The second raid two weeks later saw a heavier force (including 132 Pathfinder aircraft) briefed and routed in to the target over France, nearly as far as the Swiss border, before making their approach to the target. Whereas the first attack opened on time, on this occasion the Pathfinders were unfashionably late and the subsequent marking described as 'spasmodic'. Although the weather was clear, the winds may have affected the marking and bombing, for two clusters began to emerge, one in the southwest and the other to the northeast of the city, with a wide corridor in-between where nothing much was happening.

Although the German defences were late to respond, when they did they inflicted considerable casualties. Four Pathfinders out of a total of twenty-seven aircraft were lost, one each from 7, 35, 97 and 405 Squadrons. Flying Officer Arthur Ganderton (whose crew included a forty-one-year-old air gunner, Sergeant Arthur Weller) was flying the first Lancaster to be lost on operations since 35 Squadron converted to the type. The 97 Squadron crew of Flight Lieutenant William Meyer DFC were all decorated.

The planners switched their attention to Frankfurt for the next two major raids, and both were successful from a Pathfinder perspective. On the night of March 18/19, a large force of Pathfinders ensured that the attack was opened on

2B OR NOT 2B

"We were on our way to Leipzig, and I was working my radar plot, when I could sense someone looking over my shoulder. Without looking to see who it was, I said, 'look if you've got nothing better to do then bugger off!' At that point an arm appeared with the clear rank of an air commodore on the sleeve. It was Bennett, who immediately asked why I was drawing a track with a 2B pencil. It was so I didn't get a thinner line confused with one of the lattice lines on my Gee chart and said so. Bennett was not impressed, and told me that if my eyesight was that bad I shouldn't be doing the job! Bennett's standards were such that he expected every nav chart to look like it had been drawn by a draughtsman!"

BORIS BRESSLOFF DFC
NAV TWO. 635 SQUADRON. FIFTY-THREE OPS.

time, but the ORB reports various challenges that prevented the visual markers from being able to see the target, and a good number retaining TIs in their bellies – for the rules were that if you were not certain of the target, you did not mark. Although the immediate post-raid report is pessimistic, the actual damage done was considerable. Two PFF aircraft were lost, including a 692 Mosquito flown by a Canadian pilot, Flying Officer John Leithead who, with his navigator (Warrant Officer Joseph Burke), was apparently the victim of a nightfighter, although no claims for any twin-engined aircraft were made that night.

The bombers went back to Frankfurt on March 22/23 with a similar-sized force, and benefited from a mine-laying diversion that kept the German controller distracted for some time. The damage on this occasion was even greater than inflicted previously; visual identification of the river and the built-up area was sometimes possible and this, no doubt, contributed to the large fires that were reported by Mosquitoes over the target some time later. Half of the city was without gas, water and electricity and well over 100,000 civilians were bombed out of their homes.

While it was a good night for Pathfinders in terms of the bombing, it was unfortunate for them in terms of casualties, with six aircraft missing. The biggest blow, without doubt, was the loss of Group Captain Kenneth Rampling DSO, DFC, the commanding officer of 7 Squadron. His aircraft was known to have bombed and cleared the target area when it was suddenly hit, and equally quickly caught fire and exploded. Three of his crew made it clear. Rampling had been in charge of the squadron for almost six months, and was well loved by his crews. His shoes would, almost immediately after, be filled by one of the true Pathfinder 'greats', Wing Commander Guy Lockhart DSO, DFC & Bar, a man whom Bennett describes in his autobiography as 'fanatically courageous'.

Bomber Command, and Pathfinders in particular, had impressed with their last two raids. Two more attacks awaited Berlin and Essen, with mixed results and the loss of a further six Pathfinders – all on the trip to Berlin. One of those killed, 97 Squadron Pilot Officer William Coates, had cause to remember the capital well for it had been after his heroic return from Berlin in a heavily-damaged bomber in January that he had won an immediate DFM – a feat all the more remarkable considering it was his first ever operational sortie. Now commissioned, his bravery was not sufficient to protect him from the Grim Reaper at the second time of asking.

While the existing stations and squadrons had been busy, there had been further changes to the operational structure of 8 Group. On the 1st of the month, as the bombers prepared to attack Stuttgart, the formal handover of the airfield at Little Staughton in Bedfordshire by the USAAF to the RAF was concluded. A few days later, 3 Group ceded control of Downham Market in Norfolk, thus providing Pathfinders with two new bases from which to operate.

Pathfinders were expanding their strength to cope with increased demand on their services. To this end a new heavy-bomber squadron was formed, 635 Squadron, to occupy the newly-acquired airfield at Downham Market. It had been created by hiving off two whole flights from existing squadrons – 97 and 35 – in order to create a nucleus that could be effective immediately. In command was yet another Trenchard Brat, Wing Commander Alan Cousens DSO, DFC, MC (Czech).

Elsewhere, work began on constructing new runways at Marham, obliging 105 Squadron to move from there to Bourn; 156 Squadron uprooted itself from Warboys for the short trip to Upwood, effectively swapping homes with the Pathfinder NTU.

With its new organisation in place, and a new heavy-bomber squadron on line and ready to commence operations, the planners chose the historic city of Nuremberg as the target to test their mettle. It led to a tragedy of Shakespearian proportions.

Nuremberg was by all means a legitimate target, the embodiment of Nazi Germany made famous as the venue for the Nazi's pre-war showpiece rallies. Now the intention was to smash that heart with a force of almost 800 bombers led by 110 Pathfinder Lancasters and nine Mosquitoes. Just about everything that could go wrong, did, although the principal blame must be laid at the feet of the planning staff.

Very unusually, they chose to route the bombers from the east coast of England to Charleroi, the first turning point, and then a single long leg without deviations of some 250 miles. Bennett maintained afterwards that he had no say in the planning, and that his objections were overruled. The route would take them directly in-between two well-known fighter beacons where the enemy would congregate. There was little in the way of any significant diversions, and those that were undertaken to Aachen, Cologne and Kassel, as well as a small mine-laying trip to Heligoland, were unsuccessful. The weather, too, once again played its part.

The nightfighters were quick to assemble, and swift to take advantage of near-perfect conditions at high altitude. For this was a period of full moon when the bombers would usually have stayed at home but with predicted high cloud the planners had taken a risk – a gamble they lost in spectacular fashion. The bombers were visible to the naked eye at distances of more than half a mile. The Luftwaffe could see their prey, follow them, and virtually attack at leisure. In a running battle that lasted more than ninety minutes, the Nachtjager chopped down around eighty heavies on their way to the target (estimates vary from seventy-nine to eighty-two), with numerous other combats being reported.

Pathfinders were involved in at least eight nightfighter engagements at this stage, although none of them proved conclusive. Some eighty-eight Lancasters and eight Mosquitoes claimed to have attacked the primary target, with five Lancasters and one Mosquito abortive. The raid was late to start, and marking and the subsequent bombing was scattered. The strong winds here didn't help, with most of the markers and therefore the majority of the bombs falling to the east, with more than ten miles of creepback being reported. There were also reports of bombing to the north in the areas of Bamberg and Schweinfurt.

The facts were brutal. Although most of the killing had been done before the bombing took place, a further group of bombers were shot down on their return and further aircraft crashed in England, bringing total losses for the night to 108. One of those who crashed with his aircraft written off landing in fog at Feltwell was Flight Lieutenant A.H. MacGillivray. He survived Nuremberg only to be shot down over Düsseldorf the following month. His was one of three Lancaster crews from 7 Squadron that were missing, the others skippered by Flight Lieutenant Stanley Evans (all killed flying their twenty-sixth operation together) and Squadron Leader Colin Wilson DFC, a thirty-eight-year-old whose flight engineer was half his age.

The squadron to suffer the most was 156, with four crews missing, including a Lancaster flown by one of the handful of Norwegian pilots in Pathfinder Force, Captain Finn Johnsen. All eight of the crew onboard were killed. Also missing was Pilot Officer L. Lindley. He was the only survivor of his crew that included a Nigerian, Sergeant Bankole Vivour.

From Downham Market, 635 Squadron suffered its first casualties since forming a week or so earlier, with three of its captains missing (Flight Lieutenants Charles Lyon and Hugh Webb, both killed, and Johnny Nicholls DFC captured. Nicholls' crew was on their thirty-fifth operation).

The two remaining casualties were from 97 Squadron: Flight Lieutenant Leonard Hyde DFC was lost with his entire crew on their twenty-ninth operation. Flight Lieutenant Desmond Rowlands DFC and his crew, all on their second tour, were also missing. Noteworthy among them was the rear gunner, Flight Lieutenant Richard Trevor-Roper DFC, DFM. Trevor-Roper had only recently joined 97 Squadron from NTU, having spent six months at Central Gunnery School. Completing his first tour with 50 Squadron in 1941, he was later posted to the famous 617 Squadron, joining Guy Gibson's crew and being further decorated for his part in the dams' raid. By 1944, he was a very experienced air gunner, with more than fifty operations to his name. His was knowledge and skill that was difficult to replace.

The losses suffered that night were horrendous by any measure, and yet such is the way of things that of the forty-two Lancasters despatched by 35 Squadron, 83 Squadron, and 405 Squadron, not a single aircraft was missing. The heavy squadrons had, of course, fared worst throughout the month, but that is not to say that the Mosquito squadrons did not take their fair share of casualties. To add to a 1409 Met Flight loss in February (both Flying Officer Arthur Powell-Wiffen, who had been twice mentioned in despatches, and Pilot Officer Harry Ashworth DFM were badly burned and died following a crash landing), the unit lost another crew on March 27, killed in a training flight.

A bizarre accident befell the crew of a 105 Squadron aircraft on their return from Deelen on March 22/23. As the Mosquito came into land, all appeared well, until an explosion that killed the pilot (Flight Lieutenant Charles Boxall) and seriously injured the navigator (Flight Lieutenant Trevor Robinson DFC). Robinson lost a leg in the incident, which may have been caused by striking a bomb on the runway that had fallen from another aircraft by accident, or from one of their own bombs that had 'hung up' and broken free on landing.

The extraordinary decision to count an operation to northern France as only one third of a trip caused considerable confusion and did not last long.

Russ Yeulett, Bert Nundy, Bill Lanning, 'Tex' Barron and Dick Newman of 582 Squadron with a furry friend, winter 1944. Yeulett was the only one of his crew to make it out of Bob Palmer's aircraft on the day it was shot down.

APRIL

March had been a nadir for Pathfinders, and Bomber Command as a whole. Conversely, the German nightfighter force was reaching its zenith. Of the thirty-one aircraft missing from operations of PFF, two thirds were from only three raids. March will always be remembered for the disaster at Nuremberg, and tends to overshadow a host of other changes that went on at PFF during this time.

Although Harris's plan to wreck Berlin from end to end appears to have failed, his broader ambition to win the war (or at least contribute significantly to it) through area bombing and destroying the morale of the German people was still clearly in his mind. For a time, however, such ambitions would have to be put on hold, for powers even more senior than the Bomber Command commander-in-chief had call on his resources, and their objectives trumped his own. In just a handful of weeks, Harris was to find himself subordinate to the supreme allied commander to implement a new plan – the so-called 'Transportation Plan' – to prepare the way for the invasion of Europe.

In truth, the plan, or at least elements of it, was already underway. A feature in March remarked upon by the author of the ORB 'was the marking by our Oboe Mosquitoes for heavy attacks by aircraft of other groups'. These attacks were on seven different marshalling yards and an aircraft factory, all in France. All but a raid on Aulnoye were considered a success, and the town will feature later as a particularly tough nut to crack. The threat posed by the V1 menace, the first of Hitler's weapons of revenge, was also being countered with a series of raids on constructional works in northern France, with Oboe Mosquitoes again playing their part leading aircraft in 2 Group on risky daylight sorties.

More new squadrons were created and placed on the order of battle. A new heavy-bomber unit – 582 Squadron – was created by combining two flights (one each) from 7 and 156 Squadrons, and placed under the command of Wing Commander Charles Dunnicliffe DFC who until recently had been the temporary OC of 97 Squadron. They occupied the newly-acquired airfield at Little Staughton. A new Mosquito Squadron, 571 Squadron, was also added to the roster, originally formed at Downham Market but moving, almost immediately after, to Oakington. Its commanding officer was Wing Commander Mike Birkin, who had taken a step up in rank having earlier commanded 1409 Met Flight. In a move that was now becoming familiar (i.e. 'twinning' a heavy-bomber and a Mosquito-bomber squadron on the same station) 109 Squadron moved from Marham to Little Staughton to join their heavy colleagues.

Mid-way through the month, a move was forced upon Bennett that in his eyes all-but amounted to betrayal. Three of his squadrons – 83, 97 and 627 – were to be 'attached' to 5 Group for Pathfinder duties, and on April 15 the station merry-go-round began. A fierce rivalry existed between Bennett and the AOC of 5 Group, the Honourable Sir Ralph Cochrane. Both men thought they knew best, and held the panacea for successful target marking. Bennett believed he had already proven his point that properly-trained, fully-equipped squadrons could successfully achieve what was required of them, even in the most challenging conditions. He had, he felt, turned a 'wasteful and ineffective force into a mighty and successful one'. Cochrane believed that

MASTER BOMBER – 'MIKE' BIRKIN

James 'Mike' Birkin was one of the most exceptional of a brilliant band of Mosquito master bombers. Born in April 1912 in Chilwell, after Harrow and Cambridge (where he joined the university air squadron and RAFVR) he entered the stock exchange.

On the outbreak of war he served as an instructor and in 1942 was awarded the Air Force Cross for his endeavours in teaching a new generation of pupils to fly. Always badgering his superiors for an operational posting, his wishes finally came true at the end of 1943 when he was sent to 28 OTU (Wymeswold) and thence onward to 1409 Met Flight as officer commanding. His first Mosquito dual was with a young flying officer, Joe Patient, and his first 'Pampa' at the end of January 1944 when he had the excitement of the port engine cutting out on him. He completed a further ten Pampas (mainly in the company of Flight Lieutenant Colin Cowan DFC, DFM, a navigator with c100 ops to his name) before being promoted wing commander and posted to command the newly-formed 571 Squadron in April 1944.

A sustained period of bomber operations followed where Birkin very much led from the front. Awarded the DFC, he followed this soon after with an immediate Distinguished Service Order for planning and leading the attack on the Dortmund-Ems canal in which a handful of Mosquitoes managed to deliver a success that more 'prestigious' bomber command units with considerably larger ordinance could only imagine.

Mike handed over the reins to Wing Commander 'Jerry' Gosnell but continued to fly the occasional operation whilst officially attached to 8 Group HQ in August/September, 1944. He was finally 'rested' in November, being posted to the Empire Central Flying School (ECFS) at Hullavington.

1409 Met Flight with its mercurial commanding officer, Mike Birkin (seated centre).

the only way a target could be accurately marked was at extremely low level, and he had been working on his thesis for some time with a number of his 'pets', the famous Wing Commander Leonard Cheshire among them.

Whatever the rights and wrongs of either man's position, Cochrane had the ear of his commander-in-chief, and Harris ordered Bennett to surrender his squadrons to his equal (in fairness, Bennett was returning 83 and 97 from whence they came). Bennett later described the move as 'a slap in the face' for it meant in the eyes of the rest of the command their C-in-C believed the Pathfinders had failed.

A volume in its own right could be written about the feud that festered between these two men, although Bennett himself insisted that no such argument existed and that the two were in fact personal friends. It is difficult to believe how such a friendship could exist, however, given the harsh criticism of Cochrane that followed in Bennett's autobiography, describing him as having done 'great damage' to the PFF 'to the benefit of his own independence', and pointedly writing that if Cochrane had been given the opportunity to operate fifteen or twenty raids as the captain of a heavy bomber before being given a group, he would have been a wonderful group commander. It is surely stretching the bounds of credulity to believe that Bennett was not comparing his own position, as a former heavy-bomber squadron commander, with that of his rival.

Bennett worked with what he had – but what he had was fewer heavy-bomber squadrons at precisely the time when more were needed to keep pace with demand for their services. New targets called for a return to previously tried tactics, and he reverted to the use of a master bomber and deputy master bomber to control the accuracy of future raids.

The month started with an eventful few days for the Mosquito boys and the loss of two 139 Squadron aircraft in a week, the first in a crash and the second on operations to Hamburg. Two crew members, Flying Officer Andrew Howden RCAF and Flying Officer Frederick Stevens were killed. A 109 Squadron Mosquito (flown by Flying Officer Richard Pattison and with Jack Watts in the navigator's seat) successfully crash landed on its return from Essen on April 8/9 – the aircraft damaged by flak over the target – and the next day the pilot and navigator of a 105 Squadron aircraft were killed during an air test.

The 'heavies' were called into action to attack a goods yard at Lille, losing a 35 Squadron Lancaster flown by Flying Officer Ronald Bordiss. Further casualties were reported on raids to Aachen (three lost), La Chapelle (one missing) and Ottignies (one lost). Killed on the last of these raids was Squadron Leader Donald Mansbridge AFC of 635 Squadron (who had already completed forty-two operations) and a crew who were nearly all on their second tour. There was some excitement at Little Staughton on April 22 when the aircraft of one of its senior captains, Gerald O'Donovan, detailed for a training sortie, failed to make sufficient height on take-off, clipped the top of a nearby church and was obliged to force land at Woodbridge.

GOD AND THE CHURCH STEEPLE

Gerald O'Donovan was one of the very best. Known as 'GOD' on account of his initials, some believed it referred more to his excellence as a master bomber. Educated at Port Talbot Grammar School, his English teacher was called Burton, the adoptive father of a certain Richard Burton who gained some fame in the acting world.

Mr Burton persuaded the young Gerald to take elocution lessons to lose his accent reasoning that an Irish name and Welsh accent could cause him problems in later life. It was good advice, for having been trained initially as an apprentice aircraft mechanic, he was selected for a commission in 1942 and sent to the USA. Returning to the UK at the start of 1943, he went from OTU to 12 Squadron and thence to 156 Squadron. When his flight was earmarked to form the nucleus of 582 Squadron, he moved to Little Staughton, and completed around ninety operations, winning the DSO and DFC in the process. Even experienced men, however, could make mistakes.

On the day in question, O'Donovan's crew was joined by an experienced set operator, Syd Johnson, tasked with teaching them about the latest H2S variant (the Mark III), leaving one of the regular

Gerald O'Donovan (right) in a post-war photograph.

crew, Jeff Chapman, on the ground. For reasons best known to O'Donovan, at the intersection of the two runways he turned the aircraft so that it was facing the wrong way – lining up with the shortest part of the runway from which to take off. Rather than turn about he called for 'full power'. Remarkably the Lancaster managed to gain enough speed to make it into the air but within moments there was a sickening crash as the undercarriage wheel clipped the top of a church steeple.

O'Donovan immediately tried to lock the whole undercart down; the port wheel locked but the starboard wheel swung lifelessly in the slipstream. Rather than try to land with only one wheel in the correct position, he attempted to retract the port wheel, but without success. Flying control directed O'Donovan to make for Woodbridge, near Ipswich. After giving the crew the option of baling out, he approached the emergency landing ground with the escape hatches open and the crew in their crash positions. The aircraft was just a few feet above the ground when it stalled. O'Donovan managed to hold the unsupported starboard wing above the tarmac in a brilliant piece of airmanship before the whole aircraft finally fell to earth.

Whilst 'transportation' was the order of the day, this did not prevent Harris from turning his attentions to his favourite targets whenever he had the chance. On April 22 he sent nearly 600 aircraft to bomb Düsseldorf, causing widespread damage and resulting in two Pathfinders being shot down. That same night he sent a further 238 aircraft to attack Brunswick, a notable raid for it was the first attempt by the AOC 5 Group to prove his pet theory in low-level marking. Cochrane, like Bennett before him, found that theory and practice did not always happily coincide, and despite the best efforts of the formidable 617 Squadron the raid was not a success.

On what was a busy night for the bomber boys, Harris also ordered a further attack to be made on the marshalling yards at Laon. The attack was divided into two waves with a northern and southern aiming point (AP), both of which were well marked and the bombing well concentrated. The master bomber for the northern AP did a good job, but he paid for it with his life. Although the defences were described as 'negligible', they still accounted for three Pathfinder and six other

'FOR YOU THE WAR IS OVER'

When war came, Reg Parissien couldn't join up quickly enough. After wireless op training at Yatesbury, he arrived at HCU at Faldingworth via 5 AOS Jurby and 30 OTU where he crewed up. Posted to 626 Squadron at Wickenby the crew started operating on the night of December 3/4, 1943 and completed ten ops in total, including four trips to Berlin, before volunteering for Pathfinders and finally joining 156 Squadron. On the night of April 22 they were briefed to attack Düsseldorf:

"We were told that we would be part of a diversionary raid. That was the irony; we weren't even attacking the main target. Ray Keating, our usual nav two was sick, and we had a new navigator, an Australian, in his place to work with Derek Chase, our nav one.

"There was nothing untoward about the trip out; the usual flak and searchlights, but nothing to concern us. But after we had dropped our bombs, I heard our skipper (John Higgs) suddenly swear on the intercom. It was most unlike him. It was obvious we were lost, and the next thing we know we're coned. It was so bright in the aircraft that I could have read a newspaper.

"The skipper started to take evasive action, corkscrewing all over the place. Then we were hit. I looked out of the astrodome and could see that the starboard wing was on fire. Ducking back down into the aircraft, I could also see flames to the rear, beyond the mid upper's position. George (George Woodhead) was still in his turret. The electrics had gone; our hydraulics were shot. I tried to go

Reg Parissien (third from right). His skipper, John Higgs, is precariously perched on the engine!

aft but it was too hot. I heard the skipper on the intercom again: 'That's it. Everybody out!' I clipped on my 'chute, tapped John on the shoulder and dropped out of the escape hatch on the floor. John followed soon after.

"I don't remember pulling the rip cord – no-one does apparently, as you are only semi-conscious because of the lack of oxygen – but I do remember a sharp jolt as the 'chute opened. I floated down into the dark for what seemed like an age, at one point being caught in the searchlights and convinced

Kriegie photograph of Reg Parissien at the start of his captivity.

that they would start shooting at me. I could hear the crackling of the fires and my nostrils were soon filled with the smell of burning. I started pulling the lines above my head to try and steer me away from the target. Then there was a 'bang' as I hit the ground. Forget all that nonsense about 'bend your knees' – there simply wasn't time.

"I had landed in an open field and by the time I had recovered my senses, I was surrounded by a party of troops from the local searchlight unit who had followed my descent. One of them was standing over me, rifle in hand, and uttered those immortal words: 'For you the war is over!'

"There were seven of us in the crew, and we know that six got out for certain. Of those six, the first three out – Maurice Fowler (our flight engineer), Derek Chase and our replacement bomb aimer – whose name was Thomas – were all killed. Me, John and George, the mid upper, survived. Our rear gunner, Bill Webb, died in his turret.

REG PARISSIEN
WIRELESS OPERATOR. 156 SQUADRON.

FRIENDLY FIRE

Flight Lieutenant Bob Lasham came to 97 Squadron Pathfinders having completed seventeen operations with 9 Squadron and was very soon in the thick of it. His crew called him 'dad' on account of his age. He was twenty-three. On April 24, his crew was one of fifteen detailed for operations against Munich. It was a beautiful spring day with clear skies and excellent visibility. All went well on the approach to the target, and then suddenly disaster struck:

> *"We had just completed our marking run when we were coned by searchlights for the first time. The tactic then was to put the Lancaster into a dive and apply full power; it was the only way to shake them off. Just as we did there was an almighty thump and a bang. Although we didn't know what had hit us, the fuel pipe was severed and we lost the port outer. I managed to keep control of the aircraft – a Lancaster could easily fly on three when it needed to – and headed for home, landing at Tangmere.*
>
> *"When we inspected the aircraft, there were seven holes in the wing that we discovered had been caused when they had been struck by incendiaries falling from one of our own aircraft."*

This was not the only occasion that Bob and his crew had first-hand experience of the dangers of a crowded sky: *"On a daylight to Deelen – a trip they all thought was a doddle – one of my gunners had a grandstand view as a bomb from above fell past and hit the aircraft below, completely severing the rear turret. He remembered clearly just seeing the aircraft break apart, and the turret tumbling over and over as it fell through the sky, no doubt with the rear gunner still trapped inside."*

BOB LASHAM DFC & BAR
PILOT. 97 SQUADRON. FIFTY-THREE OPS.

aircraft being destroyed.

The dead included Pilot Officer Percy Aslett of 7 Squadron and his crew; all seven men on board the 582 Squadron aircraft of Flight Sergeant Bernard Wallis – the first squadron casualties since being formed; and the 635 Squadron Lancaster of Wing Commander Alan Cousens. In an unusual entry in the ORB, Cousens' name is singled out for special mention as 'foremost amongst missing aircrew during the month'. His voice was heard over the target during the raid, and it was assumed he had been shot down once his duties had been carried out.

Karlsruhe, Munich and Essen were all given the main force treatment in the days that followed, and four more aircraft were lost. One was a 692 Squadron Mosquito, a Mark XVI, the first of its kind to be written off by the unit. Coming in to land at Graveley, the pilot, Squadron Leader Edward Saunderson DFC, ran slap bang into the back of a 35 Squadron Lancaster that had yet to fully clear the runway. The damage to his own aircraft was terminal but so too, sadly, were the injuries caused to the rear gunner and mid upper gunner in the Lanc. Sergeant Walter Crawford was killed instantly and Sergeant Thomas Nainby died two weeks later in Ely hospital.

The ball-bearing factories at Schweinfurt managed to avoid serious damage from a raid on April 26/27 when the attempted low-level marking, once again, failed to hit the spot, this time by the Mosquitoes of 627 Squadron. More than nine percent of the attacking force was shot down, including three from 83 Squadron, among them Squadron Leader Albert Collett AFC. But worse was to follow.

When the planners chose certain vital factories at Friedrichshafen as the primary target for an attack on April 27/28, they were acutely aware of the challenges they faced. The target was deep in enemy territory, it was a moonlit night, and the memory of the disaster at Nuremberg was still firmly in their minds. Pathfinders would contribute fifty-nine Lancasters, and the first flares and green TIs fell on time and were promptly backed up. The marshalling yards and sheds could be clearly identified in the light of the flares and marking was especially accurate.

'Low-level Mossie' – a painting commissioned by Ken Oatley of 627 Squadron shows the distinctive 5 Group marking method.

Although main force was slow to arrive, the pace soon quickened and a large weight of bombs fell on the eastern part of the town. The raid might have gone very differently. The zero hour was changed while the aircraft were on their way to the target, but because of w/t failure, the master bomber, Squadron Leader Keith Cresswell, failed to receive the message. He made up for being late by putting in a sterling performance in guiding the later stages of the attack, and considerable damage was achieved. Harris described the night's efforts as 'one of the most outstanding raids of the war'. All six factories of importance were destroyed.

It did not all go the Pathfinders' way, however. Three aircraft were shot down and two senior officers killed: the officers commanding 7 Squadron and 156 Squadron.

It must have seemed to some of the men at Oakington that their CO was immortal; to others, he had already pushed his luck too far and was living on borrowed time. Either way, the death of Wing Commander Guy Lockhart DSO, DFC & Bar was a serious blow, made doubly worse by the loss of other senior leaders including Squadron Leader John Martin DFC & Bar, the navigator, and the mid upper gunner, Squadron Leader George Gyle DFC – another who had lied about his age for fear of being too old for active service (Gyle's wife would later write *Missing in Action* – a moving account of the days following her husband's loss).

Lockhart's post was immediately filled by the diminutive Wing Commander J. Fraser Barron – a Kiwi of immense experience. Barron had earned a DFM on operations as a sergeant pilot flying Stirlings with 15 Squadron in 1941/42 and by the beginning of 1944 he was a wing commander with the DSO and DFC to add to his collection. And he was only twenty-three. He would later earn a Bar to his DSO, but would not live long enough to receive it.

At Upwood, experienced crews were similarly disbelieving at the loss of their CO, Wing Commander Eric Eaton DFC. At thirty-two, Eaton was somewhat older than Barron, and a pre-war regular. He already had command experience, having been CO of 101 Squadron two years earlier, gaining the DFC as a 'very capable operational captain'. Having succeeded Group Captain

MASTER BOMBERS – THE NEW ZEALANDERS

Wing Commander James Fraser Barron was the giant among the master bombers in the Royal New Zealand Air Force whose exploits earned him many distinctions before his untimely death in May 1944. He achieved all of his awards for gallantry while flying heavy bombers.

Alfred Cochrane DSO, DFC & two Bars was a similarly highly-decorated master bomber who won his first DFC flying Wellingtons with 150 Squadron in 1942. His second Bar highlighted the attack on Goch in February 1945 when he brought his aircraft home despite severe damage to the port wing and displaying 'a magnificent example of fearlessness'.

Wing Commander Thomas Horton DSO, DFC & Bar was another superlative Pathfinder who won his first DFC in 1942 with 88 Squadron flying Bostons in daylight, a bar with 105 Squadron in August 1944 and the DSO before the war ended. He was an extremely popular pilot and flight commander. Making the transition from four engines to two, Flight Lieutenant Valentine Moore DSO, DFC, DFM was a seasoned campaigner and inveterate 'press-on' type who had won his DFM with 57 Squadron in 1942, having been shot down and surviving thirty-seven hours in a dinghy. Squadron Leader Graham Mandeno DSO, DFC, whose citation for his Distinguished Flying Cross refers to two separate trips in which he brought his bomber back having been attacked by enemy fighters, also moved from four (156 Squadron) to two (139 Squadron).

Moving in the other direction from two to four, Squadron Leader George Patrick DFC was an early Oboe navigator with 109 Squadron, who had flown some 118 sorties at the point that he was awarded the DSO while serving with 35 Squadron.

Other notable New Zealand Pathfinders with the DSO included: Squadron Leader Stephen Watts DSO, DFC, the commanding officer of 692 Squadron; Flight Lieutenant Nicholas Matich DSO, DFM, who was shot down, evaded, and won both his awards while serving with 35 Squadron; Squadron Leader John Wright DSO, DFC, another 156 Squadron stalwart described as 'an inspiring leader'; Squadron Leader John Hegman DSO, DFC, who need not have served in the war at all; and Squadron Leader Charles Kelly DSO, DFC, a navigator of exceptional skill and fortitude. These can only be passing vignettes, but the bravery of the New Zealanders – and indeed all of the commonwealth aircrew – has never been in doubt.

'Fatty' Collings as CO of 156 in the January, he had been in charge for nearly four months, and on this particular trip had taken the regular crew of Flying Officer Gilmore that included the bombing leader, Squadron Leader Leslie Glasspool DFC. (In June, while still officially missing and awaiting news of his fate, Eaton was granted the acting rank of group captain.) On May 5, Wing Commander Thomas Bingham-Hall DFC, another pre-war pilot and veteran of 150 Squadron, arrived to assume command.

Friedrichshafen was not the only target for that night. Ops to the railway yards at Aulnoye and Montzen were also undertaken, the former with little grief and much success, the latter resulting in the loss of the deputy master bomber, Squadron Leader Teddy Blenkinsop DFC, CdG. Blenkinsop emerged unscathed, only to lose his life fighting for the resistance almost a year later.

April ended with further attacks on the railway yards at Somain, Achères, and Maintenon, all involving less than 150 aircraft and each controlled by a master bomber. The difficulties some master bombers began experiencing at this time were not only related to finding and accurately marking the aiming point, or in keeping a tight concentration of bombs. One of the biggest challenges was in getting main force to obey instructions, for like disobedient children they occasionally tested the patience of Pathfinders to the limit.

Fraser Barron had struggled to get the Halifax crews supporting his raid on Tergnier to do anything he directed. Another 7 Squadron master bomber, Wing Commander Philip Patrick DFC, had the same experience at Somain. The first Oboe markers had fallen inaccurately, and although Patrick ordered the bombers to wait while he remarked, more than a third started bombing at

FROM PATHFINDING TO THE RESISTANCE

Several Bomber Command and Pathfinder airmen, finding themselves alone and on the run, eventually teamed up with the local resistance. Teddy Blenkinsop was one such man.

Born in Victoria, British Columbia in 1920, Edward 'Teddy' Blenkinsop was a chartered accountant before the war, enlisting in the RCAF in June, 1940. After training, he served first with 425 Squadron in North Africa in 1943, before volunteering for a second tour with 405 Squadron, Pathfinder Force.

On the night of April 27/28, Teddy was detailed as deputy to the master bomber, Wing Commander Reg Lane DSO, DFC & Bar. Lane recalls the markers being dropped, and instructing Blenkinsop to head home. Moments later he saw the flash of an aircraft exploding and realised at once it was his deputy. On returning to base he reported that Blenkinsop had been killed. But he had not.

Miraculously, Teddy survived to team up with the local Belgian resistance. On his way one day with a group of men determined to blow up a German garrison in Meensel-Kiesegem, they ran into a group of more than 200 men armed with machine guns. Teddy fled into a wood, unarmed, and was captured. Threatened with torture he refused to speak, but the Germans said he had been implicated in an act of terrorism and would be shot. He was held at St Gilles prison in Brussels, managing at one point to 'transmit' his identity to an American officer POW by tapping in morse code over steam pipes.

It is believed that Blenkinsop was sent to work as a forced-labourer in a factory in Hamburg and may have spent time in Bergen-Belsen. He died of heart failure in late January/early February 1945 (official death records state January 23) in a concentration camp at Neuengamme.

THE WIRELESS OP

Ernie Patterson attended Madley and Yatesbury for wireless op training (he achieved a speed of eighteen words per minute and the coveted 'S' brevet), before moving to Evanton for air gunnery where he qualified 'above average' – an unusual accolade. He flew first as wireless operator to 'Jack' Harrild DFC and then Alex Thorne DSO, DFC. His tour of operations included five master bomber trips and two as deputy.

"As the wireless op I would listen in to HQ (Huntingdon) at ten past and twenty to the hour. We would be sent the frequencies of German nightfighters and tune in to listen to them. We had a microphone attached to the brushes of the generators, so if we found a transmission we would clamp down the morse key and in doing so drown out the broadcast. The fighters would then be obliged to change frequencies and so we could disrupt their attack.

"Certain aircraft within the stream would be tasked with sending back wind speeds and transmit those speeds back to HQ so they could in turn re-transmit that information to the rest of the attacking force.

"When we were fifty miles from home, I would call to get the barometric pressure at base which the skipper would then feed into his altimeter. The WAAF controllers were always spot-on. They were constantly in control – even when you could hear other aircraft in the circuit, low on fuel or coming in on three engines or with wounded on board, there was never any panic.

"When we were master bomber, my role would also be to record every word transmitted by the skipper. Afterwards, my logs were then used to plot the precise details of the raid. Our call sign as master bomber was 'Portland One' – I have never been able to look at a bag of Portland cement without being reminded of those times."

ERNIE PATTERSON DFM
WIRELESS OPERATOR. 635 SQUADRON. FIFTY-ONE OPS.

the first opportunity. At Achères, however, Squadron Leader Keith Cresswell enjoyed rather more success, visually identifying and marking the target himself and marshalling a rather fine example of concentrated bombing.

The attack was a more upbeat finale for a month of mixed fortunes. Pathfinder resources were being stretched to the limit, making their achievements all the more remarkable. Master bombers had returned, and the accuracy they were delivering on relatively small targets was exceeding expectations, and warnings from Harris himself.

The role of the Mosquito squadrons and their payload also changed during this time: it was now commonplace for attacks to be mounted by comparatively large (forty or more) formations of Mosquitoes, many carrying 4,000-pound bombs. These contributed to an overall weight of bombs dropped of approximately 4,000 tons for the loss of thirty-one aircraft.

MAY

The generals knew it and the Pathfinder aircrew suspected that the invasion could not be far off. The opening of the long-awaited 'second front' was only a few weeks away and the target list continued to reflect the primary objective of destroying the enemy's rail and transport infrastructure. Also added to this list were various ammunition dumps and known troop concentrations as well as coastal gun emplacements and other military hardware such as radar.

The location of these targets is most interesting: the exact position of the invasion was, of course, still shrouded in secrecy. Berlin still guessed at Calais, and Bomber Command and Pathfinders played their part in keeping up the pretence. For every genuine target selected in and around Normandy and the transport links that would feed reinforcements to the beaches, two spoof attacks would also have to be made.

It is not surprising, therefore, that the number of sorties carried out by Pathfinders rose from 1,608 in April to some 2,271 in May. But this was also helped by the weather: only eleven nights during the month of May (as compared to eighteen nights during April) were some or all operations cancelled because of unfavourable weather, and of those on only two nights were they scrapped altogether.

The full moon period – usually a 'no no' for bomber operations for obvious reasons – was also used to help with precision attacks controlled by master bombers, the need for accuracy outweighing the inherent risk of being seen in the dark. The Mosquitoes were especially busy, either leading heavy raids or sometimes working alone for aircraft of other groups. Targets read like a roadmap of towns and villages across northern France from Cap Gris-Nez to St Valery-en-Caux.

Railway marshalling yards also received considerable attention, two attacks being made on Achères, Hasselt, Louvain, Le Mans, Aachen, Les Aubrais-Orléans, and Boulogne, and one attack each on St Ghislaine, Chambly, Haine-St-Pierre, Lens, Ghent and Trappes among many others. Heavy raids were also mounted on various airfields, including a particularly destructive attack on Montdidier by 84 Lancasters and eight Mosquitoes for the loss of four Pathfinders: one from 35 Squadron (Pilot Officer Colin Elton); one from 405 Squadron (Flight Lieutenant Stanley McDonald); and two from 582 Squadron (Flight Lieutenant Frederick Bertelsen and Warrant Officer Charles O'Neill – both Canadians). There was only one survivor from the four crews.

The main event that night (May 3/4), however, was elsewhere on the ammunition dump at Mailly-le-Camp. This raid, like the Nuremberg debacle in March, is remembered for all the wrong reasons. Pathfinders within 8 Group were only involved on the fringes, contributing two Mosquitoes. Their Pathfinding colleagues in 5 Group, however, were very much in the forefront of the attack, notably the officer commanding 83 Squadron, Laurence Deane.

Deane, in his memoirs, is in no doubt as to who was to blame for the disaster: Cochrane.

MASTER BOMBER – SQUADRON LEADER JOHN DENNIS DSO, DFC

John Dennis while serving in the North African campaign.

Whilst the eyes of the world focused its attention on Britain in the summer of 1940, the RAF was fighting another forgotten campaign in sunnier but no less hostile climes and against a different enemy.

Benito Mussolini had made no secret of his ambitions to extend his new Roman Empire in Africa. With the British on the point of collapse, he declared war on His Majesty's forces on June 10. The RAF in Egypt went immediately on the offensive, attacking Italian troop concentrations in Libya. Five Blenheim squadrons were engaged on operations: four were 30, 55, 211 and 113. The fifth was 45 Squadron; one of its pilots was a regular RAF officer, now in the reserve, John Mervyn Dennis.

The 45 Squadron to which Dennis belonged had been in Fuka on the day war began, moving to Helwan on June 20, 1940. It had no fewer than eleven bases in the next twelve months as the battles in North Africa ebbed and flowed. The extent to the squadron's involvement, and specifically John's part in it, can be appreciated by the citation for his richly-deserved DFC that recognised the completion of no less than sixty-eight operations since the fighting began, including sixteen raids in just twenty days. In the course of his bombing he'd obtained hits on a destroyer and a submarine, and on at least two fighters on the ground.

John completed one further operation before a well-earned rest. It was to be 18 months before he was again flying operationally, this time as a flight commander of 7 Squadron. Dennis flew his first Pathfinder sortie on Christmas Eve, 1943, a seven-hour trip to Berlin. By the following spring he had attained master bomber status, and on the night of May 1, 1944 was detailed as master bomber for an attack on the

The Distinguished Service Order and Distinguished Flying Cross awarded to John Dennis - killed on the same night as Fraser Barron, possibly in a collision.

Chambly marshalling yards.

Dennis was leading a group of Pathfinders and a hundred or so four-engined heavies from 3 Group. The recommendation for his immediate DSO said that the almost complete destruction of this target 'can be attributed very largely to this officer's enthusiasm and determination in marking the target and giving accurate directions to the remainder of the force'.

Chambly was out of action for ten days. Three weeks later, on the night of May 19, 1944, the target was another complex of marshalling yards, this time in the French town of Le Mans. Again, John was assigned to be in the vanguard of a mainly 3 Group force, this time playing deputy to his CO's master bomber role.

What happened that night is not clear; what is known is that both master and deputy were lost. Le Mans was a relatively innocuous target. To have lost one senior pilot was bad enough; but to have lost both a squadron commander and a flight commander from the same

ROYAL AIR FORCE

PATH FINDER FORCE

Award of
Path Finder Force Badge

This is to certify that

ACTING SQUADRON LEADER J. M. DENNIS, D.F.C.
41783.
is hereby

Permanently awarded the Path Finder Force Badge

Issued this 24th day of   MAY   in the year 1944.

Air Officer Commanding, Path Finder Force.

The permanent award of the Pathfinder Force Badge issued to Squadron Leader John Dennis. The permanent award was automatically issued to any PFF aircrew killed in action or otherwise earned upon the personal sanction of the AOC.

unit on the same night, was nigh on a catastrophe. Whether they were lost to flak, fighters or a collision is almost an irrelevance: the result was still the same.

The dead in John's crew included the air bomber Flight Lieutenant William Porteous DFM (later DSO), a twenty-three-year-old Scot from the Isle of Skye. He had won his DFM as a flight sergeant on a return from Hannover in September 1943 after his aircraft – piloted by Flying Officer Granville Wilson DFC, DFM – had been badly knocked about by flak. (Wilson was to receive the DSO for the same action.) Dennis's navigator was similarly highly experienced: Flight Lieutenant Ronald Hewett DFM was a VR officer who at thirty-five was comparatively old for aircrew. He had flown his first tour with 9 Squadron on Wellingtons.

The documents sent by the authorities to John Dennis's next of kin are typical of the thousands of letters that were received by at first hopeful and later despairing wives, parents, brothers or sisters throughout the war.

Although much is known of John's operational career, there is one mystery that still remains. Within his ribbon medals is a 1939/45 star. In the middle of the ribbon is a gold rosette, a feature usually included to denote service in the Battle of Britain. The name of Dennis, however, does not feature in any official lists of Battle of Britain aircrew. It remains a mystery to this day.

Cochrane, he says, had persuaded 1 Group to join him in the attack. This created a problem that ultimately led to catastrophe. Lancasters in 5 Group were equipped with the TR 1196 (VHF) for speech intercommunications between aircraft; 1 Group Lancs were not. As main force controller to Leonard Cheshire's marker leader, Deane was obliged to transmit bombing instructions via morse, rather than speech. Unfortunately for Deane, his wireless transmitter was wrongly tuned and so the attacking force heard nothing. Squadron Leader Neville Sparks took over, and a heavy weight of bombs fell on the target, but the delay had proven deadly. German nightfighters accounted for nearly all of the forty-two aircraft shot down, including the Lancaster of Neville Sparks. Happily Sparks evaded capture, along with five of his crew.

Targets in northern France were generally considered 'softer' than those in Germany. The distance travelled was greatly reduced, and less time in the air meant less opportunity for the Germans to muster their defences. For a brief period, it was even decided that targets across the Channel should only count as one third of an operation – though fortunately this ludicrous policy did not last for long. (In at least one Pathfinder squadron at this time they adopted a 'points' system where a French target was three points and a target in Germany five points. Crews needed to accumulate 150 points to complete a tour.)

If the 'wingless wonders' truly believed that 'soft' targets were in any way less lethal, they were sorely mistaken. They still claimed the lives of many an experienced airman. Flight Lieutenant Henry Churchill DFC & Bar of 156 Squadron, for example, was shot down and killed on May 6/7 over Mantes-la-Jolie. He'd won his first DFC in January 1944 with 103 Squadron for pressing on and bombing on three engines, and a Bar (gazetted after his death) for bringing his severely-damaged aircraft home after an attack on Karlsruhe. Also lost on the same raid was Pilot Officer Robert Borrowes DFC, a Canadian with 405 Squadron. He had flown not less than forty-four operations.

Two days later, Flight Lieutenant Allan Whitford DFC, RAAF was shot down over Brest on his fortieth trip, his aircraft being caught by light flak and exploding in mid air killing all on board. That same night three Pathfinders were lost attacking the railway yards at Haine-saint-Pierre. (Among them was the Lancaster of Pilot Officer Arthur Darlow of 405 Squadron – one of two 405 Squadron aircraft missing.)

Flight Lieutenant John Meredith DFC of 83 Squadron fell victim to flak and fighters during an attack on Gennevilliers. Making for home but with his starboard wing on fire, Meredith attempted to land, losing his life in the process. Two aircraft were also missing from 97 Squadron further to an attack on Lille. There were no survivors from either crew.

For the raid on Le Mans – another 'simple' target – on May 19/20, twelve Lancasters and four Mosquitoes of 8 Group were in charge of a force of 100 Lancasters from 3 Group. The Oboe Mosquitoes dropped their green TIs accurately, and the master bomber, the recently-appointed commanding officer of 7 Squadron, assessed one of the markers as being on the aiming point. Cloud, however, was obscuring the target, so the master bomber instructed the bombers to go beneath the cloud base.

A few minutes later, Wing Commander Barron called on his deputy, Squadron Leader John Dennis DSO, DFC, to reinforce the marking, and the resulting white TI fell bang on the aiming point. Several large explosions were reported on the ground, lighting up the target area and creating a pillar of smoke that rose through the cloud to a height of 9,000ft.

What happened next is still not known; what is understood, however, is that both the master and the deputy master bomber failed to return. John Dennis had flown ninety-one operations; Fraser Barron had completed seventy-nine. Oakington was obliged to find yet another squadron CO, which it did in the guise of yet another Halton apprentice, Wing Commander Reg Cox DFC, AFC. Cox had played a key role in helping to introduce the Stirling to operational service and served his first tour with 7 Squadron in 1941. It was a happy return and his steady hand in restoring confidence to a squadron whose morale had been seriously dented would soon after earn him a DSO.

The loss of two such highly-experienced heavy-bomber captains was difficult for Bennett to take, and after the debilitating casualties suffered during the Battle of Berlin, Pathfinders were in need of some respite. While the number of aircraft missing may have fallen, the quality of the crews missing, killed or prisoners of war was of the highest calibre, and their task appeared to be becoming even more dangerous.

Four crews, for example, were lost over Duisberg on May 21/22 including two from 156 Squadron. Luck – and tenacity – were on the side of Flight Sergeant 'Ralph' Temple and his crew who fought off not only two fighter attacks (for which the mid upper gunner, Sergeant Leslie Reynolds was awarded an immediate DFM for refusing to leave his position even after being seriously wounded) but also then survived a crash landing at RAF Dunsfold.

The second crew to go missing was captained by Flight Sergeant William Ward, a relative novice. Ward somehow survived when their aircraft was blown out of the sky at low level, but the rest of his crew was killed. They included the squadron gunnery leader, Squadron Leader Jack Blair DFC, DFM who was on his sixty-second operation.

Further losses were reported from the raids to Brunswick (two missing, one – a 97 Squadron aircraft – in a collision), Dortmund (one 35 Squadron aircraft missing), Aachen (three missing, one each from 7, 405 and 582 Squadrons) and Rennes (another 582 Squadron aircraft).

Flight Lieutenant George Crew DFC of 7 Squadron was more than halfway through his tour when he fell victim to German defences over Aachen; he was a mere beginner, however, compared to Squadron Leader Gordon Bennett DSO, DFC of 405 Squadron who had already logged his forty-five that included nine to Berlin. Bennett was particularly unlucky; he was, theoretically, tour expired, his total including two 'second dickey' trips. Not wanting to leave his crew to finish their last two trips with a different skipper, he volunteered to stay on, his loyalty being rewarded with his death. Somewhat ironically, the rest of his crew survived.

Bennett's experience was perhaps equalled by Squadron Leader 'Pat' Heney DSO, a master bomber with 582 Squadron shot down and killed on his fifty-ninth sortie. Heney and Bennett indeed shared a common experience, albeit almost a year apart. Both had won awards for gallantry for bringing home damaged aircraft after they had been hit by incendiaries dropped from above. Heney won the immediate DSO and Bennett an immediate DFC.

Strange, unfortunate and wasteful accidents appeared to be the order of things in May, particularly affecting the Mosquito boys. On May 10/11, Flying Officer Geoffrey Lewis of 139 Squadron was killed when a flare that had not released ignited in the bomb bay of his Canadian-built Mk XX Mosquito and the aircraft crashed. His navigator, Flying Officer Alan Woollard DFM survived, only to crash land again precisely a month later, and spend a period of internment in Sweden.

An even more bizarre incident befell the crew of a 105 Squadron Mosquito returning from a successful trip to Châteaudun. A Very pistol discharged in the cockpit, killing both pilot and navigator (Flight Lieutenants Norman Clayes DFC and Frederick Deighton) in the resultant crash. To complete the unwelcome hat-trick, Flying Officer Bernard Knight and his navigator, Flight Lieutenant Alexander Baldwin DFM were returning from an otherwise uneventful trip to Berlin and on their approach to land when the bomb doors suddenly flew open, dramatically altering the flying characteristics of their aircraft. Not surprisingly the Mosquito rapidly lost height and the pilot equally rapidly lost control. They thus became the first 571 Squadron casualties since the unit had formed five weeks earlier.

The German nightfighter force also enjoyed a number of successes that month, their most notable scalp being the 109 Squadron Mosquito of Squadron Leader Harry Stephens DFC and his navigator, Flight Lieutenant Norman Fredman DFC. They fell victim to Oberleutnant Werner

Macabre nose art – the personal mount of Wing Commander 'Slim' Somerville – 109 Squadron OC.

Baake for his twenty-seventh victory; Stephens himself had flown sixty-eight trips. (Although not a Pathfinder, Stephens's brother, Wing Commander John Stephens DFC, also lost his life with Bomber Command.)

The ORB states that Pathfinders lost twenty-seven aircraft in May, almost half of which were Mosquitoes – a reflection of the huge strain placed upon the crews and the large number of sorties undertaken both in a 'traditional' Pathfinding role and as members of the Light Night Striking Force.

A further three Mosquitoes were lost from 627 Squadron on detachment to 5 Group. There were six attacks on Ludwigshafen, five on Berlin, three on the IG Works at Leverkusen, two each on Cologne and Hannover, and one each on Düsseldorf and Dortmund. Steel works, engine plants and motor shops were all targets. In addition, the Mosquitoes of 692 Squadron also dropped mines very successfully in the narrow part of the Kiel canal from a height of little more than 300ft, while Mosquitoes of other squadrons carried out diversionary raids. In the last two raids of the month, three Mosquitoes failed to return, one each from 139, 627 and 692 Squadrons with no survivors.

The men of Pathfinder Force flew 2,271 sorties of which – gratifyingly – only thirty-three were aborted. Anyone would have thought that an invasion was just around the corner...

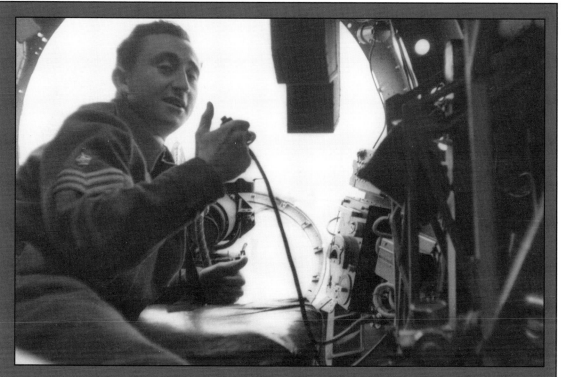

Norman Westby – one of the elite specialist air bombers.

THE SPECIALIST AIR BOMBER

After a tour of twenty-nine operations with 101 Squadron, Norman Westby volunteered for Pathfinders, flying a further twenty-six ops with a number of different pilots, including Bob Newbiggin. He was one of the elite specialist air bombers attached to crews as a primary visual marker, and flew two master bomber trips:

"My specialist role was as a visual bomb aimer. We received further training at Warboys (NTU) and had to do a number of flights and demonstrate a consistent bombing accuracy of within 100 yards of the target. There was a particular training exercise where a large photograph of an area of about five miles square was covered with a similarly large sheet of paper with a small hole cut in the centre. The instructor would move the hole around the photograph, and from what little you could see you were expected to know where you were and the heading to reach the target, and how long it would take. It was in effect mimicking the bombing run, and since many of our operations were now in daylight where the biggest obstacle was cloud, it was a very worthwhile exercise.

"As soon as we knew the target, then we would spend three or four hours studying the corresponding photographs until we knew it completely, from every direction. It was very intensive work. It had to be. It was the secret of accurate bombing. The bombs of 800 or so main force aircraft were relying on the accuracy of your markers, and although highly trained, we were all very young, and that was quite a responsibility. If I couldn't see or identify the aiming point then I would tell the skipper to go around again. Sometimes this happened three or four times until I was certain, by which stage the pilot would be shouting at me. I did not want to be up in front of Bennett, however, for allowing my markers down with such a large error. Sometimes, also, we had to bring our TIs back with us."

NORMAN WESTBY DFC & BAR
AIR BOMBER. 35 SQUADRON. FIFTY-FIVE OPS.

CHAPTER 6
INVASION

JUNE

May was busy; June proved to be even more intense as Pathfinders played their part – and a crucial role at that – in the preparation for and after the Allied landing in Normandy.

The ground work took many forms. Whilst the generals put the finishing touches to their plans, at Pathfinder air bases in the east of England security was tightened. Bennett called a defence conference on June 3 attended by a number of senior staff officers and all station commanders including such luminaries as Group Captain Paddy Menaul DFC, AFC from Graveley, Group Captain 'Digger' Kyle DFC from Downham Market, and Group Captain 'Fatty' Collings from Little Staughton. All personnel in possession of their own weapons were to keep them within three minutes' reach at all times; an inlaying picquet of one officer and fifty men was to be at instant readiness throughout the hours of darkness; grenades were to be fused and distributed where needed; and a new station password was to be implemented.

Meanwhile, the attacks on gun emplacements on the enemy-occupied coast continued with ever-increasing intensity. Bennett was asked by his superiors to guarantee that the guns would not be firing when the troops went ashore. It was not a promise he was inclined to make, but his men would do their utmost best. Between the nights of June 2/3 and 5/6, seventeen batteries were attacked, all of them first marked by Oboe Mosquitoes, assisted in some cases by a few heavy-PFF aircraft, for attacks in force by the heavy aircraft of other groups. The targets chosen were again part 'real' and part 'fiction' (so as not to give the game away as to the Allies' true intentions), two of the more important being Maisy and Longue since their guns covered the invasion beaches. Five Mosquitoes and sixty-seven Lancasters were involved in the attack on the latter that opened well and on time.

The TIs, however, disappeared quickly into cloud and only a few aircraft were able to bomb on the 'glow', the remainder resorted to H2S and Gee. Accuracy was difficult to judge, but what

---

POINTE DU HOC

Navigator 'Cam' Wallace described his war as rather ordinary and unremarkable. Perhaps it was, if being attacked by a nightfighter on your first operation, surviving two crash landings, and having your aircraft set on fire can in any way be described as 'ordinary'. After seventeen trips with 214 Squadron – during which time his crew accounted for the German ace Gerhard Friedrich – and applying to join Pathfinders, he was posted to 109 Squadron and teamed with a most capable pilot, Wing Commander Graham Foxall DSO, DFC.

On the morning of D-Day, the pair were tasked with marking the coastal battery near St Pierre du Mont (known as Pointe du Hoc) for 115 Lancasters and four Mosquitoes from 5 Group. Taking off at 03.20, the attack commenced when Cam released their target indicators from 30,000ft. The Oboe ground station estimated their green TI hit seventy yards northwest of the aiming point and their three red TIs 160 yards north. Just over one minute later two other Oboe Mosquitoes travelling in the opposite direction at 18,000ft dropped their markers 140 and 220 yards south of the aiming point. The Oboe marking was backed up by three Mosquitoes from 627 Squadron that dive-bombed from 4,000ft to as low as 500ft. Main force began bombing exactly on H-hour (04.50); the target was obliterated.

was certain was that a leading Pathfinder, Squadron Leader Arthur Raybould DSO, DFM of 582 Squadron was killed. Raybould had flown approximately seventy-eight trips, and within his crew was the squadron bombing leader, Arthur Feeley DFC.

Another senior crew, this time from 97 Squadron, was lost attacking a site at St Pierre du Mont. The squadron commanding officer, Wing Commander Eric Carter DFC, had been unimpressed with their allocation of target, but he nonetheless set off to do as he was told. He died in the attempt, along with the squadron signals leader, Flight Lieutenant Albert Chambers DFC & Bar, and gunnery leader, Squadron Leader Martin Bryan-Smith DFC & Bar, MiD.

Another 97 Squadron crew, led by Lieutenant Finn Jesperson, was also missing. Jesperson had been quite a celebrity in his native Norway before the war, and was a champion orienteer. He and four of his fellow countrymen were killed.

As the soldiers came ashore on the morning of June 6, and the free world held its collective breath, they were virtually undisturbed by the coastal batteries. With the exception of a solitary gun, the Pathfinders and Bomber Command had fulfilled their promise with ruthless efficiency.

> ## INVASION
>
> *"I remember the briefing well. Wing Commander Carter got up in front of us and said that our target – if you could call it such a thing – was a gun emplacement. He almost sneered. Ironically, of course, he was shot down and killed that night, taking with him the signals leader and gunnery leader. I understand that after the invasion they discovered that the gun emplacement we bombed had no guns."*
>
> **BOB LASHAM DFC & BAR
> PILOT. 97 SQUADRON,
> FIFTY-THREE OPS**

New tactical targets were now being fed to the bomber crews in direct support of the land battle beneath them. They comprised primarily the railway junctions and marshalling yards – all points of strategic importance to the enemy in bringing up reinforcements. Troops, tanks, ammunition, fuel etc relied on the rail infrastructure; rather than bombing single tracks or trains – a difficult and usually unproductive enterprise – far better to blitz those areas where the trains and munitions were obliged to congregate. Some thirty-two railway targets were attacked, and thirteen other strategic targets including the village of Aunay-sur-Odon – the headquarters of an SS Panzer Division – and Villers-Bocage, a major tank concentration. Both targets were completely destroyed; the army's satisfaction with the attack on Villers-Bocage was expressed in a telegram of appreciation sent by General Bernard Montgomery to Harris. (So devastating was the effectiveness of the bombing that witnesses report seeing the remains of a German Panzer sitting atop a two-storey building!)

Such raids were not without their casualties. Squadron Leader Cecil Hopton DFC, a Canadian pilot and flight commander with 156 Squadron was shot down over Versailles on June 7/8, killing all on board including the specialist air bomber, Flight Lieutenant David Wood DFC. Hopton had flown at least forty-six trips and was the deputy master bomber. An Australian, Pilot

> *"On June 6 our target was a huge gun emplacement at Longue. I was in the front turret when I spotted a twin-engine aircraft not far away. I had the guns trained on it when I realised it looked like an Oxford. As I hesitated, it suddenly dived into the clouds. When we discovered on landing that we had taken part in D-Day, I realised I may have nearly shot down a hospital plane but I will never know for certain."*
>
> **JACK WATSON DFM
> FLIGHT ENGINEER. 156 SQUADRON.
> SEVENTY-SEVEN OPS.**

Officer Bryan Giddings of 97 Squadron, was killed over Étampes on June 9/10 when his aircraft exploded, and there were casualties too over Dreux (Pilot Officer Henry Bonnett of 7 Squadron), Nantes (635 Squadron's Flight Lieutenant Cedric Ash), and Versailles (Flight Lieutenant M.P. Stronach RCAF of 405 Squadron on his twenty-seventh op). Stronach's mid upper gunner, Pilot Officer Paul Gingras, evaded capture along with his skipper, but opted to stay in France and join the resistance where he took part in a number of attacks on German communications systems. He received the *Croix de Guerre*.

The night of June 15/16 was especially deadly. Five Mosquitoes and seventy-six Lancasters of PFF took off to attack Lens, and two Mosquitoes and seventy Lancasters completed their duties. The Oboe marking was extremely accurate, and the master bomber brought the main force down below cloud to bomb. This was very successful, with several large and, no doubt, gratifying explosions being reported. Although the flak was described as 'slight', there was considerable nightfighter activity and six Lancasters were shot down: two from 405 Squadron, two from 635 Squadron, and one each from 7 and 582 Squadrons.

An interesting comparison can be drawn from two of the pilots killed that night: Flying Officer John Keenan RCAF of 405 Squadron was on his thirtieth operation; Flying Officer James Caterer of 635 Squadron had only a handful of trips to his name, having transferred to PFF in April after just three operations with 158 Squadron. (A further Lancaster was also shot down that night over Valenciennes; Pilot Officer Alan Grant, an Australian, and three of his crew were killed.)

Along with the rail targets and the concentrations of armour, Pathfinders also kept up the pressure on enemy aerodromes (Laval, Le Mans, Rennes and Flers) and radar installations. Such was the depth of the planning, and the calls on its services, that Pathfinders also marked for raids on the ports of Le Havre and Boulogne, to disrupt a co-ordinated response to the landings from the enemy's fleet of E-boats.

From the middle of the month onwards, the attention of both the Oboe and heavy squadrons was claimed by the V1s (or Doodlebugs as they had come to be known) that the Germans had started to launch from bases in the Pas de Calais. No less than forty-three attacks were made on some thirty known bases or the depots that supplied them, and on bases for 'larger rocket projectiles' that were in preparation.

The size and nature of the targets were a problem for the planners – one partially solved by ensuring each raid took place in daylight. Oboe-equipped Mosquitoes would mark the target, with the accuracy of those markers determined by a heavy master bomber who would then control the raid accordingly. Names such as Mont Candon, Oisemont, Marquise-Mimoyecques, and Coubronne would become familiar to Pathfinder Force over the coming weeks, especially the latter which accounted for four PFF aircraft including that of the master bomber, the twenty-two-year-old Squadron Leader George Ingram DFC of 35 Squadron. Two from 7 Squadron (Flight Lieutenant William Irwin DFC and Flight Lieutenant Michael Wakefield) were also lost, as was a 156 Squadron Lancaster whose

EMPTY BEDS

"At Little Staughton we slept two crews to a hut. We never thought a great deal when a crew went missing, but when it was those you shared with it gave us all a jolt, particularly seeing all of those empty beds. We shared with the crew of Norman Tutt who was shot down and killed on June 16, 1944. Only the wireless operator survived as well as his regular mid upper gunner who wasn't flying with him that day on account of cutting himself or something, shortly before they took off. It saved his life."

ALLAN EDWARDS
FLIGHT ENGINEER.
582 SQUADRON. FORTY-TWO OPS.

crew included the pilot, Pilot Officer Denis Langford DFC and the highly-experienced Flight Lieutenant Robert Manvell DFC, DFM.

Beauvoir and Siracourt were also flying-bomb bases that proved a graveyard not only for the heavies, but also for their lighter colleagues. The raid on Beauvoir, for example, on June 29 accounted for two Mosquitoes from 627 Squadron one of which – an aircraft flown by Flight Lieutenant James Saint-Smith DFC, DFM – was particularly unlucky. Having successfully found and marked the target, the navigator, Flying Officer George Heath DFC, DFM had given the course to steer for base when their aircraft was suddenly and unexpectedly blown out of the sky. Their flight path had inadvertently put them on a collision course with a flying bomb that prematurely exploded, taking the Mosquito and the two men with it.

At Siracourt, a small force of five Mosquitoes and two Lancasters led a largely successful raid that resulted in the master bomber, Flight Lieutenant Sydney Clark of 7 Squadron, being shot down on the approach to the target. The deputy realised what had happened and took over, instructing the main force to bomb half a mile east of the yellow TIs, and to ignore a column of smoke rising from an aerodrome near the target area where one or two bombs had already fallen. Clark was killed, but two of his crew survived to become prisoners of war.

With necessity proving to be the mother of invention, Pathfinders began trialing new methods of pinpointing and attacking flying-bomb targets. One such method that curried favour with the planners was for small forces of Lancasters to drop their bombs in salvo upon direction from a lead aircraft equipped with Oboe. This required the Lancaster crews to practice formation flying – a task for which they were little prepared. Bomber Command was, for obvious reasons, a night-time force, trained accordingly, and many of the crews expressed themselves terrified at the thought of having to fly alongside another aircraft rather than find their own way to the target in the dark.

Practice formation flying took its toll. On June 23, two 97 Squadron pilots – Flight Lieutenant 'Jimmy' van Raalte and Flight Lieutenant Edward Perkins – were with their respective crews over the Lincolnshire countryside when their aircraft collided with tragic consequences. One spun out of control, taking all eight men to their deaths; the other broke apart in mid-air, enabling one of the gunners to take to his 'chute and survive.

Despite the recent onslaught, Bomber Command was not yet master of the skies; the Germans could still inflict serious damage as they proved on the night of June 21/22. The target was a synthetic

MORAL FIBRE

"On one occasion we were practicing formation flying when two of the aircraft collided. There was only one survivor from the two crews. Naturally enough he was badly shaken by his experience and refused to fly again. He was posted LMF – lacking in moral fibre. It was all hushed up and he simply disappeared off the station."

PERCY CANNINGS DFM
MID UPPER GUNNER. 97 SQUADRON.
FORTY-SEVEN OPS.

Percy Cannings, pictured here with his grandfather.

"I can honestly say I was never frightened. Indeed I would go further and say that I even used to look forward to operations. It was always better than kicking around doing nothing. Whenever I went off on leave, I couldn't wait to get back. But of course there were those who were scared and some who couldn't cope.

"One morning, all of the aircrew were asked to assemble. One of the lads had been accused of lacking in moral fibre. In front of everyone, the CO tore the sergeant's stripes off his arm, and ripped off his aircrew brevet. The man was humiliated and degraded before us. It was disgraceful to watch. No man deserved that. He, like the rest of us, was a volunteer for goodness sake, that's what seemed to be overlooked, but the CO clearly wanted to make an example of him. It was like watching an execution."

REG PARISSIEN
WIRELESS OPERATOR. 156 SQUADRON.

WAR CRIMES

The bombing attacks on Germany took their toll in many ways, not least the number of civilians killed or injured as part of what today would be called 'collateral damage'. It was not surprising, therefore, that the bomber crews were nicknamed '*terrorfliegers*' and that their lives could sometimes be in danger if they fell into enemy hands. There were occasions, too, when the anger of the civilian population spilled over into something more sinister, and where the local military either turned a blind eye or even actively participated. The Geneva Convention, designed to protect captured soldiers, sailors and airmen, did not always apply. Two examples illustrate the point:

When twenty-one-year-old Flight Lieutenant Ronald Walker DFC was shot down in June 1944, he was fortunate to find himself taken in by loyal Dutchmen and part of an escape line in the home of Jacoba Pulskens, known as 'Tante (Auntie) Coba'. Hidden with two other pilots, their safety was compromised when a car containing two other airmen was stopped by the Germans, and the pair taken in for questioning. The very next morning, six Germans arrived and forced their way into Tante Coba's home, beat the three pilots to the floor and machine-gunned them to death in cold blood. Tante Coba was herself arrested and sent to a concentration camp where she died.

In another incident in early January, Flight Lieutenant Jimmy Rowland of 635 Squadron was obliged to take to his 'chute when his aircraft was in a head-on collision with a Lancaster of 431 Squadron, the impact severing the port wing and rear fuselage and probably killing both gunners. The four remaining crew members made it clear. Rowlands landed largely unscathed, save for a few cuts and grazes and was picked up twenty-four hours later. By then, however, the four others who had made it out had been rounded up and summarily shot.

In the case of Flight Lieutenant Walker, the six Germans responsible were found after the war, tried and hanged. The killers of Flight Lieutenant Rowland's crew, however, were never punished. Although the identity of the unit that carried out the atrocity was known (Ersatz Battalion 36), reports of the crime became confused with others, and those responsible were never brought to trial.

oil plant at Wesseling; 133 Lancasters and six Mosquitoes would attack in clear weather conditions, with the target marked low level in accordance with 5 Group practice. At least that was the plan. What actually transpired was that the aircraft arrived to find the oil plant covered by a blanket of thick cloud. They also found the German nightfighters up in strength, among them several experten – Schnaufer; Strüning; von Bonin; and Drewes.

Indeed more than 160 fighters were in the air, all converging on the bomber stream and ignoring a feint by thirty Mosquitoes of the LNSF

Gelsenkirchen.

to Berlin. The raid was a disaster. Four squadrons lost six aircraft each. Two aircraft were also missing from 83 Squadron, one flown by Squadron Leader Albert Dunn DFC and a second by Flight Lieutenant Ronald Walker DFC. Every member of Walker's crew had been decorated with either the DFC or DFM, depending on rank.

The Light Night Striking Force was kept busy in June, continuing its attacks on German towns and in increasing numbers, seven attacks were made on Berlin, three on Cologne, and two each on the synthetic oil plants at Homberg, Scholven and Ludwigshafen. Other targets at Gelsenkirchen (Bergwerke AG) and Sterkrade Holten (Ruhrchemie AG) were also chosen. The Mosquitoes also continued to lay mines.

Over Berlin on June 10/11, 571 Squadron posted its first casualties when Flight Lieutenant Joe Downey was killed. Downey had been operational since 1941, winning a DFM for a tour of twenty-nine ops on Hampdens with 83 Squadron, and flying a further eighteen ops with 218 Squadron throughout the winter of 1942/43. His navigator, Ron 'Wimpy' Wellington (an ex-Halton 'Brat') survived. Their aircraft was shot down by one of the Mosquito's most feared adversaries, a Heinkel He219 *Uhu* (owl), described as the Nachtjagd's only aircraft capable of meeting the Mosquito on equal terms.

The same squadron lost a second crew a few days later when Flying Officer Frank Brandwood and his navigator, Flying Officer 'Jock' Miller were hit by flak on the raid to Gelsenkirchen and killed in the subsequent crash. Brandwood and Miller were close friends who had survived a ditching off Malta in September 1941. On that occasion they had been attacking a convoy of eight merchant vessels with a strong destroyer escort and were shot down, forcing them to take to their dinghy. Adrift for nineteen hours, they were eventually rescued by a British submarine, but not before the telegrams had been sent to their respective next of kin to say that they were missing. Similar missives would be sent out again, but this time there would be no happy ending.

Another former Hampden veteran went missing on the night of June 26/27. Flight Lieutenant James Farrow, a New Zealander, had earned an immediate DFM in January 1942 as a sergeant pilot with 408 Squadron. On that particular occasion, and with his aircraft badly mauled by nightfighters, he ordered his crew to bale out. He did not know, however, that the intercom was broken, and so the order was never received. Even if it had been, the rest of the crew were so badly wounded that it was unlikely they would have made it out. Farrow was himself wounded in the leg, but despite the pain, and with no instruments to help him, he still managed to make it home, saving his aircraft and his crew with a wheels-up landing. He had added a DFC to his decorations at the time of his loss, attacking the railway workshops at Gottingen at low level. Happily he survived, although his Kiwi navigator, Flying Officer Clement Strang, was killed.

Bennett was incredibly proud of the contribution his men were making to the success of the invasion, so much so that he told them as much at a conference mid-way through the month when he assembled all officers, NCOs, airmen and airwomen at group headquarters. He stressed the point that the work was far from finished, and called for 'a united and continued effort on the part of all'.

In the matter of armaments, June was chiefly notable for the large number of changes in bombload, resulting from the diversion of effort on to tactical targets. No new weapons were brought into use, the ORB reports, but the tail-fused TI bomb (250lbs) may have proved its worth in achieving improved accuracy of marking during the month. This was due to the fact that the bomb could be burst at lower heights than the nose-fused types. A number of TI bombs were also employed fused to function on impact. In the words of the ORB: 'This somewhat uneconomical use of bombs was dictated by the need for still greater accuracy.'

There were other changes in relation to weapons. Nose turrets were re-installed in those aircraft where they had been previously removed in order to save weight. With the switch from night to daylight operations, the need for improved firepower was considered more beneficial. The ammunition was also changed, placing considerable strain on the armament staff who were, in many cases, working up to eighteen hours a day.

The number of aircraft missing for the month was thirty; the number abortive thirty-one. Both figures would have been considered acceptable given the number of sorties flown: 2,539. Happily too, the number of aircraft and men lost to accidents actually fell, which Bennett attributes to the reduction in the amount of training flying carried out by the squadrons. It was ironic, therefore, that July should start with the loss of a 156 Squadron Lancaster in an accident.

JULY

By July 1, the Allies had established a beachhead seventy miles wide and had brought around 1,000,000 men and 177,000 vehicles ashore. Yet, except around Cherbourg, their incursion was no more than twenty-five miles deep in any one place, and in most areas it extended little more than five miles inland.

Perhaps not surprisingly, therefore, Pathfinders devoted considerable time and effort into supporting ground operations, as well as continuing their attacks on the flying-bomb launch sites and depots. The daylight attacks started in June continued throughout July, and despite various cancellations due to unfavourable weather conditions either over the target or at base, there was no period of 24-hours during which no operations took place.

It was, however, a night-time operation that accounted for a true legend of Pathfinder Force, Squadron Leader Alec Cranswick DSO, DFC. Cranswick, a notable master bomber, was flying as a primary visual marker for a raid on the marshalling yards at Villeneuve St George on July 4/5 involving some 100 main force bombers. Conditions were such that Cranswick was obliged to go down to 8,000ft to get below cloud to do his job properly, but in doing so it took him in range of the light flak. Sure enough, and with his aircraft silhouetted against the cloud from the light of the flares below, it was hit. With the Lancaster on fire, Cranswick ordered his crew to bale out, but in the event only one of them – Wilfred Horner – made it, and that was by pure luck. Cranswick, veteran of well over 100 and maybe as many as 140 bomber operations, was killed. It was sad news for 35 Squadron, made sadder still with news that another of its crews, led by Squadron Leader George Lambert DFC – who had flown his first operation as second pilot to no less a man than Leonard Cheshire – was also missing. It was also a terrible blow for Bennett personally, having forged a close working relationship with Cranswick when he had been an air staff officer the previous year, and greatly admiring his determination.

Experienced men were being lost at an alarming rate. The following night, a veteran pilot of 635 Squadron, Squadron Leader Wilfred Riches DFC & Bar, was killed with his crew attacking a flying bomb site at Wizernes on a night that Pathfinders lost three of their number – two from 635 (Riches and Pilot Officer Arthur Weaver) and one from 582 (Pilot Officer Donald Manson).

Another four-engine veteran and deputy master bomber was shot down on the night of July 14/15 on a rather pointless raid to Revigny. The target was the railway junction and the attack quickly descended into farce. Although twenty PFF Lancasters took off, only one of them claimed to have identified the target by the light of the flares. The remainder, under the instructions of the Australian master bomber (Flight Lieutenant Richard Wiseman DFC), abandoned the mission and brought their bombs home. Seven Lancasters were shot down, including that of the deputy master bomber, Squadron Leader George Davies DSO.

Davies had won an immediate DSO as a twenty-one-year-old acting flight lieutenant almost exactly three years earlier with 102 Squadron, flying a tour on Whitleys, when his aircraft came under sustained attack by a number of fighters. He survived this ordeal over Bremen, only to be seriously burned in an accident while 'resting' at OTU in 1942. It was not until the autumn of 1943 that he was again fit to resume flying, having been patched up by a contemporary of Sir Archibald McIndoe of 'Guinea Pig' fame – and was finally posted to 156 Squadron in February 1944.

Over the target area near Revigny, his aircraft was intercepted and struck by cannon rounds fired by a marauding nightfighter, flown by Oberfeldwebel Reinhard Kollak. (Davies became Kollak's second victim that night, his first was the commanding officer of 550 Squadron, part of a main force squadron from North Killingholme.) The aircraft broke in two, throwing Davies clear. Somehow he survived, landing in a tree and breaking his leg. He learned later that only one other member of his crew escaped unharmed. Even with his injuries, Davies managed to evade capture for several days before eventually discovering that a 'safe house' was not as free from danger as the name had suggested. He spent the rest of the war in a POW camp.

Before the month had reached the mid-way point, the Mosquitoes too had lost two of their most exceptional pilots. Squadron Leader Bill Blessing DSO, DFC, was one of the first Australian airmen to arrive in England and his exploits with 105 Squadron as a low-level specialist had reached near-mythical proportions. It was Blessing, indeed, who had flown the squadron's first Oboe sortie, dropping heavy explosives on Gelsenkirchen on July 9, 1943. On July 7, nearly a year to the day after history had been made, Blessing was again in the news.

With the Allied troops camped around Caen and being held at bay by a series of fortified strongpoints, Blessing was detailed as a primary marker for a huge attack controlled by Wing Commander 'Pat' Daniels (of 35 Squadron) in which almost 2,500 tons of bombs would be dropped around two aiming points. Blessing was allocated Aiming point 'A', and just as he was on his marking run his aircraft was intercepted by a fighter. Like a scene from a film script, his navigator was leaning forward to pick up his charts just as the cannon shells ripped through the cockpit. A fraction earlier and they would have ripped through his body.

Blessing put the aircraft into a dive and lost his assailant, but the damage had been done. The starboard engine was overheating and three feet of his starboard wing had been shot away. Attempts to keep control of the Mosquito long enough to execute an emergency landing proved

August 1943

Date	Hour	Aircraft Type and No.	Pilot	Duty	Remarks (including results of bombing, gunnery, exercises, etc.)	Flying Times Day	Night
		HALIFAX					
2·8·43	1220	819	S/Ldr Cranswick	NAV	AIR TEST	40	
3·8·43	2310	819	— " —	NAV	"OPS" HAMBURG. SEVERE ICING. JETTISONED AMMUNITION. ALL FOUR ENGINES CUT OVER TARGET		5·45
5·8·43	1430	907	— " —	NAV	LOCAL FLYING.	·50	
7·8·43	1530	907	— " —	NAV	AIR FIRING.	1·30	
8·8·43	1030	907	— " —	NAV	BOMBING.	1·00	
9·8·43	2200	"P"	— " —	NAV	"OPS" MANHEIM. 3 ENGINES CUT OVER LUXEMBURG.		4·30
10·8·43	2200	"P"	— " —	NAV	"OPS" NÜRNBURG.		7·10
12·8·43	1100	926	— " —	NAV	BOMBING.	1·20	
12·8·43	2100	906	— " —	NAV	"OPS" TURIN HIT BY FLAK "MACK" KILLED		8·00

TOTAL TIME ... 922·00 263·35

The pages of William McRobbie's logbook suggest a hair-raising week of flying with his skipper, Alec Cranswick, including the loss of four engines over Hamburg.

CRANSWICK'S NAVIGATOR

Within the Pathfinder Museum's collection is the original logbook of William McRobbie who, for the greater part of 1943, was Alec Cranswick's regular navigator. McRobbie is an excellent example of the huge diversity in experience of the men who made Pathfinder Force, for his early flying career suggested nothing of his future endeavours.

A regular airman trained as an air gunner, he flew with 102 Squadron before the war, later qualifying as an observer. He then flew Vickers Vincents, Bristol Blenheims and Martin Marylands with 8 Squadron in Khormaksar for three years fighting the Italians, during which he was awarded the DFM. Returning to the UK in the summer of 1941, a two-month stay with 24 Squadron flying VIPs was followed by a spell as an instructor before being posted to 29 (Fighter) Squadron at West Malling, conducting nightfighter patrols.

As navigator/AI (radar) operator to Flight Sergeant (later pilot officer) Ronald Densham, the two made a successful pair, attacking a Heinkel He111 on the night of May 31 and claiming a Junkers 88 as probably destroyed three nights later. Two confirmed victories followed – an He111 on June 8 and a Junkers 88 on June 19. Further patrols followed without success until he was, at last, rested at the end of September.

His 'rest' did not last long, for in December he reported to 1659 Conversion Unit at Leeming and became one of the first members of Cranswick's new crew. Although Cranswick was quick to volunteer for Pathfinders, the move was not immediate; they were first posted to 419 (Canadian) Squadron, flying an eventful trip to Lorient on January 29 where the undercarriage collapsed on landing. Posted to Graveley at the beginning of February, the crew was operational within ten days, flying their first Pathfinder trip to – coincidentally – Lorient again.

McRobbie's logbook provides a wonderful snapshot of that time, and the perils faced by Pathfinder crews: 'April 10. Ops Frankfurt. Hit by flak; April 14. Ops Stuttgart. Port inner feathered; April 16. Ops Pilsen. Coned for five minutes. Nearly collided with Me110; April 20. Ops Stettin. Hit by flak over Kiel and Sylt; May 1. Ops Bocholt. Returned due to severe icing. May 4. Ops Rheine. Landed in fog.'

In those few short weeks, McRobbie and Cranswick had to overcome the very worst that the Germans and the weather could throw at them. Terse, matter-of-fact lines written in red ink go little way to hide the enormous dangers these men confronted on an almost daily basis. Three entries, nine days apart need no further articulation: 'August 3. Ops Hamburg. Severe icing. Jettisoned ammunition. All four engines cut over target; August 9. Ops Mannheim. Three engines cut over Luxembourg; August 12. Ops Turin. Hit by Flak. "Mack" killed.'

McRobbie's tour ended in October 1943, navigating Cranswick (by now a squadron leader) to Frankfurt on a trip that for once held little to report. Indeed Cranswick was himself also due for a compulsory rest, having completed thirty PFF trips and ninety-six in total. The pair parted company, McRobbie to an operational training unit (OTU) and thence to BOAC and Cranswick to 8 Group Headquarters. Only one would survive the war.

Alec Cranswick (standing left with wings and DFC & Bar) with one of his first PFF crews. William McRobbie, the navigator, is kneeling right.

NEVER VOLUNTEER FOR ANYTHING

George Cash lived a charmed life. He flew first with Archie Mellor, a former instructor, and survived a hair-raising trip to Düsseldorf on only his sixth operation. Shaken by his experiences, Mellor was rested and George found himself posted to 1409 Met Flight where he teamed up with Flight Lieutenant Wally Talbot, also ex-139. They too nearly met their end on Wally's forty-fifth and final operation when they were intercepted in the Pas de Calais by four FW190s and only escaped by some daredevil flying. Finding himself once more without a pilot, George was posted to 571 Squadron as the unit was expanding from two flights to three, where he was reunited with Terry Dodwell, a pilot he had known earlier on Met Flight. On the night of July 18, 1944, Terry volunteered to take the place of a less experienced crew for a trip to Berlin:

"After briefing, we made our way out to our aircraft to prepare for take-off. While I was checking my flight plan and the maps and charts, my pilot was carrying out the usual engine tests etc. Unfortunately, he found one of the engines u/s (unserviceable). This meant that we had to clamber out of our aircraft and get transport to take us to the reserve aircraft that was on the other side of the aerodrome.

"When we were finally airborne we were some ten minutes behind, at least. Time we could never make up, which meant that we would be 'tail-end Charlies'. In other words, we were in a very vulnerable situation.

"We found our way along the required route and at one stage, we were supposed to take a dog leg round Göttingen, which was heavily defended. To try to catch up some time, we decided to go straight across and take a chance. The ground defences must have been surprised by our manoeuvre and for most of the way, there was no opposition until just as we thought we had got away with it, we suddenly found ourselves in a box of heavy flak. Shells burst all round us and suddenly a large piece of shrapnel smashed through the back window and lodged in the Gee box by my left shoulder.

"Fortunately, there was no other apparent damage so we were able to continue. Very soon we reached Stendhal which was our last turning point to the target. Ahead of us we could see that the raid was in full swing with searchlights and flak bursting in the sky and we were heading straight for it. We still had a further ten minutes flight to reach the target area when suddenly we were caught in searchlights. Doddie took evasive action to try to get out of the terrific glare. Then, unexpectedly, the searchlights dipped. We thought we had thrown them off, but we ought to have known better. Unknown to us a nightfighter had seen us and was now tracking us. As we were preparing to bomb the target, we were flying straight and level when the sudden salvo of cannon shells smashed into the port engine and wing tanks setting them ablaze. The aircraft began to circle down out of control. "Come on," said Doddie, "we'll have to get out of here." I bent down to pull up the flap which covered the escape hatch but when I got up to my seat, I found that I was alone. Doddie had baled out of the top hatch. His side of the cockpit was ablaze.

"The normal exit in emergency was below the navigator's position and the top hatch was not to be used in flight because there was always the danger of striking the tail fin and rudder or the tail-plane. We decided between ourselves that in an emergency, if ever, we would go out of the top despite the hazard.

"There I was, sitting in a blazing aircraft going down in circles. I did what any other man in my position would have done — a quick prayer. Suddenly the aircraft seemed to steady. I was able to reach behind my seat to retrieve my parachute where it was stowed. In those few seconds I remembered reading about a Mosquito navigator, who had baled out at the top of the aircraft and had rolled onto the starboard wing before letting go, and had safely parachuted to the ground. I did exactly the same. As I was swept away by the slipstream I

pulled the ripcord. Then suddenly, there was a large white canopy above me and I was floating gently down. Just below I could see our aircraft in a field blazing away, and it still had a 4,000lb bomb on board! If it had gone up, then I would have gone up with it. But there it is. It wasn't to be. My number wasn't up.

"It was only many years afterward that I learned that my pilot had been killed by striking the tail of the aircraft when he baled out. Coincidentally, the man who shot us down – Heinz Strüning – accounted for the 'sprog' crew that we had replaced in the Battle Order. Perhaps more ironically, he was later killed in exactly the same way as Doddie – striking his head on the tail of his Heinkel."

GEORGE CASH DFC
NAVIGATOR. 139 AND 571
SQUADRONS AND 1409 MET
FLIGHT. FIFTY-EIGHT OPS.

fruitless as the aircraft suddenly flicked into a spin. Although the navigator made it out, on his captain's instructions, Blessing was killed. He had been 'A' Flight commander at the time and one of the squadron's finest pilots.

Three days later and another noteworthy Mosquito 'baron' and antipodean was also killed: Wing Commander Stephen Watts DSO, DFC, MiD, the twenty-eight-year-old commanding officer of 692 Squadron. It had been Watts who, in February 1943, had taken the honour of dropping the first 4,000lb 'cookie' from the belly of a Mosquito in a modified MkIV.

Watts, along with his fellow Kiwi navigator Pilot Officer Archibald Matheson DFM, took off from Gransden Lodge at 23.36 on the night of July 10/11 to attack Berlin and were never seen again. It is now known that he was intercepted on his homeward journey and shot down by Major Hans Karlewski of 2./NJG1 for his fifth kill.

The Mosquitoes were having a rough time of it. Three aircraft were lost following a raid on Berlin on July 7/8, one each from 139, 571 and 692 Squadrons. Another 105 Squadron aircraft was written off in a crash on July 13/14 having been seriously damaged by flak, and a few nights later over Berlin, yet another 571 Squadron aircraft, piloted by Squadron Leader Terry Dodwell DFC & Bar was shot down.

The new method of attacking smaller targets covered by cloud by having one or more formations of heavy bombers led by a 'musical' aircraft to achieve greater accuracy was gaining currency. The tactic usually meant a pilot and navigator from the Oboe squadron joined the crew of the lead Oboe Lancaster (hence the term 'heavy Oboe'). The 'regular' pilot and navigator would be

Above: Bombs gone!
Below: George Grant – one of Canada's best.

in charge until they were within a short distance of the target, at which point the 'guest' pilot and navigator would literally swap seats and take over for the bombing run. The main formation was accompanied by a reserve Oboe Mosquito that would take over the run should something go wrong.

The first to put theory into practice were Wing Commander Keith 'Slim' Somerville DFC, AFC and Flight Lieutenant Harry Scott DFC & Bar of 109 Squadron. It would be difficult to find two more experienced Pathfinders. Somerville had been part of the wireless development unit (later 109 Squadron) at Boscombe Down from the winter of 1940, by which time he had already completed a tour of ops on Whitleys. His experience with Oboe was second to none, and he had taken part in the first Oboe raid in December 1942.

Harry Scott's track record was similarly impressive. A Halton apprentice, Scott had already completed two tours of operations by the time he joined 109 Squadron, and had been one of five crews that marked Essen on the night of March 5/6 – the attack that signalled the start of the Battle of the Ruhr. Both men went on to complete more than 100 bomber operations and be awarded the DSO. For this particular raid, however, they took the regular crew of Squadron Leader Thomas Ison DFC (later the OC 156) including his navigator Flight Lieutenant Harold Morrish in a 156 Squadron Lancaster, tasked with attacking Gapennes. It achieved modest success.

Another pioneer, Wing Commander George Grant DSO, DFC (and later Bar to his DSO), the commanding officer of 109 Squadron, joined in a similar attack, this time with a crew from 582

Squadron. Results were mixed, but generally promising, and certainly considered worthwhile trying again. The concentration of bombs achieved was more than satisfactory.

On July 20, another daylight 'heavy Oboe' was scheduled for an attack on the construction works at Forêt du Croc. The official report on the ORB is functional: 'Three Mosquitoes and seventeen Lancasters took off but all were abortive and one Lancaster [is] missing.' The actual events, however, were far more dramatic.

The attack once again called for a 109/582 Squadron combination (the two squadrons 'shared' the airfield at Little Staughton). The regular skipper, Squadron Leader John Weightman, changed seats with the 109 Squadron Oboe specialist, Squadron Leader James Foulsham DFC, AFC, for the bombing run, and all went well until they were just a few seconds from releasing their bombs. Then the heavy flak found its mark, setting the lead Lancaster ablaze. At virtually the same time, the aircraft behind inadvertently dropped its bombs, causing

THE PERILS OF HEAVY OBOE

Flying Officer Jeff Chapman had completed a tour with 70 Squadron in the Middle East in 1942, and after a spell instructing was posted to Pathfinders, joining the crew of Gerald O'Donovan:

Jeffrey Chapman.

"On July 20, twenty Lancasters of 582 Squadron took off at 14.20 to attack the flying-bomb site at Forêt du Croc, just across the channel. We were going in to attack in a twin line-astern formation with slight variation in height to avoid the slipstream of the aircraft in front. We were in the second aircraft and flying about fifteen to twenty feet above the leader with our port wing just over and slightly behind his starboard wing. (We had been practicing this but this was the first time that we had done it operationally.)

"The leader opened his bomb doors; we opened ours and so on down the line. It would be about thirty seconds to the drop. I was standing up next to my seat with my head in the astrodome and could see it all: the leader just slightly below us and others staggered at different heights behind, each swaying slightly as in some slow, macabre elephantine dance in the sky – sinister yet fascinating to watch. It was a perfectly clear day and I felt reasonably comfortable with our situation. If fighters attacked they would get a rough time from a total of 120 Browning machine guns each firing 1,000 rounds per minute!

"And then it happened. One did not usually hear the bursts of flak above the roar of the engines. If you did, then it was very close indeed. We heard this. A 'whoof' and a ball of flame, instantly gone as we flew through it. Our aircraft was spattered with small bits of exploding shell, some of which went clean through us and out the other side, filling the fuselage for the moment with a cloud of pulverized aluminium dust. One piece on its way through tore the sleeve of my flying jacket.

"The port wing of the leading aircraft, however, was a mass of flames which streamed back as far as the tailplane in the slipstream having, I judged, received a direct hit on or near the port inner engine or one of the fuel tanks. It was obvious they would have to bale out, and quickly, if they were to survive.

"I saw a face in the astrodome, no doubt the wireless op, and the rear and mid upper gunners looking from their turrets and the blazing wing. The leader kept on, straight and level, waiting for the electronic signal to drop his bombs, still with some twenty seconds to go. After what seemed like a very long ten seconds the whole of the port wing folded upwards at a right angle and completely broke off; the aircraft turned on its back and went into a crazy downward gyration. I watched it for some time. I saw no parachutes open and did not expect to; centrifugal forces would see to that.

"When the shell burst our flight engineer, who was stretched out horizontally in the nose with his eyes glued to the open bomb bay of the leader, was temporarily blinded and because his thumb was hovering over the bomb release 'tit', he inadvertently pressed it. The rest of the gaggle behind us saw our bombs fall away and let go their own. Down went the whole lot, missing the target by at least a mile.

"None of us spoke and it was the skipper's, somewhat measured, 'course for home please, navigator' that broke the silence."

JEFF CHAPMAN DFC & BAR
WIRELESS OPERATOR. 582 SQUADRON. SEVENTY-SIX OPS.

confusion throughout the rest of the formation, some of whom began releasing their bombs in salvo. The lead Lancaster then exploded, giving the crew no time to bale out. The raid was a complete disaster, and the bombs were dropped well short of the target. Weightman, Foulsham, and all of the crew were killed. 'Heavy Oboe' became two words at Little Staughton never to be spoken.

On the same day as the failed attack on the Forêt du Croc, a small group of dissident Germans also failed to kill their führer, with disastrous consequences for the conspirators and their families. A few days later, Bomber Command, with Pathfinders in the lead, once again turned its attentions to more substantial targets involving more bombers than usual. The raid on Kiel, for example, on July 23/24 involved more than 600 heavy bombers delivering, as it happens, the biggest RAF raid on Kiel of the entire war. The hard-pressed 8 Group Pathfinders were reunited for the raid with their 5 Group Pathfinding friends from 83 Squadron, operating from Wyton, much to their mutual enjoyment.

Cloud conditions over the target made visual identification and assessment of the results impossible, but the crews were confident that the centre of the TI concentration, as checked by H2S, was well over the aiming point, and a number of large explosions were reported. Substantial damage was indeed done to the port areas and the critical U-boat yards and naval facilities.

Defences were weak, the fighter controllers having been duped by various radio countermeasures deployed, spoof raids and feints, as well as the very fact it was a surprise return to a German target. Four Lancasters were shot down, including the 582 Squadron aircraft of Flying Officer Ray Rember, an American serving in the Royal Canadian Air Force. A further three Lancasters crashed in the UK, including another 582 Squadron aircraft piloted by a young South African, Lieutenant Ted Swales. Swales was injured but was soon back on operations.

Harris next turned his attention to Stuttgart, attacking the city three times over five nights, causing significant damage. The German defences, however, had recovered from their earlier stage fright and fought back hard, accounting for seventy-two bombers – the biggest losses (thirty Lancasters) were inflicted in the final attack on the night of July 28/29. Pathfinders escaped relatively lightly: two were lost on the first attack (one each from 35 and 83 Squadrons including Australian Flight Lieutenant Raymond Banfield DFC); and one from 582 Squadron (Squadron Leader V. Coleman) on the last. They also gave as good as they got, claiming a number nightfighters in return. The ORB makes mention of two Junkers 88s, one Me410 and one unidentified aircraft being claimed as damaged.

Awards for gallantry were commonplace among Pathfinder crews, usually by dint of operational experience and longevity. The crew of Squadron Leader Robert Eggins DFC for example, one of two Pathfinders missing from the attack on the Givors railway yards, had one DSO, one DFM and five DFCs between them. The most experienced was the navigator, Wing Commander Gordon Georgeson, who had won the DFC with 12 Squadron and a DSO, promulgated after his death. He had also served for a time on Bennett's staff.

Though awards for gallantry could be a lottery, pilots on main force could almost always guarantee a DFC at the end of their first operational tour – assuming they lived that long. Indeed not for nothing was it known as 'the survivor's gong'. But alongside the non-immediate awards for sustained periods of bravery, there were also those immediate awards to recognise a specific act of gallantry. Two such awards to illustrate the point were made in very different circumstances on the night of July 28/29, when Harris opted to return to yet another favourite target of his, Hamburg.

The C-in-C allocated around 300 bombers to raid Hamburg, sending a much larger force to Stuttgart that same night as well as some 100 or so aircraft to the Forêt de Nieppe. Mosquitoes dropped Window ahead of the attacking force, and the sequence of attack proceeded as ordered. Skipper in one of the 53 Pathfinder Lancasters that took off that night was Flying Officer Keith Perry of 7 Squadron. Among his crew was his navigator, Sergeant Leonard Riddle, flight engineer, Sergeant Richard Bostock, and mid upper gunner, Sergeant Bernard Loosley.

MASTER BOMBERS – THE SOUTH AFRICANS

Ted Swales VC in his distinctive khaki uniform poses for the camera with his air and ground crew. Ted's hands are on the shoulders of his navigator, Clive Dodson.

With their distinctive Khaki uniforms, South African Air Force aircrew were immediately identifiable against the predominant blue of their RAF colleagues. Their number was comparatively few compared to other commonwealth members, but they were nonetheless brave.

Captain Edwin 'Ted' Swales is without doubt the most well known, and one of only three members of PFF to be awarded the Victoria Cross. Originally a soldier, Swales fought in the desert and at El Alamein before transferring to the SAAF. He was unusual in being posted directly to Pathfinders, joining 582 Squadron in July 1944. By the time of the Cologne/Gremberg disaster, in which he won the DFC for fending off countless fighter attacks, he had flown thirty-three operations, and shortly after conducted his first master bomber trip. He was killed on his forty-second operation as master bomber to Pforzheim, staying at the controls of his aircraft to give his crew enough time to bale out.

Another notable, but rather more obscure, Pathfinder was Flight Lieutenant Bernhorst Botha of the RAFVR. Botha might never have joined the RAF, or indeed fought on the side of the British. His parents were strongly anti-British, and wanted him to join the Luftwaffe! Fortunately he chose to ignore his parents' wishes and sailed for the UK. Botha had a remarkably varied career, starting out as an air gunner and winning the DFC with 50 Squadron while on his third tour of operations. Later qualifying as a pilot, he was awarded the DSO in September 1944, the citation crediting him with helping to maintain the high standard of morale in his squadron, and having completed 'a very large number of sorties'. His operational tally at that time stood at 105. Transferring to PFF, he flew with 35 and 582 Squadrons, adding the DFC (US) before the war ended. An unconventional officer, Botha was often in trouble with his superiors, and the whiff of court martial was often in the air. His crew was known as 'Botha's Bastards' because of their reputation for breaking the rules.

Their flight out had been unremarkable until they reached the target and were on their bombing run. Shortly after dropping their bombs, there was a 'whoomph' as the aircraft was hit by flak and a fire broke out in the cockpit and the fuselage. Loosley was trapped but began fighting the fire with an extinguisher. When that ran out, he took off his jacket and began beating the flames by hand, with some success. Meanwhile, Riddle and Bostock also managed to quell the fires towards the front of the aircraft and give assistance to their pilot who had been injured and overcome by smoke and fumes. Despite all three men suffering burns, their pilot being wounded, and their aircraft down to two engines, they made it back to the Suffolk coast where they crash landed at Bungay.

The three NCOs received immediate Distinguished Flying Medals and their skipper, a well-

A NIGHTMARE TRIP

Despite its neutrality, Eire produced a good many soldiers, sailors and airmen who were prepared to overlook the niceties of diplomatic convention and fight for a cause that they still viewed as just. One of the most noteworthy in Pathfinder circles was Dubliner Michael Finlay. 'Paddy' Finlay conducted most of his flying training in Texas in late 1942/early 1943, returning to the UK in the spring to go through the usual AFU, OTU and heavy conversion before joining 101 (Special Duties) Squadron in May 1944 and flying his first trip on the 24th.

Singled out as a talented pilot with an equally accomplished crew, he was selected for Pathfinders, passing through NTU in July 1944 (under the tutelage of the incomparable Squadron Leader Ernest Rodley DSO, DFC & Bar, AFC) before joining 582 Squadron. He would later fly as deputy master bomber to Captain Ted Swales over both Pforzheim and Chemnitz and complete fifty-six operations, earning the DFC & Bar all before the age of twenty-one. And yet he nearly came to grief on one of his first Pathfinder trips to the Mercedes-Benz factory at Stuttgart on the night of July 24/25, as his mid upper gunner recalls:

"In the rear turret, Freddie Jones thought he noticed something. Then he confirmed it. It was a burst of tracer fire from a marauding Junkers Ju88, and it was aimed at him. At exactly the same time, another Ju88 attacked from the starboard low, and put in another burst. It was all a blur. We had Ju88s attacking us from the front and from behind. I saw one come in from the starboard quarter. I kept him in my sights and had a go, but as a gunner you knew that actually your only hope was that he missed you. If he missed with his cannon, he would then come in range of our .303s, and you could fill him. At close range they were lethal.

"As I fired Freddie gave the command to his skipper to corkscrew – a violent form of evasive action. As he did so, the aircraft rose, and Freddie fired and hit one of the German nightfighters in the belly. Immediately it broke away to the port quarter up, and dived away from sight. In the corkscrew I was thrown out of my seat and out of my turret, finishing up in a heap at the bottom of the aircraft, all jumbled up with intercom leads, suit-heating cables and the oxygen hose.

"It seemed like we had been mortally hit. We all waited, fully expecting to be told to abandon the aircraft that now seemed to be falling and tumbling in a most erratic fashion. The navigator grabbed his 'chute and made for the escape hatch in the nose, where he found the flight engineer, Jock Dicerbo, slumped over the exit. He had been killed instantly by a cannon shell.

"The aircraft was in a parlous state. Paddy asked for something to help hold the control column back. We cut a length of the dinghy rope that was housed in its position near the rest bunk, tied the rope to the control column and then around Paddy's right-hand arm rest, but Paddy wasn't happy with that because he thought it might get in the way if he had to get out in a hurry. So we tied it around the back left-hand side of the seat instead with a couple of hitches around the arm rest.

"On Paddy's instructions, we made for the emergency field at Woodbridge. By now it was clear that the hydraulics had been damaged, and the emergency air that would be essential for the undercarriage, flaps, brakes etc. was also non-operational. The skipper ordered us all into our crash positions, except the navigator who had had pilot training before being remustered and so might be able to help. On Paddy's instructions he pulled and slackened the rope as we came in for a beautifully smooth belly landing without the help of flaps.

"No one else was injured in the crash landing, but Paddy looked like a chimney sweep from all the dirt and sand that had come in through the broken nose."

ROY LAST
AIR GUNNER. 582 SQUADRON. c.FIFTY OPS.

Paddy Finlay (third from right) and his crew deputised to Ted Swales on the night the latter was lost over Pforzheim. Teenage air gunner Roy Last is far left.

earned DFC for 'displaying great coolness and courage'.

Squadron Leader Herbert Slade of 156 Squadron was also taking part in the Hamburg raid, one of sixteen Lancasters from Upwood despatched. Slade, a popular and experienced Australian bomber captain, was on his fifty-eighth operation, and on his return could look forward to a long rest from operations. He was in good company: also flying that night were Flight Lieutenant Richard Wiseman DFC on his seventieth operation, and Squadron Leader Thomas Godfrey DFC & Bar on his sixty-first. Both were also completing their respective tours.

It was before the target had been reached that Slade's aircraft was hit by flak, causing substantial damage. Although able to keep the bomber steady and drop his bombs, the aircraft suddenly went into a slow spiral out of control, and he ordered the crew to grab their parachutes and standby to bale out. A large part of the port wing was sticking up, making the Lancaster virtually unflyable, but somehow Slade managed to regain some semblance of control, carefully adjusting the rudder and throttle until the aircraft was on an even keel.

Slade asked his flight engineer to check the engine temperatures and fuel capacity, with a view to making it over the sea to the emergency field at Woodbridge. He also told his navigator that all

Thomas Godfrey, a professional in every sense.

was well, comparatively speaking, but that he would have difficulty making any turns to port; sudden turns were certainly out of the question. On reaching the enemy coast, they were again engaged by flak. Still mindful that his aircraft was, at best, unpredictable, Slade kept about twenty-five miles out to sea and flew parallel to the coast so that he could cross the sea to England at the narrowest point, or return to the enemy coast to crash land.

He then ordered a bombing check and found that four TIs and two 1,000lb bombs were still hung up. Opening the bomb doors proved problematic with the aircraft losing valuable height, so he decided against releasing the bombs by hand. The flight engineer then suggested using the fuel from the port tanks first to lighten the load on the damaged side, which they did and flying conditions slightly improved. Slade checked the condition of the undercarriage and the associated stalling speed with the wheels down, and calculated his approach speed accordingly. Ordering the crew to assume crash positions, with the exception of the flight engineer, Slade approached Woodbridge at 150 knots, reducing this to 145 knots and touching down just as the aircraft stalled. The undercarriage collapsed and the aircraft skidded to a halt. Slade was awarded an immediate DSO.

(There was one other Pathfinder aircraft lost that night: a 139 Squadron Mosquito skippered by Flying Officer Balfour Hay DFC, killed with his navigator Flying Officer James Dunn DFC, DFM.)

By July 30, Allied ground troops had yet to effect the success originally envisaged, although news from the front was improving. Bomber Command despatched nearly 700 aircraft that day to attack various German positions, although cloud seriously hampered operations and only half managed to successfully carry out their duties. Flight Lieutenant Hugh Baker, a Jamaican pilot from 97 Squadron who had completed fifty-one operations, was probably the most notable loss. His crew had four DFMs and three DFCs between them.

AUGUST

The month started with some good news for the over-worked Mosquito crews: the formation of a new squadron to swell the ranks. On August 1, 608 Squadron, comprising two flights, and 9608 Servicing Echelon were formed at Downham Market. The squadron was placed under the command of an Australian, Wing Commander Walter Scott (later DFC).

Operations throughout the month proved a mirror image of July: planners were focused on flying-bomb sites, oil installations, railway marshalling yards and stores, airfields, and tactical targets in support of the commanders on the ground. The Light Night Striking Force went in ever-increasing numbers to the usual favourites – Berlin, Cologne, Essen etc – in such force that the Germans, according to the ORB, had been forced to admit they were now more than simply nuisance raids. Main force raids were also mounted on Rüsselsheim (twice), Stettin (twice), and one each on Bremen and Kiel.

August was effectively a month of two halves: in the first two weeks, the targets were almost

NO SOFT TARGETS

"There were no 'easy' targets, not in our experience. Take the daylight to Bordeaux (August 18) to attack oil installations that fed the U-boats; another 'doddle', we were told, only it wasn't. They were short of a crew and so we were told to report, which we did. The weather was clear and the attack seemed to be going well. Then on the run up to the target we were hit by heavy flak. They'd managed to hit the pitot head so that I had no airspeed indicator and which also rendered the bombsight u/s. More importantly they hit and wounded my mid upper gunner who received facial injuries. He might have been blinded but fortunately he was wearing his goggles and they protected him.

"On further inspection we realised just how badly we had been hit: the high frequency radar equipment and intercom were both u/s, the mid upper turret and gunner u/s, and I was obliged to feather the port outer. We made for Manston and landed without further incident. I believe afterwards they counted more than 100 holes, but I didn't get involved in all that. I just know that our aircraft was category A/C."

BOB LASHAM DFC & BAR
PILOT. 97 SQUADRON. FIFTY-THREE OPS.

SNAGS AND GLITCHES

No-one within Pathfinder Force or Bomber Command generally could ever say enough about the quality and support given by the ground crews – a dedicated team of men and women without whom the aircraft would never have left the ground and the night assault on Germany could never have taken place.

While every pilot, flight engineer, air bomber, navigator, wireless operator and air gunner was obliged to maintain a record of their service in a corresponding log, there was no such history for the ground crews. There was, however, a record attached to the individual aircraft they maintained, and two such 'snag books' are included in the RAF Pathfinder Museum's collection.

They belonged to 'B' Flight, 35 Squadron, for the six months from July to December 1944, and then from January until the end of the war and provide a graphic illustration of the stresses and strains placed upon aircraft and men. From the smallest 'snag' such as a faulty light bulb through to major engine overhauls and repairs due to damage inflicted by flak or fighters, all is recorded, as are the names of pilots and numbers of aircraft that failed to return.

They also serve. Without the commitment, dedication and support of the ground crews, the Pathfinders would never have taken to the air. The young engine fitter top centre seems to have mischievous intentions for his hammer!

The 'snag book' for 'B' Flight, 35 Squadron – a fascinating history of squadron life recorded in a school exercise book. Simple words speak volumes. The aircraft of Flying Officer Grainger (sic) and Flying Officer Campbell are recorded as missing.

exclusively flying-bomb sites, oil-storage depots, and German army positions in and around the Normandy battle area. They were particularly called upon to support two specific operations whose codenames begin to appear in the logbooks of crews operating at that time: Totalise and Tractable.

Operation Totalise opened on August 8 with the objective of breaking through the German defences south of Caen and capturing the high ground north of Falaise. Operation Tractable, which commenced on August 14, involved Canadian and Polish troops tasked with capturing the town of Falaise itself. (The latter was devastatingly successful, trapping some 150,000 German troops in a gap that narrowed and eventually choked the last semblance of resistance from the German commanders in northern France.)

The number of aircraft deployed in these attacks was often large (a case in point being August 5 when well over 1,000 heavy bombers were engaged in raids against flying-bomb sites and oil installations and then again two days later when a similar number attacked five aiming points ahead of the Allied ground troops) but the losses were comparatively small. That's not to say, however, that they weren't significant.

When Troissy St Maximin was selected as one of two flying-bomb sites (the other L'Isle-Adam) to be attacked on August 4, no-one could have foreseen how dramatic the events of that afternoon would turn out. Included among the five Mosquitoes and sixty-one Lancasters detailed for the raid were fourteen crews from 635 Squadron who would provide the master bomber

(Wing Commander David Clark) and deputy (Flight Lieutenant Bob Beveridge DFC).

Although the raid was a success, Beveridge was shot down and so too was one of the Canadian supporters, Squadron Leader Ian Bazalgette. Bazalgette managed to keep his burning bomber aloft sufficiently long enough to mark the target accurately and allow his crew time to escape. In trying to land and save two of his crew who were too badly injured to leave the aircraft, he crashed and they were all killed. For Bazalgette's heroic action, he became the first of three pilots from Pathfinder Force to be awarded the Victoria Cross (VC). All of them were posthumous.

Not all the attacks achieved the results anticipated or desired by the commanders who planned them. One example of a good plan going badly wrong was an attack on German troop positions blocking the advance of the 3rd Canadian Division as part of Operation Tractable. There were seven aiming points, each marked by Oboe

Above: Ian Bazalgette – the first of the three PFF VCs.

Right: The logbook of Lionel Wheble records heavy predicted flak for the daylight raid on Troissy (daylight ops were recorded in green ink, night ops in red) and the loss of Ian Bazalgette. Wheble was himself shot down a short time after over Kiel. A change in handwriting tells its own story.

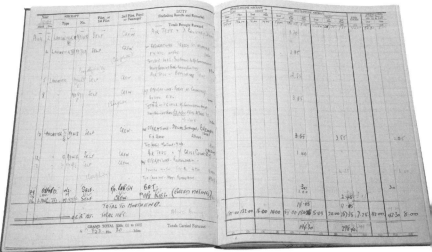

Allan Craig and Stafford Harris (right) during their goodwill tour of the US after the war. Craig flew as master or deputy master bomber on no fewer than thirty occasions with 7 and 156 Squadrons, winning the DSO and DFC. Craig still wears his Pathfinder eagle beneath his medal ribbons.

Mosquitoes and each with its own master and deputy. All went well until mid-way through the attack when a small number of main force aircraft dropped their bombs on a large quarry in which parts of the Canadian forces were sheltered. They claimed to have bombed 'yellow markers'. Despite the best efforts of the Pathfinders directing the attack, and the constant remarking of the correct aiming points, a further group of bombers also dropped their explosives on the quarry, and in doing so killed thirteen men, injured another fifty-three, and destroyed a good many guns and vehicles.

There were reasons why this unprecedented 'black' by Bomber Command occurred, but in the inquiry that followed, the master bombers (Wing Commander 'Howie' Morrison, Wing Commander W.T. Brooks, Squadron Leader Allan Craig, Wing Commander Thomas Bingham-Hall, Wing Commander 'Dickie' Walbourn, Wing Commander 'Tubby' Baker, and Flight Lieutenant Jack Ford) were all exonerated. They had done everything in their power to control where the bombs had fallen but their instruction had been – in part – ignored. It has been suggested that the reason for the mistake was the use by the Canadians of yellow flares to identify their position, and these had been taken to be the yellow target indicators used by the Pathfinders. In the 'fog of war' such mistakes are understandable, but rarely forgiven. Scapegoats were still

THE FOG OF WAR

"It was a 'simple' daylight in support of Canadian troops who had stalled north of Caen. With the target close to the UK, we had been briefed to make use of Gee for blind marking. This effectively involved 'sliding' down one co-ordinate from roughly north to south until crossing another co-ordinate, at which point the bombs and the TIs would be released some 6,000 yards in front of the Allied lines.

"The co-ordinates had to be set up manually in flight by the navigator who would then give directions to the pilot to maintain track on one co-ordinate until crossing the 'release' co-ordinate. The co-ordinates were delineated on the cathode ray tube (CRT) by two green lines about four inches long, sub-divided by ticks at decimals. My navigator, a Canadian, must have set up the wrong release point, for the TIs and the bombs fell amongst his own countrymen.

"'Butch' Harris was rightly aggrieved, having assured the generals of accurate support and took us off marking duties to be sent to a main force squadron. Bennett appealed against this but Harris was adamant, so Bennett compromised by letting us (the navigator and I) go on to Mosquitoes, within PFF but not on marking. We were on 128 Squadron at Wyton, I as a flight commander. November came and 608 needed a new CO so Bennett let me take over the squadron at Downham Market where I saw out the war."

CLIFF ALABASTER DSO & BAR, DFC & BAR
NAVIGATOR AND PILOT 97, 582, 128 AND 608 SQUADRONS. 100+ OPS

MASTER AND DEPUTY

A nicely-composed photograph of Fred Phillips (left) and his 7 Squadron crew.

Fred Phillips joined the RAAF in 1941, and after training in the US he finally arrived in the UK in January 1943. After OTU and converting to Stirlings he commenced operations with 622 Squadron, completing twelve ops before being invited to join PFF largely, Fred believes, because of the skill of his Kiwi navigator Dave Goodwin. The crew arrived at 7 Squadron in April 1944, and swiftly became a senior crew:

"We'd done about thirty trips as a Pathfinder and on numerous occasions we had been obliged to make three or four runs over the target to ensure it was accurately marked. Most of us, it is fair to say, did not want to be over the target area any longer than was needed, but if it was a long, large raid you could be circling the target for twenty minutes. In preparation for becoming a master bomber I was allotted a specialist map reader and bomb aimer, 'Steve' Harper, who was the sole surviving member of a crew blasted by a night intruder over Oakington. His skipper had been a good friend of mine.

"My first master bomber trip was a daylight raid to Oisemont, a flying-bomb site, on June 30, followed by two more on July 4 and August 28. On the latter we were engaged by very

A young Fred Phillips with 622 Squadron, main force, prior to joining PFF. Fred is third row, circled, near centre right of the photograph. The huge size of the Short Stirling is immediately apparent.

Fred Phillips. His youthful looks belie his experience as a devastatingly effective master bomber, or deputy to Brian Frow and Allan Craig.

heavy and accurate flak.

"Perhaps the trip I remember most though was in early August. Montgomery had requested bomber support for his troops around Caen. I went with Squadron Leader Brian Frow DSO, DFC to group headquarters to be briefed personally by Bennett (Brian had taken over the master bomber role from Fraser Barron); we were told to fly over the battle area to observe some special artillery shells that would indicate our aiming point. On the following night, August 7, more than 1,000 aircraft were despatched to attack German positions facing the Allied advance. Brian was master and I was his deputy, and I remember we bombed from around 4,000ft. Afterwards it was described as 'carefully controlled' and very successful. Another similar raid was carried out on August 12 when I was again Brian's deputy. Two days later I celebrated my twenty-first birthday.

"I flew three raids as master bomber and seven raids as deputy to Brian Frow, followed by a further seven with Squadron Leader Allan Craig DSO, AFC after Brian had been stood down. I received my first DFC from the king; the second arrived in the post."

FRED PHILLIPS DFC & BAR, CDG
MASTER BOMBER. 7 SQUADRON. SIXTY-FOUR TRIPS.

NO-ONE LIKES A SPARE

Rupert Noye flew with some of the best master bombers of the time.

Rupert Noye was no stranger to lucky escapes. While training and on detachment doing coastal sweeps from St Eval in aged Whitleys, he survived a crash landing on the Scilly Isles following a glycol leak and another when a propeller feathered mid flight. Posted to 166 Squadron on Wellingtons, after a series of mishaps and adventures he eventually crewed with an Australian skipper who had been operational in the Middle East. The adventures still continued – their Wimpey was badly shot about at low level over a German airfield, one shell striking the port engine, splitting the engine cowling ring from top to bottom.

When the squadron converted from Wellingtons to Lancasters, those with twenty or more trips were screened, and Rupert found himself 'rested'. After six months' instructing, he was posted to 12 Squadron at Wickenby to replace a rear gunner injured in an attack by an enemy intruder. The crew, led by Pilot Officer Frank L'Estrange, had already volunteered for Pathfinder Force, and after three trips they were posted to 156 Squadron via NTU at Warboys. When L'Estrange was posted after being involved in the accidental deaths of several Canadian soldiers, Rupert found himself once again as a 'spare'.

"I did eighteen trips as a spare with nine different crews. No-one liked to fly with a spare; some thought we brought bad luck and they'd end up getting the chop, but I was very lucky. I flew with two wing commanders (Wing Commander Richard Burrough DFC who later went on to command 128 Squadron and Wing Commander Kenny Lawson DSO & Bar, DFC) and three master bombers (Squadron Leader Alfred Cochrane DSO, DFC & 2 Bars, Squadron Leader John Wilson DFC, and Squadron Leader Peter Clayton DSO, DFC). Although I was an NCO flying with comparatively senior officers, there was absolutely no 'bull'. When we were in the aircraft, they were just ordinary chaps – just people in the crew. The skipper."

RUPERT NOYE DFC
AIR GUNNER. 156 SQUADRON. SEVENTY-TWO OPS.

needed, and a number of Pathfinders found themselves posted with immediate effect.

The revisiting of major targets in the second half of the month meant a return to multiple losses for individual squadrons. Three crews, for example, were lost from 83 Squadron during an attack on Brunswick – a raid that is interesting because it was experimental. Known as Operation Hackle, the purpose was to show whether or not 'regular' navigators and bomb aimers could execute a successful raid without Pathfinder support, only using H2S. The answer was a resounding no. Only a poor concentration was achieved and some areas twenty miles distant were mistaken for Brunswick and bombed. If ever there was a shining example of why Pathfinder Force had been created, it was surely this.

The attack on the Opel motor factory at Rüsselsheim that same night, August 12/13, was also somewhat experimental. The blind illuminator force was divided: the blind illuminators went in first and dropped flares, with the visual markers close behind. If the visual markers were able to identify the target, then the blind markers held on to their TIs. This was in effect a variation on the Newhaven form of attack that greatly helped both main force and the backers-up because it was easier to bomb a small, compact group of TIs. As it happened, the show didn't quite go according

THE MOST WONDERFUL FEELING EVER EXPERIENCED

Elmer 'Al' Trotter had commenced his operational duties with 101 Squadron at Ludford Magna, winning the Distinguished Flying Medal on only his fourth sortie for bringing his severely-damaged Lancaster back to base after seeing off a nightfighter attack. Earmarked for Pathfinders, he flew first with 156 Squadron at Upwood, then with 582 Squadron, Little Staughton, when his flight was hived off to form the nucleus of the new unit.

"On August 12 we were once again on the battle order. This time the target was the Opel factory at Rüsselsheim. It was to be our forty-fourth operation.

"Around 01.30 while on the return trip, all hell broke loose when an undetected nightfighter suddenly attacked us from below. There were numerous explosions and both starboard engines caught fire. There was little or no feel on my control column and although the aileron controls seemed capable of keeping the aircraft laterally, more or less level, the elevator and rudder controls were completely non-responsive. The aircraft seemed to be in a series of stalls and subsequent recoveries. It was apparent that our only possibility of survival was to abandon the aircraft.

"I gave the order immediately which was followed by John (John Rawcliffe), the engineer, and Bart (Bart Mathers), the navigator, quickly proceeding to the forward escape hatch. I remember Bart squeezing my shoulder as he hurried past. As Bernie (Bernard Pullin DFC) was already down in the nose position, it was reasonable to assume he would have opened the escape hatch and be the first to leave the aircraft.

"The aircraft was now gyrating wildly, almost completely out of control, and it was becoming

Parachute pack with D-ring in place

obvious that I must leave this burning mess; however I had not heard or seen anything of my gunners (Walter Parfitt and Kenneth Archibald). I looked back at what was left of the now burning fuselage, and it appeared 'Corny' (John Broad), the wireless operator, was dead or severely wounded. Because of smoke and other wreckage, neither Walter nor Archie's positions were identifiable. There was absolutely nothing I could do under the circumstances but I still found it extremely difficult to abandon the rest of my crew.

"I unbuckled my seat belt and was bouncing around like a tennis ball. For what seemed like an eternity, I struggled and finally reached the forward escape hatch. I spotted Bernie, still sitting up forward. I think it is possible he was not about to leave the aircraft until he knew I was safely out.

"Once free of the aircraft I tried to reach the 'D' ring to deploy my parachute. For a millisecond I could not find it and panicked, actually clawing through some of the leather on my flying jacket. I finally found it and pulled. The sudden opening jolt plus the billowing noise of the deploying 'chute was certainly the most wonderful feeling and sound I have ever experienced. The next remarkable incident was the sudden stop as I landed in trees on the side of the mountain."

ELMER 'AL' TROTTER DFC, DFM
PILOT. 156 AND 582 SQUADRONS. FORTY-FOUR OPS.

to plan. Haze prevented the visual markers from identifying the target and many of the bombs fell some way away.

Two crews were lost from 156 Squadron that night. Squadron Leader Garrard Hemmings and Flight Lieutenant James McDonald DFM, RAAF (the latter a veteran of the Middle East) were the two pilots among fifteen dead. A third aircraft flown by Flight Lieutenant Al Trotter DFC, DFM, a former 156 Squadron pilot now flying from Little Staughton, was also shot down. Trotter and two of his crew survived.

There was better luck later in the month when a strong force of Lancasters (preceded by 'Windowing' Mosquitoes, who flew on to attack Frankfurt) headed for the Opel works again to see if they could do any better using the same technique. They certainly did: the ORB makes mention of 'the hooded flares which provided excellent illumination over the target enabling crews to clearly identify the aiming point.' Red and green TIs soon followed as did the bombs from almost 400 aircraft.

The whole raid was over and done with in only ten minutes, by which time the forge and the gearbox assembly lines had been put paid to. The bombers were more than satisfied with their night's work, and would never have guessed that the factory would be up and running again within forty-eight hours. Unfortunately for 7 Squadron, Flight Lieutenant T.H. Strong DFC, RNZAF failed to return, though he would later turn up safe along with five others in his crew.

SHOOTING DOWN AN ENEMY FIGHTER

"We shot down an FW190 on our way home from Rüsselsheim (the Opel motor factory) on August 25, 1944. We had completed our duties as a blind marker illuminator when our rear gunner, Eddie Brackett (a Canadian), spotted an FW190 that was trying to creep up on us from behind and underneath. He called 'corkscrew' and as we did he opened fire. As the aircraft twisted and climbed, the mid upper gunner, John Turner, scanned the skies for a second fighter, just in case, before he then also opened fire. With both of the gunners shooting, the German fighter suddenly burst into flames and fell away. They were both able to claim it as 'destroyed'."

TONY HISCOCK DFC & BAR
PILOT. 156 SQUADRON. SIXTY-EIGHT OPS.

By marked contrast, the bombers of what had become known as Cochrane's independent air force executed their own attack on Darmstadt that night, using the '5 Group method' of low-level marking. It was a total failure, as the markers were unable to locate the target. The master bomber was obliged to return early and the two deputies were shot down. Squadron Leader Stuart Parkes DSO of 97 Squadron was killed and two pilots from 83 Squadron – Flight Lieutenant Oliver Meggeson DFC and Squadron Leader Arthur Williams DFC – were missing. More than thirty Lancasters opted to bomb other targets rather than return with nothing to show for their night's endeavours, including thirteen aircraft who were lured to the fires at Rüsselsheim. The irony would not have been lost on Bennett.

August 25/26 was indeed a busy night for Bomber Command in general, and Pathfinders specifically. Those aircraft not designated for the Rüsselsheim attack were directed to no fewer than eight coastal battery positions in and around Brest, and acquitted themselves admirably. Most of the bombing was accurate and only one Lancaster and one Halifax was lost out of some 334 aircraft taking part. Perhaps not surprisingly, given the risks they undertook, the one Lancaster was a Pathfinder from 7 Squadron – Squadron Leader Ralph Chopping DFC. Among his crew was the rear gunner, Flying Officer Chester Marchand who had journeyed more than 5,000 miles from British Honduras to serve his king.

The Mosquitoes of the LNSF, meanwhile, as well as supporting the main effort, also went on to Frankfurt and Berlin. The Berlin contingent comprised thirty-six Mosquitoes, of which twenty-eight attacked the primary target, one was abortive, and seven were outstanding. Of those seven, two crashed over the UK, both from 692 Squadron.

The attack on Kiel the following night was one of mixed fortunes for the PFF Mosquito and Lancaster crews taking part. German defences put up a successful smoke screen that frustrated the

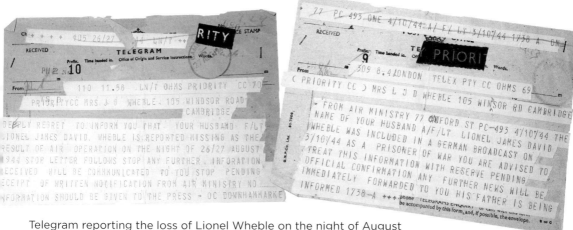

Telegram reporting the loss of Lionel Wheble on the night of August 26/27 1944. Ten weeks later, the Germans announced that he was safe.

visual markers' chances of identifying the aiming point, despite all of the crews reporting that the illuminating flares had been extremely well positioned.

The crews had been briefed to approach the target at 2,000ft, below the radar screen, and climb to height only before bombing. The tactic was then to reduce height for the flight home in the hope of rendering the German controllers blind. It wasn't wholly successful, it was thought many had climbed too early. The net result was combats reported aplenty, and six PFF aircraft were shot down, three from 635 Squadron (Flight Lieutenants Reginald Barker and Lionel Wheble, and Warrant Officer George Shirley) and one each from 7, 35 and 156 Squadrons (Flight Lieutenant William Smaill DFC, Flight Lieutenant D.L. Knockloch, and Flight Lieutenant Robert Etchells respectively. Etchell's crew at least had the satisfaction of shooting down their attacker, and spent five days afloat in the North Sea before finally being rescued. Etchells was awarded the DSO.)

There were two further raids of note that occurred in August. The first was a relatively modest show by the Halifaxes of 4 Group led by a combination of Mosquitoes and Lancasters from Pathfinder Force. The target was Gewerkschaft Rheinpreußen, a synthetic oil facility in Homberg; it was historically significant being the first major raid by Bomber Command to Germany in daylight for more than three years.

Musical Mosquitoes opened the attack with red TIs that fell accurately on the aiming point. The master bomber was more than satisfied, and called in main force to bomb. A little while later, he dropped his own green TIs,

Lionel Wheble.

which slightly overshot, and therefore instructed the Halifax bomb aimers to bomb the centre of the reds and greens. While the cloud made any assessment of the results difficult, the target was smothered with bomb bursts, and the crews returned home, congratulating themselves on a job well done. They also managed to come away without losing a single aircraft, helped no doubt by the protective shield of nine squadrons of Spitfires.

The second noteworthy attack was by sixteen Mosquitoes on the heavily-defended Dortmund-Ems canal, on the night of August 9/10, led by the 571 Squadron commanding officer Mike Birkin. The canal was an essential transport route for materials to and from the Ruhr and the North Sea. It had been a favourite target of Bomber Command almost from the start, and had indeed been the venue for one of Bomber Command's first Victoria Crosses. Newspaper reports at the time describe the attack as 'one of the most daring and important mine-laying operations of the war', and correctly detail the method of attack as being a timed run from markers dropped by Pathfinder Mosquitoes (two out of the four 109 Squadron aircraft completed accurate drops). All of the attacking aircraft returned home safely and the canal was closed for the better part of six weeks.

MINE-LAYING IN THE DORTMUND-EMS CANAL

Aubrey Strickland was an electrical engineer before the war, working for the North Met Power Company. Trained to fly in the United States, he spent more than two years in Training Command before being earmarked for a heavy-bomber squadron but actually converting to Mosquitoes and being posted to 571 Squadron in May 1944.

"The briefing prior to the Dortmund-Ems canal raid was to drop the parachute mine at about 150ft to 200ft; we did not have any practice runs of any significance, prior to this trip, nor did we have any special training other than normal flying exercises such as bomb-aiming practice, low flying and one-engine landings.

"The marking was by Mosquitoes; the method was ground marking by red burning flares. We made a timed run from these (flares) and sure enough, there was the canal. I remember that Dave (my navigator, 'Dave' Davidson) and I were a bit lower down from the actual area specified to drop the mine but as it turned out, it was actually better for us because we had a nice run up letting down to the right height, round a bend, over a bridge and there we were.

"To fly low was just a matter of keeping your eyes on the instruments as you would blind flying or at night, anyway, when there is nothing to see outside. There was plenty of flak, of course, but we missed the lot."

AUBREY 'STRICK' STRICKLAND DFC
PILOT. 571 SQUADRON. FIFTY OPS.

The month ended with a return to Stettin on the Baltic, a round trip of more than nine hours. It was the second of two attacks on the port and industrial areas, and more successful than the first. Many thousands of houses and industrial premises were destroyed or badly damaged, and a number of ships sunk or holed. Bomber Command lost twenty-eight aircraft across the two nights, three of which were Pathfinders.

One of those missing, from 582 Squadron, was Squadron Leader Allan Farrington, a pilot of some 'celebrity', having featured in a well-known book published during the war entitled *Wings of Olympus*. He had only just arrived at Little Staughton after a long period instructing, and on the night of his death was flying with the regular crew of Wing Commander Peter Cribb. One of the other pilots missing was Flight Lieutenant Francis Healey DFC of 635 Squadron. Healey had flown forty-two trips and was in line for promotion.

692 Squadron, May 1944.

The losses suffered by Bomber Command were falling and in Pathfinder Force they had stabilised: twenty-nine aircraft were reported missing in August.

Of the Mosquito Squadrons, 692 suffered the worst, losing five aircraft – four out of those five in crashes, albeit that some were no doubt battle damaged. Only one (the Mosquito of Flying Officer S.G.A. Warner) was actually shot down. The new boys at 608 Squadron also suffered their first casualties since becoming part of PFF: Flying Officer S.O. Webb RCAF wrote his aircraft off in a crash having been caught and attacked by a nightfighter and seriously damaged. He was lucky; his would-be victor was Hauptmann Friedrich-Karl Müller, squadron commander of 1./NJG10 who attacked the home-bound Mosquito on four occasions and was confident enough of the damage inflicted to claim a 'kill'. His twenty-fourth victim, however, actually made it home, albeit not quite in one piece. The first person to be killed was Flight Lieutenant Charles Darby DFM, navigator to Flying Officer Millard Coles DFC. The two Canadians were shot down on operations to Mannheim on August 27/28.

Allan Farrington was a pilot of some fame, having fought in the Greek campaign before finally joining PFF in the summer of 1944.

The LNSF was indeed being stretched, even with the arrival of 608. Two crews were lost from 139 Squadron in the same night early in the month, part of a nuisance raid to Castrop-Rauxel. One was shot down, the navigator Flying Officer John Stevenson losing his life; the second overshot and caught fire attempting to land at Upwood, in thick fog. Both the pilot, Flight Lieutenant John Kenny DFC & Bar and his navigator, Flying Officer Martin Levin DFC, were killed.

Of the heavy bombers, the biggest loss that month was outside of 8 Group but still a member of the Pathfinder 'family' – Wing Commander 'Ted' Porter DFC & Bar of 97 Squadron. Porter had been commanding officer of 9 Squadron throughout the Battle of Berlin and was now leading an especially daring raid, to mine the Stettin-Schwinemünde channel, on the night he was shot down (August 16/17). He was last heard reporting that his aircraft was on fire saying that he had 'had it' and would have to bale out. In the event, none of the crew made it out and all were killed. Porter was not flying with his regular crew that night and all, ironically, survived the war.

On its second anniversary, Bennett spent the morning at RAF Graveley where he held the investiture of one of his most notable captains, Major Johan Christie of the Royal Norwegian Air Force. Christie, who had fled to London after the fall of Norway in 1940, was presented with the Distinguished Service Order, and there was a DFC for his fellow Norwegian, Lieutenant Wang.

Later that same day, Bennett and his men afforded themselves a small celebration of their achievements. By the end of August, Pathfinders had flown some 2,802 sorties, bringing the total number of sorties carried out since August 15, 1942 to 26,841 (or 105,509 operational flying hours). The total number of bombs (including heavy explosive, incendiaries and TI markers) dropped amounted to 5,662.38 tons. A dinner was held to mark the occasion at which the great and the good assembled, including the 'father' of the RAF, Viscount Trenchard, and Lieutenant General James H. Doolittle of the USAAF – himself a 'master bomber' in the truest sense of the word.

It was then back to business.

CHAPTER 7
FORTRESS EUROPE

SEPTEMBER

September marked a turning point both on the ground and in the air.

The Battle for Normandy was effectively over, and Allied troops had reached Paris. Brussels was liberated soon after and the Germans were in full retreat, although not everywhere. In certain quarters they dug in and refused to surrender. Pockets of resistance were left that seriously hampered the flow of fuel, ammunition and other essential supplies to the front line. Indeed the Allied advance, when it finally happened, almost came about too quickly and their supply lines were alarmingly over-stretched, so much so that General Dwight D. Eisenhower – who had assumed control of Allied ground operations in northwest Europe from General Bernard Montgomery on September 1 – was obliged to order a halt.

While Cherbourg was in Allied hands, and providing a critical re-supply route, the Allies were in desperate need of further port facilities closer to the advancing armies. The Canadians were unable to capture the Channel ports quickly because Hitler had declared them *festungen* (fortresses) and the dock facilities that did fall into their hands had been largely destroyed. Montgomery captured Antwerp, but the town was of little use without control of the Scheldt that remained resolutely in German control. In the short term, these *festungen* were simply ignored, but they could not

---

A QUESTION OF CONVENIENCE

Called up at eighteen in 1942, Percy Cannings began training as an air gunner at Llandwrog (9 AGS) in the winter of 1942, eventually 'crewing up' at 1656 HCU, Lindholme. Screened in July 1943 having flown twenty-two ops at 100 Squadron with Ken Harvey DFC, he spent more than six months instructing at OTU before being ordered to report to 97 Squadron at Bourn. Reporting to the guardroom on arrival, he was told to leave his kitbag and find Flying Officer Bill Reid in the briefing room as he would be flying that night.

"As the mid upper gunner, there was not a great deal of space inside the turret and so I had to stow my parachute inside the aircraft, rather than have the seat-type 'chutes that the pilot and rear gunners wore. I never left the turret for the duration of the flight, and given that they could last up to ten hours, this could be a problem.

"We had an Elsan chemical toilet in case of emergencies. It was no good for the gunners, of course, as we were not allowed to leave our positions, not that the thought of using the toilet in temperatures of minus forty degrees centigrade was especially appealing, and the smell was foul. On one occasion when we were caught in a searchlight – we all hated those – our pilot threw the aircraft around so violently I am sure that we looped the loop! As a result, the contents of the Elsan were spilled around the fuselage and the poor old ground crew had to clear up the mess after we landed. What they said could not be repeated here. They were exceptional: they were there when we left, and there when we got back, always on hand to service and repair our aircraft."

PERCY CANNINGS DFM
MID UPPER GUNNER, 97 SQUADRON, FORTY-SEVEN OPS.

be dismissed forever. The ports – running from St Nazaire in the south to Dunkirk and the approaches to Antwerp in the north, contained more than 140,000 German troops.

One of these fortresses was Le Havre and for a period of seven days Bomber Command undertook a series of heavy raids intended to dislodge the stubborn German defenders from their perch. Nearly 2,000 aircraft carried out these attacks and dropped more than 9,500 tons of bombs before their objective was finally met, and the garrison commander, Oberst Eberhard Wildermuth, surrendered.

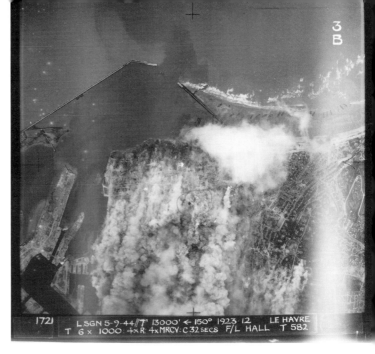

The clarity in this bombing photograph of Le Havre is exceptional. The German garrison surrendered after a sustained onslaught.

The most elaborate of all these attacks was on September 10, when eight separate coastal batteries were earmarked for destruction and each individual aiming point was given a codename and number after a make

THE CHALLENGES OF OBOE

Tony Farrell began his flying training in the early summer of 1940, and became somewhat of an expert in blind approach training (BAT), commanding 1534 BAT Flight at Shawbury from December 1942 until March 1944. After being graded 'above average' by Wing Commander Roy Ralston at 1655 MTU, he eventually joined 105 Squadron in the summer of 1944, flying his first op whilst attached to 'B' Flight, 692 Squadron, to Berlin on July 10. Returning to 'A' Flight of 105, he flew his first Oboe sortie later that same month. The marking accuracy recorded, notably for raids on Le Havre and Calais in September 1944, suggests errors of only thirty yards.

"The deeper the range, the less reliable it (Oboe) became. With line of sight reception the range was limited by the height we could reach (about 36,000ft was the maximum). Unless signals were clear we had to abort; also if our flying was not accurate we had to abort and/or we would get a washout signal. Getting the bomb doors open and maintaining accurate flying at extreme altitude was very difficult – we usually ended up at full power at long ranges.

"We operated in pairs so if the first aircraft aborted the second took over. We flew as close as possible in daylight and at night at times we felt the other's slipstream. It has to be remembered that the approach was along an arc, so the beam wasn't straight! The closer the range the greater the change of angle. There were a lot of technical difficulties, mostly in the aircraft's equipment I believe. One night I was detached to one of the ground tracking stations at Kingsdown, near Deal, and watched a raid from the other viewpoint. It taught me to respect the hard work and technical ingenuity of the ground controllers."

TONY FARRELL DFC, AFC
PILOT, 692 AND 105 SQUADRONS, SEVENTY-EIGHT OPS.

AN ABSOLUTE SECRET

'Cam' Wallace both flew and led a large number of Oboe operations, and therefore had first-hand experience of its strengths and weaknesses:

Alexander Wallace

"[Oboe] was incredibly accurate within its range, but this was only about as far as the east end of the Ruhr. If you flew higher you increased the range, so we did experimental ops at up to 38,000ft which gave us the bends and blew out valves. When we got the pressurised Mark XVI 'planes it was better. The other trouble was that only a few 'planes could use it at a time, thus excluding the main force; we either marked for them in the PFF role or went out ourselves, alone, doing accurate but small jobs. When marking for heavy-bomber forces, they would kick you off the channel and call in your reserve if they saw you were going to miss by more than about 100 yards.

"Oboe was absolutely secret; we were not allowed to talk about it except behind closed doors, and when we landed away we had to demand that a guard be put on the 'plane and couldn't even discuss it with the people who interrogated us on another station, which made us unpopular."

ALEXANDER 'CAM' WALLACE DFC
NAVIGATOR. 109 SQUADRON. EIGHTY-NINE OPS.

of car (Buick I and II, Alvis I to IV and Bentley I and II). The significance in Pathfinding terms was that it effectively introduced a new lead player to the cast – a 'long stop' – to control the whole attack. The man chosen for the task was the commanding officer of 582 Squadron, Peter Cribb, and his role was to cancel any inaccurate marking or bombing by dropping yellow TIs. The lessons of the previous month had been learned, and nobody wanted a repeat performance given the proximity of Allied troops. At one stage of the raid he was indeed obliged to intercede to show main force not to bomb beyond a particular point, and he also instructed the master bomber at one of the Buick targets to abandon his attack.

The Pathfinders came through these raids virtually unscathed. The only loss came from the attack on September 8, when Wing Commander 'Howie' Morrison DFC of 405 Squadron (and later its commanding officer) was shot down. Morrison, controlling the third of five aiming points, made no less than three runs over the target, and on the fourth was so low that he attracted the attentions of the German 37mm light flak which set the aircraft on fire. The crew, including Flight Lieutenant Reg Swartz, successfully baled out and evaded capture. Shortly after, Morrison received the DSO.

Boulogne proved easier to bully into surrender,

Peter Cribb as commanding officer of Little Staughton, home to 109 and 582 Squadrons.

This 405 Squadron Lancaster was lucky to make it home. The damage fore and aft is extensive.

HIT THREE TIMES IN TEN SECONDS

"At only 2,000ft over Le Havre, and amid fierce flak, our Lancaster was hit three times in ten seconds: the first hit set off the TIs in the bomb bay and fired a header tank which filled the aircraft with smoke and flames; the second tore off 10ft of our starboard wing; and the third hit what was left of the wing, leaving a huge hole."

REGINALD SWARTZ DFC & BAR, RCAF
NAVIGATOR. 405 SQUADRON.

helped by a huge force of more than 750 bombers executing an early morning attack on September 17. Once again there were multiple aiming points with several master bombers and the long stop technique was similarly deployed with good effect.

Calais proved somewhat more problematic. A large attacking force of almost 650 aircraft was assembled for a raid on September 20, but the Germans stubbornly held on. Indeed they continued to resist even after five further attacks between September 24-28. These raids went largely uncontested, at least in the air, with only very small numbers of main force aircraft being lost. The highest casualty rate was recorded on September 24, when the weather forced a number of bombers to descend beneath the cloud and come into range of the deadly light flak. One of those shot down was the 156 Squadron Lancaster of Flight Lieutenant Ken Doyle DFC, the former NCO pilot who was acting as long stop. Doyle and his crew – including two who had been with him back in February when their rear gunner had been awarded the CGM as well as Harold Morrish, the regular nav to Thomas Ison – were all killed. It was a huge loss of a vastly experienced crew. Doyle had flown some forty-four operations since arriving at 156 at the start of the year.

Several other aircraft were badly damaged, including the 35 Squadron Lancaster of another of PFF's Norwegian pilots, Lieutenant Svein Hausvik. Hausvik was the son of a wealthy ship owner and had originally embarked on a career in the navy, but the war had changed his plans. Rated an 'above average' pilot, he gained a reputation as an outstanding Pathfinder captain, and had many scrapes along the way. He would survive this experience, only to be killed the following month over Cologne.

The Calais defences also claimed the life of another master bomber, Wing Commander Charles Palmer DFC, on September 26. Palmer was the commanding officer of 405 Squadron, and was

2335 L.8GN 6-10-44/8" 19000'←121° 1657·45 SCHOLVEN
J 18 X 500   C40SEC F/O BROWN J582

The synthetic oil facility at Scholven from 19,000ft.

shot down three miles south of the target and crashed behind Allied lines. Within his crew and one of the survivors was the navigator, Flight Lieutenant Hugh Anderson DFM, RCAF.

In the middle of September, the C-in-C was freed from control by supreme headquarters of the Allied Expeditionary Force and once again took his orders direct from the Air Ministry. Operations in support of the ground forces remained a priority; indeed Pathfinders led two raids to support the landing of British forces in and around Arnhem and Nijmegen in the ill-fated Market Garden operation. But this only took up a small fraction of Harris's overall strength, and so the question remained as to how the rest of his command could be best employed.

Sir Charles Portal and the Air Ministry favoured attacks on synthetic oil production, they argued the German military's ability to wage war without fuel would be seriously hampered. On Eisenhower's staff, his deputy – Air Chief Marshal Sir Arthur Tedder – preferred an all-out attack on the German transportation system, having witnessed at first hand the destructive power of British and American bombers in preventing a co-ordinated German response. A directive of September 25 gave a clear priority to oil, with the German rail and waterway transport system, tank production and motor vehicle production coming a close second.

The synthetic oil facilities at Dortmund, Castrop-Rauxel, Kamen, Gelsenkirchen and Scholven-Buer therefore appeared on the target list on consecutive days/nights with mixed results and a disappointing number of casualties. They were heavily defended and tested the mettle of Pathfinder and main force crews alike.

One aircraft fell victim to intense accurate heavy flak over the Klöckner-Werke AG plant at Castrop on September 11, the 582 Squadron Lancaster of Flight Lieutenant 'Tiny' Shurlock, so-called because of his massive frame. Shurlock and his crew – on their twentieth operation together – made it out in one piece to survive as prisoners of war with the exception of the flight engineer, Warrant Officer Victor Davis DFM. 'Davy' Davis, who was on his ninety-seventh operation in total, was killed instantly by a flak burst that exploded in the front section of the aircraft. Five other squadron 'planes returned with battle damage.

That same afternoon, two Lancasters were shot down over Gelsenkirchen, one each from 35 and 156 Squadrons, though it could have been many more. They had been among ten Mosquitoes and nineteen Lancasters from PFF that had set out, but only three Mosquitoes and twelve Lancasters later claimed to have attacked the primary target. A well-laid smoke screen was responsible for disrupting the raid, supported once again by heavy flak that hit no fewer than ten out of the thirteen Lancasters operating from 156 Squadron. Squadron Leader Tony Raw DFC, AFC, who

AN ACT OF CHIVALRY

Ernie Patterson attended Madley and Yatesbury for wireless op training before moving to Evanton for air gunnery where he qualified 'above average' – a highly thought of accolade for any 'trade'. He completed twenty-nine trips with his first pilot, 'Jack' Harrild DFC, one of which was particularly memorable:

> "It was September 13, and we had bombed Gelsenkirchen as part of an attacking force of 140 aircraft. Not long after leaving the target, however, our aircraft was hit by flak in the wing and the starboard outer was put out of action. While a Lancaster could fly comfortably on three engines, it made for a slow and arduous journey home and there was always the danger that further damage had been caused to the aircraft controls. It also left us more vulnerable to fighter attack.
>
> "As if sensing the danger, another Lancaster approached us and flew alongside, taking station on our starboard wing. They could see we were in trouble and obviously wanted to give us some moral support. It remained alongside until Jack was able to land the damaged aircraft safely at Downham Market.
>
> "Jack told me to make a note of the aircraft's squadron code and identifying letter and the next day, he wrote to the pilot to thank him for his action. The following week, Jack received a reply from the pilot in question, Flying Officer Lindsay Cann of 156 Squadron, RAF Upwood. In it he thanked Jack for taking the time to write – something no one had ever done before – and said: 'I was determined to see you home… it was our duty to support you and, if necessary, call for help. The age of chivalry and good will has not passed,' the letter concludes: 'Let us hope our good will spreads.'"

The following month, Cann was awarded an immediate DFC and his navigator an immediate DFM following an attack on the oil refinery at Sterkrade in which he was badly wounded. Sadly, this gallant officer did not survive the war.

ERNIE PATTERSON DFM
WIRELESS OPERATOR. 635 SQUADRON. FIFTY-ONE OPS.

was on his thirty-fourth operation, was one of the unlucky ones. Raw had only recently returned to operations after a long spell as an instructor for which he added an Air Force Cross to the DFC he had earned for completing a tour of operations with 61 and 144 Squadrons in 1942. Raw, a flight commander with 156, was one of three brothers who served in the RAF during the war; two others – John and Peter – were also killed.

Scholven/Buer on September 12 also proved to be well defended as did the Krupp Treibstoffwerk plant at Wanne-Eickel. On approach to the latter, the Mosquitoes' task was hampered by yet another effective smoke screen, but one at least was lucky to see a gap and drop its 4,000lb high capacity (HC) bomb right onto the target. Other Mosquitoes used their precision devices to ensure the aiming point was accurately marked, and the rapid rise of thick black smoke that followed the main force bombing suggested the raid was a complete success. It may well have been, but success came with the loss of three aircraft, two from 35 Squadron (Flight Lieutenant Peter Granger and Flying Officer Donald Campbell – both killed in action with their crews) and one from 405 Squadron (Flying Officer A. Sovran who survived as a POW, despite his aircraft receiving a direct hit). The Canadians escaped relatively lightly given that six other squadron aircraft were also damaged, at least one having to make an emergency landing at Woodbridge without power on any of the four engines.

Within the new directive, bombing of German cities was to be undertaken only when weather or tactical conditions were unsuitable for attacking priority objectives. Such vague directions only served to further Harris's ambition to demonstrate how his bomber boys could force Germany to collapse from within, and the month is punctuated with the names of familiar cities appearing on the battle order, as well as some that were being raided for the first time.

Emden, Frankfurt, Kiel and Neuss were all on the receiving end of heavy attacks and each interesting in its own way.

The attack on Emden, for example, was the first in more than two years and, as it transpired, the last. Of the forty-two PFF Lancasters taking part, all but two carried out a successful attack. The ORB remarks that the red TIs were well placed from the beginning, and main force bombing was well concentrated, so much so that the aiming point was quickly obscured by clouds of brown and black smoke. In the end, the master bomber was obliged to instruct those yet to bomb to aim at the centre of the smoke with a two-second overshoot.

Several large explosions left the target well ablaze, including the dock installations and industry harbour, the inner harbour, bridge, lock gates and railway yards. A 9,000-ton merchant vessel was also reportedly hit. Defences were only moderate and spasmodic, but sufficiently accurate and timely to claim the life of the deputy master bomber, Flight Lieutenant Granville Wilson DSO, DFC, DFM of 7 Squadron. Wilson, an extremely popular twenty-four-year-old Northern Irishman, was killed instantly together with his navigator and air bomber. Five others made it out and survived.

The attack on Frankfurt was similarly the last major RAF raid directed at that city and followed within only a few hours of a highly-destructive raid by 5 Group on nearby Darmstadt. Cochrane's 'independent air force' had long-since overcome its earlier disappointments and now, not for the first time, their marking produced an outstandingly accurate and concentrated attack (though for the death of Wing Commander Jesse Walker AFC, DFM of 83 Squadron; he had been flying operationally since 1940). Frankfurt was also heavily hit, as the primary visual marker did an especially good job in the first instance, and a heavy attack quickly developed with numerous explosions, fires and the inevitable smoke reported. Flight Lieutenant Robert Banks and his 7 Squadron crew failed to return.

Kiel was the next major target on the list involving almost 500 aircraft. It illustrates perfectly the dangers still faced by Pathfinder crews above and beyond those experienced by main force. Only six aircraft were shot down during the attack: four Halifaxes and two Lancasters. The two Lancasters were both PFF aircraft – one from 405 Squadron (Flight Lieutenant Ronald Long DFC, RCAF) and the second from 582 Squadron (Flight Lieutenant Graham Nixon).

Remarkable in both crews were the gunners. The flight sergeant rear gunner in Long's crew, Alan Gowdey, was only a teenager, and given that he had enlisted in 1941, that means he probably completed his training while he was still under age. The rear gunner in Nixon's crew, Pilot Officer John Norris DFM, was a recognised ace. His DFM, gazetted in December 1943 while serving with 158 Squadron, credited him with two enemy fighters confirmed, and having assisted in the destruction of two more enemy aircraft. He had started operating in the autumn of 1943 after initial training at 4 AGS and crewing up at 10 OTU.

Of the four heavy attacks mounted on German towns, the largest that month was directed at Neuss. Although the main force contingent was significant (more than 500 aircraft), the PFF contribution was comparatively light (seventeen Mosquitoes and fifteen Lancasters) and the effectiveness of the raid was difficult to gauge. Interestingly, only seven of the Mosquitoes attacked the primary; ten were abortive. All PFF aircraft returned safely.

Alongside the heavy raids, the LNSF were kept busy as usual with six attacks on Berlin, three on Brunswick and Karlsruhe, two on Bremen and Hamburg, and one each on Hannover, Nuremberg, Osnabrück, Bochum, Mannheim, Frankfurt and Kassel. Smaller raids were also mounted, often as training and occasionally experimental. The strain upon the LNSF crews was increasing, but their ranks had at least been supplemented at the start of the month with the arrival of 128

A TOUR OF OPS BEFORE HIS TWENTIETH BIRTHDAY

Ray Wilcock (left) and Allan Edwards (second right) with 'Irish' Miller (right). Ray always found his way home.

Allan Edwards was a flight engineer with C.J. 'Irish' Miller. He flew a number of sorties with 514 Squadron at Waterbeach to such targets as Brunswick, Stuttgart, Magdeburg and Berlin, before being posted with his crew to 582 Squadron at Little Staughton to continue operational flying:

"Flying daylight operations was certainly an experience and given the choice I always preferred to fly at night. During the day you could see the anti-aircraft fire reaching up to hit you. You not only saw the flash but also the smoke that followed, and it could be quite disturbing. We flew a number of daylights, attacking airfields, bomb dumps, railway junctions and marshalling yards, usually in a loose formation unless on an Oboe run over a flying-bomb site in which case we would close up tightly on the leader and drop our bombs when he dropped his.

"I recall on July 18 being briefed to attack a railway yard at Vaires-sur-Marne to the east of Paris. I remember it especially as we were well and truly clobbered by flak, and our rear gunner – [Sergeant Loseby] – was temporarily blinded by splinters. He came on the intercom and simply said: 'Miller, they've got me!' We patched him up and carried on. I remember that raid also because I was aiming the bombs and managed to get an excellent aiming point photograph.

"On another occasion I flew as a spare bod with Flying Officer Magee. It was an eventful trip for we were attacked by a German fighter but escaped. I didn't enjoy the experience. Still, I survived to complete my tour, finishing up in September 1944 ahead of my twentieth birthday."

ALLAN EDWARDS
FLIGHT ENGINEER. 582 SQUADRON. FORTY-TWO OPS.

Squadron at Wyton, under the command of Wing Commander Richard Burrough. A former flight commander with 156 Squadron, he would soon have his unit fully operational.

The high intensity of flying took its toll, both on operations and whilst training. The Trinidadian, Philip Cross, almost came to grief on the night of September 11/12 over Berlin when his aircraft was hit by flak and his pilot was obliged to execute an emergency landing at Woodbridge. Though they both walked away unscathed, a second 139 Squadron crew – piloted by Flight Lieutenant James Halcro RCAF – failed to return.

Indeed the attacks on Berlin led to a serious number of Mosquito casualties: 571 Squadron lost one of its aircraft on September 12/13, though the crew escaped unharmed; Squadron Leader Charles Barrett DFC, with more than sixty operations to his name, failed to return on September 13/14, along with his 608 Squadron navigator; that same night, a crew from 692 Squadron (Pilot Officer Gwilym Thomas) were also killed. Two nights later, 608 Squadron lost Flight Lieutenant Bert Smith RCAF and his navigator, and later in the month, Flying Officer Leonard Brennan

RNZAF and his navigator of 692 Squadron went missing over Mannheim.

Pathfinder Mosquitoes attached to 5 Group also took casualties, 627 Squadron losing four crews, including that of Wing Commander Guy Gibson VC, DSO & Bar, DFC & Bar on the night of September 19/20. It is still unclear why Gibson should be flying in a master bomber role, especially since he had little experience of target marking or the Mosquito. What happened to him and his navigator, Squadron Leader Jim Warwick DFC, has been the subject of enormous debate for many years.

In 2011, a documentary producer claimed to have uncovered the 'truth', which was that Gibson was the victim of friendly fire, having been shot down by the mid upper gunner of a 61 Squadron Lancaster. The evidence, though compelling, was still a little way short of conclusive. Whatever the truth, Bomber Command lost one of its true legends, with few equals.

And so September drew to a close, with the Bomber Command chief once again in his element enforcing his own agenda. With the forces at his disposal, he could more than meet the demands of his peers while still having enough aircraft left over to pound the Germans into submission, even changing the bomb loads so that each aircraft carried less incendiaries and more heavy explosives on the basis that there was little left to burn.

Harris sought a new battle, and he found it.

OCTOBER

The second battle of the Ruhr opened on October 6/7 with an attack on Dortmund. It was a most satisfactory affair, both in terms of the accuracy of the Pathfinder marking and the subsequent destruction caused, especially to the railway network and local steel plant. A reconnaissance aircraft flying over the target only forty minutes after main force had departed reported a concentration of fires burning fiercely in an oval from the northwest to the southeast.

But Dortmund was a mere sideshow compared to what Harris had planned for Duisberg. A glance in the logbooks of any Pathfinder or main force crew operating at this time will show the remarkable feat of two heavy attacks carried out on the target within a twenty-four-hour period, with the downtime filled by a raid by the American 8th Air Force involving more than 2,000 bomber and fighter aircraft.

The raid was given a codename: Operation Hurricane. Why Harris should choose Duisberg has again been the subject of much debate, but it certainly took careful planning. In advance of the attack, no heavy bombers had flown on operations for two nights, so they were clearly being rested for something special. The attack, when it happened, was complicated by having five aiming points; drifting patches of cloud, however, made identification difficult and three out of the five master bombers instructed their charges simply to bomb visually on any built-up areas they could see. Only on the 'special' aiming point did thirty-four out of the thirty-five PFF Lancasters successfully attack the primary target.

The devastation caused by this daylight attack was substantial and was followed by a night-time assault that added to the terror the people of Duisberg must have already been experiencing. Again there were multiple aiming points, but this time the crews were more easily able to find their way, primarily because the fires in the city were visible from a distance of more than 100 miles. A large number of explosions were reported, one said to last several seconds, and as the departing crews looked back they could still see the glow of the flames from the Dutch coast.

In twenty-four hours, Bomber Command had flown 2,647 sorties and dropped 10,300 tons of bombs, of which more than 9,000 had been allocated to Duisberg. Not content with Duisberg, Harris next turned his attentions to Essen, marshalling two huge attacks within forty-eight hours. The first, on the night of October 24/25 was the heaviest raid on Essen attempted, thus far, and the number of aircraft despatched – 1,055 – the largest number ever assembled for a single target.

THREE RAIDS IN THIRTY-SIX HOURS

Doug Reed arrived at 166 Squadron in March 1944 as the wireless operator for Flying Officer Peter Legard, but was allocated a new pilot when Legard was shot down and killed over Nuremberg on his first trip as a 'second dickey'. He flew more than half a dozen trips with his new pilot, Bill Peedell (ex-Kings Royal Rifles who had fought at Dunkirk) before volunteering for Pathfinders. The crew arrived at 156 Squadron on May 24, 1944 and flew that night to Aachen. After twenty ops, Bill was posted and Doug was given yet another pilot, Tom Williams, who he knew from OTU and with whom he would complete his tour:

"The Ruhr was always 'hot', especially in daylight. I remember one raid where, I believe, we were one of five aircraft from 156 Squadron operating that day, and we were primary blind marker for the raid. But when we got there, the main force was nowhere in sight. This meant we had to stooge around until they arrived, and of course that meant that we had all of the defences in the Ruhr opening up on us. Not surprisingly we were hit in the nose, and a piece of Perspex wedged in the pilot's head. The aircraft went into a near-vertical dive and I admit I thought it was bale-out time. Tom managed to pull her up at around 10,000ft, with his head bleeding from the wound, and managed to get her level. We still had a full load of bombs and target indicators on board and so we slowly started to regain height in order to finish the job. Then we limped home.

"We did three raids in thirty-six hours, one of which was a daylight when we got thumped by flak. Predicted flak you could avoid by judging the height and timing of the bursts and altering your altitude accordingly. But when you had a combination of predicted and barrage flak, it was more difficult. On this occasion we were peppered by flak in the wings and fuselage and lost an engine. After we landed at Upwood, our ground crew inspected the damage and counted more than forty holes. One was the size of a fist, and a piece of shrapnel had lodged in a fuel tank and acted like a cork."

DOUG REED DFM
WIRELESS OPERATOR. 156 SQUADRON. FIFTY-TWO OPS.

Nine out of ten bombs of the 4,538 tons that were dropped that night were heavy explosive, destroying huge numbers of buildings. A smaller force (771 aircraft) did even more damage on October 25, especially to the Krupps steelworks that was virtually brought to a standstill.

Remarkably, the number of aircraft lost on these four enormous raids was again so small that they were expressed in numbers rather than as a percentage of the attacking force. Only one PFF Lancaster was lost over Duisberg, a 7 Squadron aircraft piloted by Flying Officer Christopher Crawford. The twenty-year-old was killed along with his crew, having completed thirty-two trips. Similarly only one Lancaster was lost coming back from Essen, a 635 Squadron aircraft that overshot and crashed on its return. All of its crew were safe.

Aside from the major attacks on Duisberg and Essen, Harris also chose Saarbrücken, Cleve, Emmerich, Wilhelmshaven and Stuttgart for major raids. In addition, and to ensure he kept faith with his masters' bidding, he also mounted four attacks on oil targets (Scholven, Sterkrade-Holten, Wanne-Eickel and Homberg) and five on the sea wall and defences of Walcheren Island to effectively flood the areas believed occupied by the Germans.

In defence of their oil targets, the Germans put up a fierce resistance. Two Lancasters from Oakington were shot down over Scholven on October 6, although happily, all but two out of the fifteen men from 7 Squadron survived as prisoners of war. (Flying Officer R.G. Beaune, one of the pilots, had only just joined PFF, having transferred from 90 Squadron after seventeen ops.) Two aircraft were also destroyed following the attack on Wanne-Eickel on October 12, including yet another 7 Squadron Lancaster, this one flown by Squadron Leader Brian Bennett AFC. The second

STRANGE VOICES IN THE DARK

'Pat' O'Hara, a 109 Squadron navigator at Little Staughton in the autumn of 1944, had been with the squadron for more than two years and regularly partnered with Wing Commander Peter Kleboe DSO, DFC, AFC (later to lose his life on the low-level attack on Shell House in Copenhagen):

"On October 25 I was all ready for a trip to Bedford when Peter collared me and said we were on the detail; someone had gone sick. At briefing I noticed we were the first on target (Essen), coming in from the north with red markers, five minutes before the heavies came in from the south. I said: 'we will be on our own'.

"We hit the (Oboe) beam on time; my routine was to open the bomb doors when I received the 'D' but at 'C' I heard a voice, or something, say 'open now'. I bent forward to do so and there was a loud bang as a piece of flak came through the windscreen, removed the epaulette of my battle dress, and went out the back.

"The aircraft immediately dived and I noticed Pete's face was covered with bits of Perspex. He insisted we got the bombing signal before leaving the target. By this time we were down to 20,000ft from 32,000ft; I had grabbed the stick to level off. We made it home ok; Pete made a perfect blind landing (having been a BAT flight instructor) and was rushed to hospital where, luckily, they saved his sight.

"But had it not been for that voice, or it may have been intuition – the only time in eighty trips that I opened the bomb doors at 'C' – the flak would have got me in the throat."

PAT O'HARA DFC & BAR, DFM
NAVIGATOR. 109 SQUADRON. EIGHTY OPS.

aircraft, a Lancaster of 582 Squadron, crash landed and caught fire on its return to Manston, all of the crew, however, managed to make it out in one piece.

The *festung* at Walcheren was attacked on half a dozen occasions in October in raids of varying sizes, starting on October 3. The gun batteries at Walcheren at the mouth of the Scheldt estuary were an important part of the Germans' much-vaunted 'Atlantic Wall' and effectively controlled the approaches to the port of Antwerp. So whilst the Allies held the port, they could not yet exploit its facilities to the full. Walcheren was the shape of a saucer, with its rim made up of dykes and dunes. The theory was that if the bombers could smash the rim, the saucer would flood, and the German defences would be neutered. This was put into practice with devastating effect.

The attack of October 3 on the sea wall near Westkapelle comprised eight waves of bombers controlled by a master bomber, Group Captain Peter Cribb. By the fifth wave, the breach had been made, and Cribb urged the remaining crews to come lower and finish the job. By the end of the attack, they had achieved a breach of more than 100 yards, and the water was flooding in on cue.

The Allied ground forces, however, were in no rush to advance. Indeed they waited until Bomber Command had mopped up the remaining gun positions and forced the Germans to concede defeat before finally making their move at the end of the month, the day after the final raid was led and marked by Pathfinders of 5 Group. Only two Pathfinders, a Lancaster from 8 Group and Mosquito from 5 Group, became casualties during the Walcheren campaign: Flying Officer Lawrence Croft of 582 Squadron was shot down on October 29, and his aircraft was lost without trace.

Only one Mosquito was lost, that of Flight Lieutenant Anthony St John RNZAF and his navigator Flying Officer La Verne Dick RCAF of 627 Squadron. They had been heard on R/T saying that a TI had exploded in the bomb bay and they were baling out. Both were killed, and Dick's body was never found.

Once again, however, it was really the LNSF Squadrons who suffered the worst, with 608

Squadron at Downham Market, for example, losing three aircraft and two crews in only three days. Among those killed was Flight Lieutenant Reginald Gardner whose aircraft crashed and exploded on the final approach on his way home from Wilhelmshaven. Sitting in the navigator's seat was Flying Officer Oswald Sweetman DFM, who had won his spurs fighting in the Middle East.

There was a similar air of resignation at Gransden Lodge, home to 692 Squadron. It too lost three aircraft between October 13 and October 17, including the crew of Flying Officer Norman Hornby, lost without trace. They would lose another aircraft and one more skipper, Flight Lieutenant Lawrence Shackman AFC, over Hamburg before the month was out.

The Kiel canal was the scene of a particularly heroic incident that month involving a small mixed force of aircraft from 571 and 692 Squadrons on a 'gardening' expedition. (Gardening was the name given to mine-laying, the mines themselves being referred to as 'vegetables'.)

It was a dangerous occupation, flying at low level against a target strongly defended by flak, searchlights and balloons. One Mosquito, skippered by Squadron Leader 'Johnnie' Greenleaf, had just dropped its mine when it was hit by flak. The shell splinters killed the navigator

Peter Cribb and his father at Buckingham Palace in 1942. Peter has just been given the DFC from the king – the first of four awards for gallantry he would receive in a distinguished bombing career comprising more than 100 sorties.

(Pilot Officer Ken Rendell – described by one contemporary as 'the life and soul of the crew room') and seriously injured the pilot in the face and arm. Despite intense pain and fatigue, Greenleaf made it home to an emergency landing at Woodbridge. He received an immediate DSO. There were seven other immediate awards made.

A freak accident befell the crew of a 105 Squadron aircraft on the night of October 19/20. Flying Officer Leonard Whipp was at the controls of his Mosquito when shortly after taking off from Bourn they encountered technical difficulties with the aircraft, and decided to jettison the 4,000lb 'cookie' in the bomb bay. Unfortunately they did so at such a low altitude that as the bomb hit the ground and exploded it literally blew them out of the sky. A gallant crew thus became casualties in tragic circumstances, killed by their own bomb.

That same squadron had lost another crew at the start of the month, when a Mosquito XVI was one of only five aircraft taking part in an attack on Heilbronn. The pilot lost an engine over the target, making for a long journey home and a subsequent crash upon landing. Happily both he and the navigator survived, although injured.

There was similar relief for one of the other crews (this time from 109 Squadron) taking part in the same operation when both pilot and navigator were obliged to take to their parachutes over Allied-held territory. Both the pilot – Flight Lieutenant Russell – and his navigator returned to Little Staughton a week or so later.

Pathfinders lost eighteen aircraft in October, and the trend of falling casualties would continue. It also received further reinforcements in the guise of yet another Mosquito unit – 142 Squadron

ONE UP FOR PATHFINDERS

Ted Stocker joined the RAF in 1938 as one of Trenchard's 'Brats'. As one of the new batch of flight engineers, he began the first of an astonishing 108 operations in October, 1941, with 35 Squadron and was still with the squadron when it became part of Pathfinder Force. Later posted to 582 Squadron at Little Staughton, he flew as a spare bod on a number of master bomber trips, including several with the squadron commander, Peter Cribb:

Ted Stocker. One of only a handful of aircrew to complete more than 100 heavy bomber operations and the only flight engineer to win the DSO.

"I was flying with Group Captain Peter Cribb, 582 Squadron CO at that time. It was a daylight raid, and we were briefed to bomb the island of Walcheren on the Scheldt estuary. The idea was to make the island uninhabitable for the Germans by knocking a hole in the sea wall. It wasn't a big raid as far as aircraft was concerned. We stayed over the target for a couple of hours and they were sending in fifty main force aircraft every twenty minutes or so.

"We put the markers down on the sea front and gradually the bombers demolished part of the sea wall and eventually the water came flooding in. The best bit was that the last wave of bombers included 617 (Dambusters) Squadron with their 'special' bombs called Tallboys. The Dambusters were part of 5 Group, and obviously there was quite a rivalry between them and us. The dyke was breached before they arrived, so I had great fun in telling them to go home. One up for Pathfinders!

"It was also an interesting trip because there was only one anti-aircraft emplacement at Westkapelle, right on the tip of the island, and earlier – between, I think, the first and second wave – we lobbed a few smaller bombs in their general direction. We had the pleasure of seeing the brave Hun get on their bicycles and cycle down the main road straight through the middle of Walcheren Island to the mainland. That was very satisfying, seeing the Germans doing a runner."

TED STOCKER DSO, DFC
FLIGHT ENGINEER. 35 AND 582 SQUADRONS. 108 OPS.

– to share the burden of the nightly assaults on German targets by the Light Night Strikers. Wing Commander Bernard Nathan, formerly of 582 Squadron, was posted in to command, and the squadron began operating from Gransden Lodge on October 29.

Sadly some of those killed during the month were the most experienced; many had been operating from the start. One such character was Squadron Leader Des Kay DFC, a 109 Squadron stalwart shot down and killed on his eighty-fourth op while on the outbound leg. Kay, who was said to have a fatalistic attitude to operations, had started his flying career as a fighter pilot as one of the 'Few'.

NOVEMBER

Pathfinders were plagued by a series of accidents and incidents throughout the month prompted, in part at least, by the changing weather and the onset of winter. Some fourteen aircraft were lost (and a further four from 5 Group Pathfinders), and nearly all of them as a result of crashes.

There were red faces all round in the crew of a master bomber, Squadron Leader Alfred 'Cocky' Cochrane RNZAF, taking off from Upwood for an attack on Düsseldorf at the start of the month. Cochrane and his flight engineer were rather too keen to retract the undercarriage before the aircraft had actually left the ground (the engineer was a 'spare bod' and had apparently misunderstood his pilot's instructions), thus the aircraft sank onto the runway and skidded along for several hundred yards while some members of the crew threw themselves out. They were fortunate that no-one was injured or killed.

On its return from Gelsenkirchen on the night of November 10/11, a Mosquito of 608

Squadron flown by Pilot Officer James McLean spun in and crashed, almost certainly as a result of icing; a few days later another 608 Squadron aircraft also crashed following an engine failure, taking the Canadian pilot – Flight Lieutenant Stuart Webb – to his death. The navigator survived, although badly injured.

CAUGHT IN A FLAP

"To survive, you needed experience, good training and lady luck to make sure you weren't in the wrong place at the wrong time. You ate, drank and lived as a crew. You understood one another and knew how each of you would react and respond in particular circumstances. That's why we didn't like 'spare bods' in the crew. One occasion I recall we had a spare flight engineer and it nearly ended in disaster. Our pilot and flight engineer worked as a team, so that when Tom called 'flaps' after take-off, the flight engineer took the flaps up by five degrees. When he called flaps with the spare the fool took the flaps up completely and we very nearly crashed. Apparently the ground crews watched us with their fingers in their ears and were just waiting for the bang."

DOUG REED DFM
WIRELESS OPERATOR. 156 SQUADRON.
FIFTY-TWO OPS.

Even the most senior officers and experienced flyers sometimes misjudged their landings. Thankfully for the commanding officer of 156 Squadron, Wing Commander Donald Falconer DFC, AFC, he got away with his on November 16 on his return from Düren, when his aircraft landed slightly short of the runway and was seriously damaged as a result.

Indeed the raid from which he was returning is remarked upon specifically in the ORB as being 'unusual'. The American 1st and 9th Armies were approaching the Rhine – the last natural barrier preventing an all-out assault on the Fatherland. Three towns – Düren, Julich and Heinsberg – were earmarked for destruction in order to further disrupt communications and prevent the flow of reinforcements to the front line. Described as 'fortified positions', they were believed to contain significant stores. It was, as it happens, a savage attack, involving more than 1,000 aircraft of every heavy bomber group, in conjunction with an even greater number of US Fortresses and Liberators from the 3rd and 8th US Bombardment Commands.

Pathfinders marked the first two targets with ease in almost perfect bombing conditions, although of the 30 Mosquitoes involved, only six attacked the primary targets and 24 were abortive. Düren and Julich were virtually destroyed, and 3 Group – operating alone with their G-H blind bombing system – completed the hat-trick. Ironically, the American advance could not match the success of their airborne colleagues, and the infantry took many casualties.

Pathfinders suffered only one loss, from 109 Squadron. Warrant Officer Joseph Garcia-Webb was returning to Little Staughton having attacked Julich, but arrived to find the airfield sitting under a thick blanket of black cloud. Garcia-Webb opted to use a blind landing system based on the German Lorenz beam (known to the RAF as a standard beam approach or SBA) but just as he was nearing the runway his aircraft was seen to rise suddenly to avoid some high-tension cables at which point the aircraft stalled and crashed. Both Garcia-Webb and his navigator, Warrant Officer Robert Wendes, were killed.

Three aircraft – one each from 35, 139 and 571 – were lost on the night of November 18/19, all in crashes, following operations to Hannover. Of the three, Flying Officer Norman Blackband could consider himself particularly unfortunate, especially given his undoubted abilities as a pilot, having earlier earned the Air Force Cross for his skill in the air. Blackband was returning from Wanne-Eickel, where he had been one of thirty-two PFF Lancasters who had contributed to a most-successful attack. He misjudged his first attempt at landing and was obliged to overshoot, opting to go around again. In between making this decision and a second attempt, something went horribly wrong and the aircraft crashed into some woods not far from base. The mid upper and rear gunners were injured, but both survived; the rest of the crew perished in the crash. The skipper had earlier reported a problem with the flaps.

Blackband was not the only 35 Squadron casualty that month. On November 29, Flying Officer John Thorpe had been engaged on operations to Dortmund when he and his crew were lost without trace. Thorpe, who held the DFC for an operational record of not less than forty-seven sorties, had recently married a WAAF whose first husband had also been killed on operations. Some disapproved of wartime marriages, especially to aircrew, and some WAAFs – unfairly – were seen as a jinx to a man's survival.

Four Mosquitoes were lost between November 21 and 28, three as a result of accidents. Flying Officer Jack Campbell took off from Oakington in the late afternoon of November 21 for operations to Stuttgart. It was an all-Mosquito affair comprising twenty-nine aircraft. Two had to abort, one flown by Campbell.

He was over half way to the target when his aircraft was hit by flak. Unable to jettison the 4,000lb bomb they were carrying, he made for the emergency field at Manston where he touched down perfectly, but as the aircraft sped along the runway the 'cookie' suddenly fell off. There was the briefest sound of metal touching concrete and then it exploded. Fortunately the momentum of the aircraft carried them just far enough ahead of the blast, which caused the undercarriage to collapse. The Mosquito caught fire and the two men scrambled out. Although badly shaken, both Campbell and his navigator, Flight Lieutenant Arthur Cleaver, lived to fly and fight another day.

Pathfinders were involved in two major operations on the night of November 27/28, the smaller of the two forces sent to Neuss. Only seven out of the fourteen Mosquitoes attacked the primary target but they did their job well, as did the backers-up. Main force helped to start a good many fires in the central and western halves of the town, with the raid punctuated by frequent

The distinctive bulge beneath the Mosquito, adapted to carry a 4,000lb bomb.

Close up of a 'cookie' being winched into the belly of a Mossie. Note the safety pins still in place to stop the bomb from arming prematurely.

fierce explosions. One Mosquito was shot down, that of Flight Lieutenant Norman Williamson DFC of 109 Squadron. Williamson survived, but his navigator, Flying Officer Alfred Kitchen DFC, was not so fortunate; his body was washed ashore from the Ijsselmeer some three months later.

The number of targets now within Oboe range had increased, as mobile stations were established near the Allied front lines. A new method of Pathfinder attack was subsequently trialled on the last two nights of the month. The trials comprised a large formation of Mosquitoes divided into four, with each led by an Oboe-equipped aircraft. In case of equipment failure, four reserves followed on behind. The coking plant at Duisberg-Meiderich was singled out for one such trial with encouraging results. A reconnaissance aircraft over the target after the attack reported a huge column of brown smoke turning black, and rising through the cloud to a height of 10,000ft.

DECEMBER

Weather affected operations to a considerable extent in November, with operations being cancelled on six days and nine nights. Nevertheless, Pathfinders flew 2,641 operations, taking the grand total of sorties carried out since August 1942 to 35,082. It lost only nine aircraft.

December followed a similar pattern. Unfavourable weather led to the cancellation of all operations on eight days and nights, but the total number of operations carried out remained consistent at 2,677. The number of aircraft lost more than doubled to twenty-three, although a high proportion of this figure is attributed to a single disastrous raid towards the end of the month.

Bennett started the month, however, with a large-scale Mosquito raid on Karlsruhe, and crews were reported to be 'enthusiastic about the excellent concentration achieved'. Karlsruhe was visited again a few nights later by a much heavier force of more than 500 aircraft, and although the Mosquitoes on this occasion struggled, they still managed sufficiently well to contribute to an attack that did further damage to a target already on the verge of total annihilation. One 109 Squadron Mosquito failed to return, having collided with another aircraft at 30,000ft. The pilot, Johnny Liddle, and his navigator Albert Smith both made it out safely – Smith later suffered a stroke while recuperating in hospital. Doctors attributed this to the strain of operations.

This latter attack on Karlsruhe was one of ten heavy attacks mounted on German towns during the month, two were made on Bonn, and one each on Hagen, Karlsruhe, Soest, Osnabrück, Essen, Ludwigshafen, Ulm, Duisberg (inevitably), and Mönchengladbach. These attacks were all primarily in the first half of the month, for the second was taken up by attacks on railway targets for reasons that will become clear.

Of these heavy raids, the attack on Soest on December 5/6 was especially successful, as were the raids on Essen (December 12/13) and the IG Farben chemical factories in Oppau, in the northern part of Ludwigshafen (December 15/16). Hitler's armaments minister, Albert Speer, would later remark upon the accuracy of the raid on Essen. At the time, the Pathfinders were not convinced as to the effectiveness of their marking: cloud meant the raid developed into a pure skymarking affair; the few red TIs that had been dropped could not be seen, and the visual centrers held on to their greens. One bomb aimer flying as a visual backer-up with 7 Squadron said that there couldn't have been much of Essen left to clear out, and as it happened it proved to be the last main force attack to be mounted on the city.

Harris was making sure that no German city would be safe from his bombers so long as they continued to resist. The Germans, for their part, made sure that their attackers paid for their 'terror attacks' in blood. Two PFF aircraft were lost: Flying Officer Jack Kinman and his seven-man crew from 582 Squadron were all killed when their aircraft was hit by flak and exploded; a similar fate befell the 635 Squadron crew of Flight Lieutenant Norman Shaw. Again there were no survivors.

Bomber Command's first and only raid on Ulm was directed against the city's Magirus-Deutz and Kässbohrer lorry factories and comprised more than 300 aircraft, including a component of thirteen Mosquitoes and fifty-four Lancasters from Pathfinder Force. Bomber Command dropped nearly 1,500 tons of bombs in twenty-five minutes, and a square kilometre of the city was set ablaze. The 156

Mönchengladbach in a photograph taken on a Cook's tour after the war.

Squadron Lancaster of Flight Lieutenant Lindsay Cann DFC was the only casualty. Squadron colleagues believed it might have collided with another Lancaster lost that night (a 153 Squadron aircraft) as they descended through thick cloud over France. The gallant young officer was only twenty-three.

Another collision accounted for Flying Officer William Hearn and his crew during operations to Leuna on a busy night for Bomber Command which split their forces across three principal targets: Leuna; Osnabrück; and Giessen. Leuna, near the town of Merseburg in eastern Germany, boasted significant oil facilities, and this was the first (but by no means the last) time that the towns would appear in the aircrews' logbooks. Cloud made the job of the master bomber impossible, and bombing was chiefly carried out either on skymarkers or by means of navigational aids, making the results impossible to assess.

German flak grew in intensity, and a handful of fighters also put in an appearance. It was ironic, therefore, that of the six aircraft missing, one was lost through an engine fire, one through icing, two in a collision and only two as a result of flak. Hearn, of 635 Squadron, reportedly collided with a 460 Squadron aircraft and both aircraft fell apart. There were three survivors from the two crews.

Smaller raids involving heavy bombers were plentiful throughout the month, and not just against the 'traditional' targets on Harris's obligatory list. 'Tactical' objectives in direct support of the army included three unsuccessful attempts to breach the Urft dam near Heimbach, with the intention of preventing the enemy from smashing the dam themselves if the Allies opted to advance in that direction. The attacks only succeeded in blowing a small section off the top but no breach was ever made, and the Germans were indeed able to release large quantities of water at will.

Only one aircraft went down in these dam raids, a 582 Squadron Lancaster flown by Flight Lieutenant Art Green. He had taken part on the first attack on December 3 that had ended in farce, and obliged the master bomber, Squadron Leader 'Min' Mingard, to order main force to return home. Although there is no mention in the 8 Group ORB, some of the aircraft found themselves on the receiving end of an attack by the Luftwaffe's principal jet fighter, the Messerschmitt Me262. Although Art Green's crew included a 'guest' mid upper gunner (the regular gunner had shot himself by accident!), and that was none other than the squadron gunnery leader, Squadron Leader Frederick Grillage, they were still no match for the jet and were quickly despatched. Happily, six of the crew made it out, but Grillage was killed.

While the heavies did their work, the Oboe Mosquitoes and LNSF were frenetically busy, the latter mounting raids on every night when weather allowed. Bennett argued successfully for the need to increase the scale of his Mosquito capability and added 162 Squadron to his group in December, operating from Bourn. Wing Commander John Bolton DFC (later DSO), formerly of 608 Squadron and having served on the AOC's staff, was given command. The unit began operating almost immediately.

No fewer than six attacks were made on Hannover, four on Osnabrück, three on Berlin and Münster, two on Nuremberg and Hamburg, and one each on fourteen other towns including Bielefeld, Hanau, and Koblenz. These three have been singled out in particular because they led to the losses of a number of pilots, among them Flight Lieutenant James Brass RCAF of 105 Squadron (flew into high ground near home); Flight Lieutenant Sidney Brunt of 692 (overshot, crashed and caught fire on landing); and 105 Squadron's Warrant Officer Thomas Jefferson AFC (crashed using SBA but survived – helped no doubt by the fact he had been an SBA instructor! He later went on to win the DSO).

Berlin also proved typically deadly, claiming the lives of a 608 Squadron crew on December 6/7 (Flying Officer Graeme Weir and his navigator both killed) and Flight Lieutenant Charles Harrison of 139 Squadron (December 9/10) who crashed on his return to base. Two other aircraft, one each from 142 and 692 Squadrons had an eventful night, one being obliged to jettison the

162 Squadron in April 1945. Malcolm Sewell (seated centre), former commander of the Mosquito training unit, had only recently taken over as OC from John Bolton.

bombs through technical problems and the other by running out of fuel.

On December 16, the German army caught the Allied commanders completely off-guard by launching a significant armoured attack through the Ardennes in a campaign that would later be christened 'The Battle of the Bulge'. Once the Allies had regained their composure, they turned to Bomber Command for help, and Harris duly obliged by mounting a series of attacks on German airfields to suppress the potential use of German aircraft in support of ground troops and at railway marshalling yards and depots to prevent the re-supply of tanks and reinforcements to fuel the German advance.

Bingen was a new name for the crews and resulted in an extremely accurate raid on December 22 that succeeded in preventing any further movement by rail through the area. The destructive power of the main force 4,000-pounders was particularly noted, three explosions were seen in quick succession. No opposition was reported, although two PFF aircraft were lost, both from 405 Squadron. Flying Officer Joseph Tite DFC and three of his all-Canadian crew were killed; Flying Officer Vivien Woods DFC (and later Bar) and his crew survived a crash landing resulting from a jammed undercarriage.

Two major marshalling yards at Cologne were singled out for attention, Nippes and Gremberg. Both were attacked twice in quick succession. It was the attack in daylight on December 23 to Cologne/Gremberg, however, that December will probably be best remembered, for all the wrong reasons. Only thirty aircraft took part – twenty-seven Lancasters from 35 and 582 Squadrons and three Oboe Mosquitoes (two from 105 and one from 109 Squadron) – in a classic 'Heavy Oboe' attack. It was a total disaster. Two aircraft collided at the beginning, killing both pilots (Pilot Officer Richard Clarke and Pilot Officer George Lawson) and their respective crews. Over the target they arrived to find brilliant sunshine instead of the expected cloud, and there was confusion with regards to whether the attack would still be in formation or whether the Oboe run would be abandoned to allow the bombers to attack independently.

In the confusion, and as the bombers dutifully flew straight and level, the German predicted flak had a field day. To further the calamity, a staffel of German FW190 fighters arrived on the scene, led by one of the Luftwaffe's top experten and attacked in strength. As well as the two Lancasters lost at the beginning, a further four heavy bombers were shot down and a fifth abandoned, as well as a reserve Oboe Mosquito flown by Flying Officer Eric Carpenter DFC.

Bob Palmer (right), a future VC, while at Elementary Flying Training School (EFTS).

Of those who were shot down, Flight Lieutenant Walt Reif, an American, was killed along with four of his crew; Flight Lieutenant Peter Thomas DFC was killed along with two of his crew; and Flight Lieutenant Reg Hockley DFM and his crew all survived and were captured – with the exception of the flight engineer, Pilot Officer Ken Hewitt DFM, who was surrounded by a mob upon landing and shot. Two others in his crew had a miraculous escape, being caught in the fuselage of the aircraft as it broke apart and flat spun, carrying the two of them to earth, injured but alive.

The leader of the attack, Squadron Leader Bob Palmer DFC & Bar, was also killed along with his 109 Squadron navigator, Flight Lieutenant George Russell DFC and all but one of the 582 Squadron crew with whom they were flying. Palmer, on his 110th operation, would later be awarded a posthumous Victoria Cross, the citation describing his 'heroic endeavour … beyond praise'.

Palmer had swapped seats with the 582 Squadron pilot, Flight Lieutenant Owen Milne DFC, for the Oboe run, and had never heard the order to abandon. Also decorated that day was another future VC, Captain Ted Swales, who fought off multiple attacks from the marauding Focke Wulfs to bring his aircraft and his crew safely home.

Many men were left wondering why they deserved to live when so many of their friends had died. Another squadron of Pathfinders was similarly stunned by the loss of their commanding officer before the month was out. Wing

Owen 'Jock' Milne. Jock gave up his seat for Bob Palmer to fly the Oboe run for the attack on Cologne/Gremberg.

THE BEST CHRISTMAS PRESENT EVER

When war broke out in 1939 'Nick' Nicholson was a fourteen-year-old, obliged to work after the premature death of his father. Two years later, while working at the Blackburn Aircraft factory in Brough, he decided to join the RAF. After training at 1 Gunnery School, Pembrey, he arrived at Abingdon to be crewed up. After his first pilot didn't work out, he found himself flying with a brilliant New Zealander by the name of Pilot Officer 'Kiwi' Lawson, and ultimately posted to 35 Squadron, commencing operations in July 1944. By December 1944, they were a senior crew, and one of nine aircraft flying in the third formation for the attack on Cologne/Gremberg:

"The raid got off to a bad start when two of our squadron's Lancs collided over the Thames estuary. But our troubles had only just begun. The weather forecasters had promised 10/10th, or total cloud cover all the way to and over the target area in Cologne; however, just before we started our bomb run the cloud suddenly vanished completely and the sky was clear blue for miles.

"Sitting in the rear turret I couldn't see the thick wall of flak that we were fast approaching but suddenly it seemed as if every gun in Germany had opened up on us and it was then that we received the codeword – 'Cowboy' – which meant that we were to break formation and bomb independently.

"Just as we commenced the run our bomb aimer, Alan Card was hit in the face by flak and was temporarily blinded and deafened. At the same time our wireless operator, Ted Herod, volunteered to put his head into the astrodome to look out for fighters and almost immediately fell to the floor with his head covered in blood as the astrodome was hit by flak.

"Kiwi had to circle around the target again before Alan was in any fit state to continue the bomb run and I remember saying, 'I reckon we've had it!' The sky was literally full of flak – and I mean packed, and I could see enemy fighters circling around the perimeter of the flak zone waiting to pick us off, if by some miracle we managed to get through the target.

"By now Alan had recovered sufficiently and made a perfect bomb drop. Then the flight engineer, 'Eddy' Edmonson was hit on top of the head but fortunately for him the shrapnel hit his flying helmet which deflected the impact and thankfully he was not seriously injured. At the same time I had a lucky escape too when flak burst just to the side of my turret and a piece of shrapnel shot through and impacted behind my head just above my left shoulder – six inches to the right and I would have been a goner!

"Our Lanc was by now very badly shot up and limping along on three engines so I wasn't surprised when I heard Kiwi talking to an Allied airfield in Belgium asking for permission to make an emergency landing. The next thing I recall was him saying that he would try to make it across the channel and he contacted the emergency landing base at Manston to tell them we were coming in.

"As we approached the Kent coast our predicament worsened as five German Bf109s were seen closing in to finish us off. Miraculously, a flight of Mustangs was scrambled and escorted us into Manston without any problems. Despite having no brake pressure, and only three engines Kiwi managed to land the crippled Lancaster safely, bringing it to a halt just off the end of the long runway – fortunately the longest in England!

"When I got out Eddy and I started to count the holes . . . we lost count after 100 – and that was just on one side between the wing and my rear turret. Sadly that was the end of 'J' for 'Johnny'. Alan and Ted went off to hospital and both were awarded immediate DFCs.

"The next day I remember arriving back at Graveley where only one of our aircraft had returned and heard that the CO, Group Captain 'Dixie' Dean, an experienced and battle-hardened, marvellous man, had been very upset, asking: 'What have they done to my squadron?'

"On Christmas Day I celebrated the best present I've ever had – my life!"

LAWRENCE 'NICK' NICHOLSON DFM
AIR GUNNER. 35 SQUADRON. FIFTY-SEVEN OPS.

ORDER OF BATTLE

DECEMBER 1944

HEADQUARTERS 8 GROUP – HUNTINGDON

Graveley	35 Squadron	Lancaster
	692 Squadron	Mosquito
Oakington	7 Squadron	Lancaster
	571 Squadron	Mosquito
Wyton	128 Squadron	Mosquito
	1409 (Met) Flight	Mosquito
Bourn	105 Squadron	Mosquito
	162 Squadron	Mosquito
Gransden Lodge	142 Squadron	Mosquito
	405 (RCAF) Squadron	Lancaster
Upwood	156 Squadron	Lancaster
	139 Squadron	Mosquito
Downham Market	635 Squadron	Lancaster
	608 Squadron	Mosquito
Little Staughton	582 Squadron	Lancaster
	109 Squadron	Mosquito
Warboys	PFF NTU	Lancaster

Detached to 5 Group: 83, 97 and 627 Squadrons

Commander Donald Falconer of 156 Squadron had taken part in operations to Koblenz on December 29 as a primary visual marker. In the same attacking force, Flying Officer William Cornelius had been on his bombing run when his aircraft was hit and both the pilot and flight engineer wounded. Despite being in obvious pain, Cornelius executed a successful attack and made it home, in a feat that was to lead to the award of an immediate DFC.

The result of Cornelius's injuries was to have disastrous consequences for the rest of the crew. Less than two hours after returning from Koblenz, Falconer took the Cornelius crew, supplemented by the engineer leader, Flight Lieutenant William Bingham, to Cologne. Tragically, the aircraft received a direct hit, killing everyone on board. Falconer, from Concession, Southern Rhodesia, had completed fifty-five operations and was an experienced master bomber and long stop. He had earned his DFC as long ago as 1941 with 49 Squadron, and added the AFC for his contribution in producing well-trained crews from 14 OTU with whom he took part in the first 1,000-bomber raid and survived a mid-air collision! He had been in charge of the squadron for only five weeks. His place was taken temporarily (and then permanently) by the 'B' Flight commander: Wing Commander Thomas Ison DSO, DFC.

FAILED TO RETURN

With the Lancasters and Mosquitoes at Little Staughton, Norma Watts felt that she was at last taking 'an active part in the war', even after the excitement of being at Biggin Hill and serving alongside squadrons of Spitfires under the leadership of Group Captain 'Sailor' Malan:

"None of us would forget Squadron Leader Bob Palmer and Captain Ted Swales who had been awarded VCs posthumously. They were among the many who failed to return and remained on the crew list in flying control until it was certain that they would not be returning.

"Squadron Leader Donnelly from New Zealand was another who failed to return one night after a master bomber assignment. I had often talked with him about his family and how much he missed them. When I found out that he was missing I had to give in to my emotions and found myself in the 'Gubbins Room' downstairs shedding a few tears. Jack Watts happened to come in and put his hand on my shoulder, said how sorry he was that I had lost a friend, and comforted me as best he could. Despite his notorious reputation with the WAAFs, I found this reputation was completely unfounded. He proved to be a gentleman through and through, sharing and comforting me in my personal loss."

NORMA WATTS
WAAF (FLYING CONTROL)
LITTLE STAUGHTON.

Top: Bob Palmer had flown more than 100 trips when called upon to lead the disastrous daylight in which he lost his life.
Left: Norma Watts was determined to take an active part in the war.

CHAPTER 8
TOTAL VICTORY

JANUARY 1945

A new year might have given Harris the opportunity to try new things, but he remained steadfast in his opinion that bombing the Germans into surrender was what he had been fated to do. Some thought he simply lacked imagination; others that his obstinacy would never allow him – fully – to engage in a plan in whose effectiveness he did not wholly believe.

Actually, such generalisations are not entirely fair on the commander-in-chief, since a study of targets attacked in the last few months of the war shows that he did, in fact, go some way to meeting his primary instruction of neutralising the German war effort by destroying its transport and oil-producing infrastructure when conditions allowed (this being the crucial phase). He could also, with some justification, argue that even area bombing invariably led to the destruction of certain installations directly or indirectly linked to his two 'panacea' objectives.

In January, for example, the attacks on Ludwigshafen (389 aircraft), Hanau (482 aircraft), and Stuttgart (602 aircraft) all involved the destruction – either intentionally or by circumstance – of various railway installations or infrastructure; dedicated raids were also mounted on Leuna (587 aircraft), Zeitz (328 aircraft), Brüx (239 aircraft) and Duisberg (302 aircraft) – all of which had as their primary objective certain oil or synthetic oil-producing plants.

Indeed it was both an imaginative and necessary attack that opened the month when seventeen Mosquitoes from 128, 571 and 692 Squadrons set out to attack a series of fifteen railway tunnels nestling in the woods and hills of the Eifel between the Rhine and the Ardennes battle area. The purpose was, once again, to hamper German troop and armour movements. The method of attack was brutally simple, but needed incredible skill and nerves of steel to execute. The Mosquitoes had to dive down to around 150/200ft and then effectively 'lob' a 4,000-pound 'cookie' into the tunnel entrance. For the low-flying enthusiast, among them the CO of 571, Wing Commander Jerry Gosnell DSO, DFC, the brief was a busman's holiday and the attack achieved considerable success.

There were, however, casualties: one Mosquito was shot down, a 692 Squadron aircraft flown by Flight Lieutenant George Nairn and his navigator, Flight Sergeant Daniel Lunn. They had been unlucky; the aircraft in front of them had alerted the defences, and Nairn flew into the cross-fire. Both engines were set ablaze and the aircraft smashed into the surrounding hills. They had crashed in October, but on that occasion had lived to tell the tale. At the time of their deaths, they had logged some forty operations.

A further aircraft, skippered by Flight Lieutenant Leo Wellstead DFC, DFM of 128 Squadron, took off from Wyton to join the attack but never made it. An engine failure caused the aircraft to crash, killing Wellstead and his navigator, a thirty-three-year-old Scotsman, Flight Lieutenant George Mullan DFC.

It is remarkable, in the truest sense of the word, how the Mosquito crews bore the lion's share of operations during this period and – not surprisingly – suffered an alarming rise in the number of aircraft lost and aircrew killed. It is significant also in the number and diversity of targets being attacked.

On January 1/2 Flying Officer Henry Ross and Sergeant Herbert Cook of 571 Squadron were killed when their aircraft crashed on the homeward leg from Hanau. The next night, Flying Officer Frank Watson DFM was killed and his pilot captured when their 105 Squadron aircraft came

TUNNEL VISION

Flying Officer Bill Ball flew as the regular navigator to Flight Lieutenant Norman Griffiths, a former police clerk and pilot who had flown a twenty-eight-sortie tour with 15 Squadron in 1940. Bill kept a diary at the time:

"January 1: Up at 04.30 for second and final briefing. 'Griff' and I were one of four crews selected for this low-level daylight op, to drop a 4,000-pound bomb into the mouth of a railway tunnel in the Ardennes.

"Briefing revealed that German Panzer divisions under Von Rundstedt had thrust sixty miles into Allied lines and this bulge was causing concern. Pathfinder headquarters had studied the battle area and decided to paralyse the railways thus preventing supplies reaching the German troops. The tunnels were all behind enemy lines in the Ardennes sector.

"We were due off at 07.00. We had spent a lot of time studying the route – noting the spot heights, contours and landmarks etc. We had been briefed to approach from the south at the railway junction and run up to the target.

"The bomb was fitted with an eleven-second delay fuse, so that we could drop it in the mouth of the tunnel and get away before the whole thing erupted. It was cold and dark out at dispersal with thick frost on the ground, but a crisp clear morning, free from the mist and fog which had restricted flying for the last few nights.

"We were to fly in 'K' for King. We were both keyed up and anxious to get going as the hands of my watch reached h-hour. The green Aldis flashed its signal from control and we were away. First off at 07.02, we set course for Orford Ness, at 5,000ft. As we crossed the English coast daylight was just coming up on the eastern horizon.

"At Charleville, there was bright sunshine across the countryside. We cruised at 500ft and kept a watchful eye out for enemy fighters, but I still had time to notice the tiny villages huddled around a church in the wooded country of the Ardennes. The rooftops of the houses and chalets were covered in snow. We raced on at 300mph, now at 50ft. Suddenly we swept over a high railway/road bridge with only feet to spare. An old man driving his horse and cart across the bridge must have nearly died when he saw the RAF roundels on the Mosquito racing straight for him. He dived head first over the side of the cart, probably thinking that we were going to machine-gun him.

"At 100ft the ground simply raced beneath us like lightning. From the big railway junction, dead on ETA, the tunnel came up in a flash and we just could not position ourselves in time. We overshot the target and went round again, and this time ran up, dead in line, astonished that the ack-ack batteries had not been alerted. We rapidly reached the target, dropped the bomb and soared up almost vertically to get away from the blast. When we had gained height, we looked back and saw a column of brown/black smoke amid sizeable debris rumbling upwards – a mixture of bricks, shattered masonry and jagged keystone, rising, falling and scattering. Griff and I agreed that it would be some time before trains ran up that line.

"The excitement in the cabin was intense. We were elated and felt that we'd done a good job."

WILLIAM BALL
NAVIGATOR. 571 SQUADRON.

down on a raid to Bremen. It was a case of third time unlucky for this particular crew who had already survived two previous crashes, one less than forty-eight hours earlier. Flight Lieutenant James Howard RCAF and Flight Lieutenant Derek Williams of 139 Squadron were both lost when their aircraft crashed operating to Berlin. Both men had been decorated with the DFC but were no match for their adversary on this particular night, Oberleutnant Kurt Welter, in his Me262 jet.

A trip to Berlin, three nights, later led to the loss of Flight Lieutenant Bohuslav Eichler – a Czech pilot – and his navigator when an engine on their 142 Squadron Mosquito failed while they were attempting to land. A 571 Squadron aircraft was also abandoned over France although both pilot and navigator baled out and later returned to Oakington to resume operations. Another successful bale out was conducted, after a raid to Hannover, by the crew of a 162 Squadron aircraft on the night of January 7/8, both men similarly having to take to their 'chutes as a result of engine failure. When Hannover was, again, the proposed target for night operations on January 10/11, 128 Squadron suffered the loss of one of its most experienced pilot/navigator combinations – Squadron Leader Ronald Tong DFC, MiD (ex-57 Squadron) and Flight Lieutenant Marie Lagesse DFC (ex-139 Squadron). Their aircraft was seen to bank steeply shortly after taking off at which point all control was lost and the aircraft crashed. (Lagesse, from Curepipe, Mauritius, had been a barrister before volunteering for service overseas.)

An extraordinary series of mishaps befell the 105 Squadron Mosquito crews at Bourn when they lost three aircraft in as many days, all as a result of accidents, two where the undercarriage collapsed. Fortunately all of the crews were uninjured.

The worst night of all, however, for the Mosquitoes came on January 14/15. It was a busy one for Bomber Command, with the synthetic oil plant at Leuna featuring as the main event, alongside two smaller raids on the railway yards at Grevenbroich and a Luftwaffe fuel storage depot at Dülmen. There was also a force of more than eighty Mosquitoes detailed for Berlin, and a much smaller number despatched to Mannheim.

By the end of the night, an incredible nine Mosquitoes were downed and thirteen men killed, all from the raid to Berlin. Four of that number came from a single unit, 128 Squadron. Two of the aircraft were abandoned after running out of fuel and the other two were written off in landings. All could be attributed to the weather that was described as atrocious.

Two aircraft also failed to return to Upwood, home to 139 Squadron. Squadron Leader Robert Green – formerly of 156 Squadron – and his navigator, Flight Lieutenant John Robson DFC flew into a tree, a mile short of the runway at Little Staughton where they were attempting a beam-guided landing. It was a terrible end for a gallant pilot who had been badly wounded earlier in the war in an action that earned him the first of two DFCs.

Their squadron compatriots Flight Lieutenant Peter Drane DFC and Flying Officer Kenneth Swale DFC similarly clipped a hedge and crashed trying to get down at the neighbouring field at Thurleigh.

Of the three remaining aircraft destroyed, one ran out of fuel obliging the crew to bale out, one hit a tree attempting to land in Belgium, and one was shot down over the target area. The three crews – two from 692 and one from 571 Squadrons – were all killed, including the young sergeant, John Sturrock, who was only nineteen. He had successfully left the aircraft he was navigating but for some unknown reason released his parachute before reaching the ground.

One of the 'newer' squadrons suffered the loss of two aircraft on their return from bombing the oil installations at Sterkrade. Neither crew was hurt. Sadly, two days later the unwanted privilege of being the first 142 Squadron crew lost on operations fell to Squadron Leader Ralph Don DFC and his navigator, Flying Officer George Allan DFC, RCAF. The pair had set off from Gransden Lodge in the early evening to attack Kassel and their aircraft failed to return. At forty-three, Allan was one of the oldest Canadians killed in Bomber Command in the entire war.

This bad run of form for the Mosquito boys was at least tempered in part by the creation of another unit – indeed the last to join Pathfinder Force – 163 Squadron. Bennett chose as its commanding officer, acting Wing Commander Ivor Broom. A former 571 Squadron pilot and 128 Squadron flight commander, he had won a Bar to a DFC he gained in Malta for his part in the attack on the Dortmund-Ems canal and added a second Bar for the raid on the tunnels on

THE FINEST AIRCRAFT OF THEIR TIME

After flying training in the US and the obligatory OTU, Flying Officer Les Fletcher flew twenty-six operations with 100 Squadron at Waltham, earning his first DFC. A six-month spell instructing was followed by a conversion to Mosquitoes at MTU Warboys and a posting to 571 Squadron at Oakington as part of the Light Night Striking Force (LNSF). Here he was engaged in a series of spoof attacks, nuisance raids and the occasional 'gardening' trip, dropping mines in the Dortmund-Ems canal. Although not unique, Les is certainly unusual in having operational experience as a pilot on both aircraft:

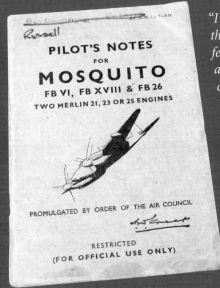

Pilot's notes were essential reading for pilots flying any new type for the first time.

"I was fortunate to fly the two finest bomber aircraft of the time – the Lancaster and the Mosquito. Of course you felt far safer in a Mosquito. It was beautiful to look at, and wonderful to fly. It was faster, very responsive on the controls and more manoeuvrable, and therefore less likely to be intercepted by German nighfighters.

"That's not to say that Mosquitoes were immune from danger; one night over Berlin I was being held in the usual searchlight cone and had just completed my bombing run when to my complete surprise I saw a stream of tracer passing over my head. My immediate reaction was to dive and turn into the direction of fire to force him to break off. I couldn't see the fighter as I was blinded by the searchlights but a black shape flashed over the cockpit uncomfortably close. It must have come within a few feet because the turbulence threw my aircraft all over the place, although he was probably as scared as we were.

"We went to Berlin thirteen times, but the target none of us fancied was Essen in the Ruhr. The Krupps works were always heavily defended. On a heavy-bomber squadron, you nearly always lost at least one aircraft on every raid, and sometimes as many as three. It was more noticeable when you lost a Mosquito crew because it didn't happen very often."

LES FLETCHER DFC & BAR
PILOT. 571 SQUADRON. SEVENTY-SIX OPS.

January 1. He brought with him as his squadron navigation officer his namesake, acting Squadron Leader Tommy Broom DFC, the pair of them being known with obvious humour as 'The Flying Brooms'.

The heavy crews of PFF were busy on nine nights across fourteen targets. Nuremberg was effectively neutralised on January 2/3, with the Pathfinders able to mark the target accurately in clear visibility and the light of a rising full moon. The centre of the city was destroyed, and severe damage inflicted in the industrial area comprising the M.A.N and Siemens factories. That same night some 500 HE bombs and 10,000 incendiaries were aimed at the IG Farben chemical factories in Ludwigshafen, causing production at the two main plants to cease.

Hannover was the target on January 5/6, the largest raid on the city for more than a year, and was followed a few nights later by Bomber Command's last major raid on Munich. The latter was spoiled for PFF by the loss of two Lancasters – one each from 405 and 635 Squadrons – that

EMERGENCY SIGNALLING

"Coming back from Hannover in January 1945, I was moving the turret from beam to beam, scanning the sky both for enemy fighters and indeed our own aircraft. There was always the risk of collision, especially if we had arrived early and were obliged to dog-leg which meant crossing the stream.

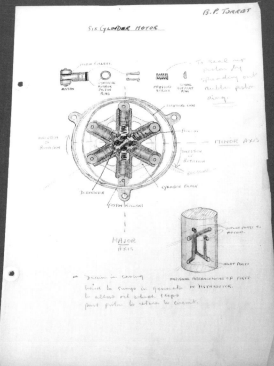

Boulton Paul turret mechanism as drawn by John Jackson during his gunnery instructor's course.

"It was pitch black outside, but even so, the ground is still darker than the skyline and I just caught sight of what I took to be a 190 or a 109 and told Tony (Tony Hiscock – our pilot) to dive starboard or corkscrew, I can't remember which, but whatever I told Tony to do he obeyed, and just as he dived the German opened fire. My turret was facing the other way at the time and I couldn't get my sights on him. The mid upper wouldn't have seen him as the aircraft attacked from below the starboard tailplane so his view would have been blocked.

"Diving or corkscrewing usually succeeded in losing the fighter but we kept looking for him. I knew we had been hit and the hydraulics damaged because my turret was put out of action and I was forced to crank the turret by hand. (The aircraft had actually been hit slightly before the main spar, shredding the port elevator, and narrowly missing the rear turret.)

"My intercom was also u/s and I was forced to use the emergency signalling lights on my control column that would flash in the cockpit to tell Tony whether to dive to port or starboard. Tony kept corkscrewing for some time until we thought we were safe, and when we were about half way across the North Sea I left my turret and made my way to the rest bed where I stayed for the remainder of the flight."

RUPERT NOYE DFC
AIR GUNNER. 156 SQUADRON. SEVENTY-TWO OPS.

collided in mid-air. There were no survivors from either crew.

The Canadians at Gransden lost another of their aircraft and the crew of Flight Lieutenant Harold Payne as it assisted in the marking of the Braunkohle-Benzin synthetic oil plant at Zeitz. And there was yet another casualty before the month was out when Flying Officer Franklin Cummer, an American, was shot down taking part in a raid to Stuttgart. PFF lost two further aircraft that night, including a 156 Squadron Lancaster flown by Flight Lieutenant James Freeman RCAF who was a little over half way through his Pathfinder tour.

Unusually, at this stage in the war, every one of the heavy-bomber squadrons in 8 Group lost at least one aircraft in January. Flying Officer Louis Friedrich, a Kiwi of 7 Squadron was shot down by a nightfighter over Hannover on January 5/6, while Flying Officer Ken Potts DFC of 35 Squadron fell victim to flak. (Potts had won his DFC on his first tour with 51 Squadron for bringing his badly-damaged Halifax back from Venlo and carrying out a nearly-impossible landing on one engine. He had been one of the pilots to survive the calamitous Cologne/Gremberg raid just before Christmas.)

Two Lancasters were lost to 582 Squadron: one, flown by Flying Officer Patrick McVerry, had to be abandoned over Allied lines on their return from a harrowing trip to Zeitz when their aircraft was hit by a combination of flak and fighters, and the rear gunner mortally wounded. McVerry and several of his crew received immediate awards for gallantry. The second aircraft fell in an accident. They almost lost a third, when the Lancaster of Flying Officer Frank Lloyd was struck by 'friendly' bombs from above over Leuna, causing significant structural damage. He gave the order to bale out but somehow regained control of the aircraft and rescinded his command, although not before one

Frank Lloyd in front of his favourite Lancaster, the veteran 'P' Peter.

of the navigators – David Mansel-Pleydell – had already gone through the hatch. With enormous physical effort, Lloyd managed to coax his bomber home and landed at Manston. He received an immediate DFC.

As well as Flight Lieutenant Robert Clarke RAAF, killed in the collision with Flying Officer Leslie Sparling, 635 Squadron also lost the crews of Flight Lieutenant Ivor 'Misty' Hayes and Flight Lieutenant Jimmy Rowland RAAF. Hayes was shot down having completed more than fifty operations and spent the remainder of the war as a guest of the Germans. All of his crew survived. Rowland also survived, possibly as a result of being thrown clear when his aircraft broke up in mid air following a collision. Four of his crew also made it out, only to be shot upon landing.

The greatest tragedy of all, however, fell to the Canadian squadron who lost four crews in January. Although ironically it was a quintessential Englishman – Wing Commander Kenny Lawson DSO & Bar, DFC – whose death was perhaps the most significant. Lawson, a supernumerary at 405 Squadron, had set out to bomb Nuremberg when his aircraft was intercepted by a nightfighter flown by Hauptmann Kurt-Heinz Weigel. In the attack, the port wing tanks were set on fire and although the aircraft flew on for a few short moments, it suddenly went into a spin and exploded in mid air. The flight engineer and rear gunner made it out safely, but the rest of the crew – including Kenny Lawson – were killed. He was believed to have been flying his ninety-eighth operation.

By the end of January, PFF had taken the total number of sorties carried out since their formation to 39,722. The pace was unrelenting.

FEBRUARY 1945

February proved to be an eventful month for Bomber Command, a month in which Harris took the decision to give a new generation of senior officers an opportunity to experience wartime command. Air Vice-Marshals Rice of 1 Group, Carr of 4 Group and Cochrane of 5 Group were all replaced in February; significantly, Bennett was not rested. The RAF, it was said, had no plans for Pathfinder Force once the war was over.

For the time being, however, there was still plenty to do. With some 3,131 sorties carried out, February was far busier than January – and far more controversial. It also spelled the end for

FIRST OUT – LAST HOME

David Mansel-Pleydell acting the clown. David began flying with Frank Lloyd after his regular skipper was killed in action.

David Mansel-Pleydell was a volunteer reserve officer who had won the DFC in May 1944 with 15 Squadron having completed 'very many sorties against strongly-defended targets such as Berlin, Hamburg and Essen'. After his first tour and a period of rest, he joined Pathfinder Force and was posted to 582 Squadron as the regular navigator to Squadron Leader Owen Milne DFC. 'Jock' Milne had been lost a few weeks earlier in the Cologne/Gremberg fiasco. The loss had unnerved him. On the night of January 14, he was flying with Flying Officer Frank Lloyd, a 'B' Flight pilot on his fourteenth trip with 582 Squadron:

"Quite honestly I had the screamers. I knew I was going to get the chop and I had locked all of my valuables in a top drawer and left the key at intelligence. I kept telling myself that I had had that feeling once before and everything had been OK.

"Fifty miles from the target we were eight minutes early; when we got there we were two minutes late. I had just pronounced the magic words 'bombs gone' when the party started. There were two heavy thuds and the intercom went dead. The aircraft went into a dive and started to vibrate quite a bit. We seemed to be diving almost vertical and away up in the corner I saw the little man with the reaper, very clearly. He was grinning and sharpening his knife!

"I grabbed my 'chute which had rested for over forty trips on the bomb sight computer box, and clipped it on without any difficulty. Then I turned and looked up into the cockpit. The pilot was wrestling with the controls but the engineer was standing as though all was well or soon would be. We went on diving for what seemed an eternity.

"Though it seemed hours since we had been hit I expect that it can't have been more than a few minutes. My thoughts were suddenly interrupted by a shout from the engineer ('Timber' Woods), and looking up I saw his face lit up by the starlight, looking very scared. 'Dave, jump, jump' he screamed. I guessed that it was no time for argument and disconnecting my intercom I pulled in the escape hatch and tried to jettison it. It stuck in the gap and before I tried to pull it clear I checked my 'chute. Then I managed to pull the hatch clear and facing to the rear I dropped out.

"As I fell clear of the aircraft to the starboard quarter I looked up. All the engines appeared to be turning and I could see no damage. The night was surprisingly bright. When I saw that I was clear [of the Lancaster] I pulled the ripcord and with a snap the 'chute tore up in front of my face and I came to a sudden stop. As my own aircraft roared into the night there was a deathly silence all around and it was obvious that we must have been the last on the target and were all by ourselves.

"I seemed to be hanging in the air and there was no sensation of descent. As I hung there a star shell came up not so very far away and lit up the sky. I felt very vulnerable. After what seemed hours I found myself in cloud and not so long afterwards I saw the ground only a few feet from me and coming up at me very fast. I just had time to draw myself into a ball before I hit the ground. It was very hard, and there was a sharp frost. I must have passed out for when I came to I was lying on my back with an agonising pain at the base of my spine.

"I must have panicked for I undid my harness and throwing my helmet away I climbed up and tried to run. However, my legs gave way beneath me and I crawled until I was exhausted."

DAVID MANSEL-PLEYDELL DFC
NAVIGATOR. 582 SQUADRON. FORTY-NINE OPS.

MASTER BOMBER – KENNY LAWSON

John Mitchell, a VR officer who completed a tour of operations with 58 Squadron, met Ken Lawson at a specialist navigation (Spec.N) course in Port Albert, Ontario in March 1941. Lawson had himself just completed a tour with 149 Squadron, and was a flight lieutenant DFC. As graduates, they could both expect to go back into the training machine of their respective commands but instead were nominally attached to the British Air Commission in Washington DC:

> "Kenny was a few years older than me. We were both Londoners and ex-VR entrants; and both of us had been in jobs before the war, so with similar interests we became friends, strengthened by our post-course meetings in Washington when our visits coincided. He lived in Ealing with his widowed mother. He also had an uncle and aunt living in Philadelphia who, in the summer months, went to their residence in New Jersey. I always enjoyed his relatives' hospitality with him, both in their apartment in Philadelphia and at Allenhurst.
>
> "Kenny returned to the UK before me and was to join 156 Squadron as a navigator, beginning his long period in the PFF. I had returned to the Air Ministry in July 1942, but sought further experience wherever I could. Later, meeting up with Kenny in London I badgered him successfully to fix me up with some supernumerary flying at RAF Warboys in March, 1943. He had a strong, outgoing personality; cheerful and optimistic, and with a strong hatred of Nazi Germany and all its works he seemed fearless in his approach to operational flying. So he proved a splendid navigator companion.
>
> "After his second tour, as a navigator, and now with his first DSO, he persuaded Bennett that he should be given a chance to become a pilot. Not content with two tours as a PFF navigator, Kenny Lawson went on to almost complete his second tour as a pilot, before being shot down and killed. He was to have been my elder son's godfather – born on December 29, 1944 – when I was in Athens at the time of the Communist uprising.
>
> "I had lost a stalwart friend. He was a powerful personality, strong leader, calm and confident and an inspiration to his crew and squadron. He would have gone far when peace came."

JOHN MITCHELL LVO, DFC, AFC
TWENTY-THREE OPS (1940/41) PLUS 1PFF WITH 156 SQUADRON.

two noteworthy master bombers, a station commander, and the award of the third and final Pathfinder Victoria Cross of the war.

But the month started with what had now become a familiar story: the loss of a series of Mosquitoes to accidents, crash landings and collisions. Only one was actually shot down: a 627 Squadron Mosquito taking part on an all-5 Group raid on Siegen on the night of February 1/2.

The next night, Bomber Command conducted its one and only large-scale attack on Wiesbaden, in complete cloud cover, although most of the bombing hit the town. Harris committed almost 500 aircraft to the attack, using the balance to raid Wanne-Eickel and Karlsruhe with only limited success. In the four raids in which the 'heavies' of PFF had taken part, they had come through unscathed. It was a blow, therefore, to lose two of their number in a comparatively small raid on the Prosper benzol plant at Bottrop on February 3/4 – both antipodeans and both from Upwood. Flight Lieutenant John Evans DFC, an Australian, was shot down by a nightfighter – and possibly by the ace of aces, Wolfgang Schnaufer. Four of his crew were killed, including Warrant Officer Frederick Parr DFM, an ex-Halton apprentice. The second 156 Squadron aircraft to go was that flown by Flight Lieutenant Maurice Spinley DFM, MiD RNZAF; only the rear gunner made it out alive.

Pathfinders lost eight aircraft over the next five days until, on February 13/14, they were briefed to attack Dresden.

OVER DRESDEN AT 500 FEET

Flying Officer Ken Oatley.

Ken Oatley's journey to Pathfinders had been somewhat eventful. Originally trained as a pilot (he had about 100 hours on Tiger Moths and Oxfords) he was eventually washed out as being, apparently, 'inclined to over confidence'. He remustered as a navigator and after training in South Africa was posted to 106 Squadron at Metheringham. Unfortunately his pilot went on a 'second dickey' trip with a crew on their last operation and all were killed.

With no pilot, the crew was split up. Ken went to Swinderby and was assigned to another pilot but that partnership didn't work out either. After one particular heavy landing, the instructor nodded to Ken and muttered 'rather you than me mate' which somewhat sealed the pilot's fate. Ken and the others refused to fly with him, and were threatened with court martial. Posted to Scampton, Ken met another new pilot, Flying Officer Jim 'Jock' Walker, and they were sent to Woodhall Spa. Their first op was to L'Isle Adam in August 1944.

On the night of February 13, 1945, Jock and Ken were one of eight 627 Squadron Mosquito crews tasked with marking the city of Dresden, in the east of Germany. The marker leader was Flight Lieutenant Bill Topper DFC:

"Climbing towards Holland and half way across the North Sea my Gee box started playing up and then packed in altogether. I had worked out the winds but did not feel confident that I could rely on them, and so decided to give Loran a go. Loran (long-range navigation) was a new device that had only just been fitted. None of us had much experience of it but I didn't have much choice. More by luck than judgment, the graticules on the Loran chart ran almost parallel to our own track, so I thought it might be reasonable to home along this line as we very often did on our return to base on Gee.

"I switched on and saw the expected picture of an uncut lawn; the trick was to pick out the longest piece of 'grass' and apply the reading to the chart. It appeared reasonably OK so when we arrived at the chosen graticule, turned onto it and, following the strobes, I gave as limited changes of direction as possible, and kept a rough air plot. Working out what time we should be at the 'stand off' point, I started to switch over to the intersecting graticule, eventually it came up on the screen and the fix was made; we should be there.

"At the appropriate moment I told Jock to do a rate one turn and to my relief I could see the first flares going down about three or four miles away. Jock went like the clappers down to 2,000ft and immediately identified the aiming point, which was the middle one of three sports'dromes. We were just turning into a dive and on the verge of pressing the R/T button to announce 'Marker Two Tally Ho' when the marker one, Bill Topper, beat us to it.

"We followed Bill in and put six markers in the stadium, and then headed for home, making a very low-level run across the city at little more than 500ft and almost hitting the cathedral spires. It was like daylight and you could quite clearly see the beautiful old buildings below us; there was no flak but quite a few bombs falling down around us.

"We flew home on dead reckoning and nearby managed to pick up a rather faint Gee signal which was sufficient to get us back safely. I never did let on to Jock how we got to Dresden."

KEN OATLEY
NAVIGATOR. 627 SQUADRON.

The background to the raid on Dresden has largely been obscured and forgotten over time, partly because of the horror that the attack evoked after the event. It is important, however, that Dresden is not seen as an attack in isolation, but rather the continuation of a policy, one part of which required Bomber Command to mount raids in support of the Allies' advance. By the beginning of 1945, this had included discussions about how the British and Americans could support their Russian allies, given that by the start of February, the Russian army was but fifty miles from Berlin.

The cities of Berlin, Chemnitz, Leipzig and Dresden – all in the east – were discussed in a series of meetings and memoranda at the very highest level. All were viable targets, singled out as major administration and control centres crucial for the deployment of troops and armour to the front. Other targets – Stettin and Zagreb – were added to the list, and at the famous Argonaut Conference at Yalta, a final list was agreed and sanctioned by the British, US and Russian chiefs of staff and fully supported by those countries' respective leaders. Operation Thunderclap – as the series of attacks was to be called – was given the green light. Intelligence suggested (wrongly as it transpired) that large volumes of troops and resources were being concentrated in and around Dresden, and so Dresden immediately rose to the top of the list.

The attack on Dresden was divided into two raids: the first was carried out in cloud by 5 Group, with Wing Commander Maurice Smith DFC – part of the specialist Pathfinder team at 54 Base – detailed as master bomber supported by Mosquitoes of 627 Squadron. Although the marking was accurate, and some 800 tons of bombs dropped on the target, the raid achieved only moderate success.

The second raid followed three hours later, by which time the cloud had cleared. Lancasters of 1, 3, 6 and 8 Groups under the direction of Squadron Leader Charles de Wesselow DFC & Bar as master bomber and Wing Commander 'Speed' Le Good AFC as his deputy (both from 635 Squadron and both later decorated with the DSO) had more success. More than 1,800 tons of bombs were dropped with great accuracy, and a firestorm tore through the narrow streets of the city consuming everything in its wake. Returning bomber crews spoke of the target area being one mass of fires, and actually being able to feel the heat from the inferno even at 18,000ft.

With the city numbers swollen by refugees fleeing the Russian advance, the number of dead may have exceeded 50,000. Only six Lancasters were lost, which was surprising given the amount of flak and fighters engaged. The aircraft of the deputy master bomber, for example, was hit several times, taking out the port engine and punching a large hole in the port wing. The one Pathfinder Lancaster missing was from 405 Squadron. The pilot survived but the rest of his eight-man crew perished.

Operation Thunderclap continued the next night with yet another two-phase attack, this time on Chemnitz and without 5 Group support. Again the bombers arrived to find the target covered in cloud, but this time it did not clear and the city was spared the damage that might have been inflicted had conditions been more benign. Many of the bombs fell in open country and thirteen aircraft did not survive.

Pathfinders emerged largely unscathed apart from one Lancaster in the first wave from 635 Squadron flown by Flight Lieutenant John Cowden DFC. Cowden, a second-tour man, who was described by his squadron commander as 'invincible', fell victim to Hauptman Kurt-Heinz Weigel (the victor of Kenny Lawson) for his fourth and what transpired to be his final victory. Every member of the crew, with the exception of the forty-three-year-old mid upper gunner Flight Lieutenant James Davidson, had been decorated, including the navigator/air bomber, Squadron Leader Robert Boddington who had twice been awarded the DFC. Every one of them was killed except the rear gunner, Flight Sergeant John McQuillan. He was under the impression that they had been shot down by a Me262 and there were indeed other reports of 'rocket fighters' in the area that night.

Minor operations and small-scale raids kept Pathfinder Force occupied for the next few

CALLING CARDS

Я англичанин

" Ya Anglichánin " *(Pronounced as spelt)*

Пожалуйста сообщите сведения обо мне в Британскую Военную Миссию в Москве

Please communicate my particulars to British Military Mission Moscow.

ID cards in Russian.

With the bomber battle moving further eastwards in support of the Russian advance, and Russian soldiers said to fire first and ask questions later, aircrew were issued with an interesting means of immediate identification should they be shot down: a Union Jack with Russian words printed on the reverse requesting that their particulars be immediately communicated to a higher authority.

days with only limited success. The raid on the synthetic oil plant at Bohlen on February 19/20 was typical of the period: damage to the target by more than 250 bombers was described as being 'superficial', probably because the aircraft of the master bomber, Wing Commander Eric Benjamin DFC & Bar of 627 Squadron was shot down by flak just as the raid was getting under way. Benjamin had converted to Mosquitoes from Lancasters, having previously flown with 61 Squadron. He and his navigator, Flying Officer John Heath DFM were both killed.

The 'heavies' continued to lose a number of crews over the next few nights: 156 Squadron lost Flight Lieutenant Des Pelly and his crew over Düsseldorf on February 20/21. Pelly survived as did four of his crew. That same night, a 405 Squadron Lancaster flown by Squadron Leader Harold Marcou DFC, AFC was shot down over Dortmund. All baled out successfully, but unfortunately the flight engineer, George Bolland DFM, was killed.

From Oakington, 7 Squadron lost the crew of Flight Lieutenant James Liddell on February 21/22 on the first and only large Bomber Command raid on Worms that destroyed much of the town's industry. Liddell and his mid upper gunner survived.

That same night, attacking Duisberg, 35 Squadron had two of their number downed, both extremely-experienced men. The Lancaster of Flight Lieutenant Frank Tropman DFC – a veteran of some sixty-two operations – was hit by flak, obliging him to crash land but only after the rest of his crew had baled out. The aircraft burst into flames and rescuers were unable to reach the pilot before the fires consumed him.

The pilot of the second aircraft, Flight Lieutenant James 'Bluey' Osmond DFC – who had survived some ninety-one operations – was more fortunate. His aircraft was attacked by a German nightfighter and the starboard engine and wing set on fire. The order was given to bale out, which all did so successfully with the exception of the mid upper gunner, Flying Officer Bert Golden, who had been killed in the initial burst of fire. (Osmond survived the war only to be killed in a tragic motorcycle accident in 1948. He was then only twenty-four.)

Indeed this was a bad night for losing experienced crews: the Pathfinders on loan to 5 Group attempted to breach the Mittelland canal near Gravenhorst, and in clear visibility believed the attack to be wholly satisfactory. But for such a small raid there were heavy casualties: nine Lancasters were shot down and a further four crashed behind Allied lines. One of those was captained by Group Captain Anthony Evans-Evans DFC, the larger-than-life station commander at Coningsby. He was in charge of an 83 Squadron aircraft and had with him most of the section leaders as his crew, including Squadron Leader William Wishart who was twenty years his junior, and had won the DSO and two DFCs in just over twelve months.

The only survivor, the rear gunner Pilot Officer Eddie Hanson DFC, recalls a thump as the aircraft was hit, followed by intense heat and an orange light. The port wing and engines were torn away and the aircraft went into a fatal spin. Hanson baled out. The aircraft crashed into a farmhouse, with the rest of the crew still trapped in the fuselage.

An accurate daylight attack on Essen on February 23 was followed that night by a raid on Pforzheim which – in the Bomber Command habit of naming all cities after fish – was codenamed Yellowfin. The raid was a controlled Musical Parramatta, carried out at low level. The blind illuminators' flares were released around accurately-placed Oboe target indicators, enabling the master bomber, his deputy and the primary visual markers to identify the aiming point with ease, and almost immediately after the first of more than 1,800 tons of bombs began falling.

Although Pforzheim has not attracted the same notoriety as the raid on Dresden just a few days before, perhaps it might have done given the catastrophic damage wreaked in such a terrifyingly short space of time. More than eighty percent of the town's built-up area was destroyed in a little over twenty minutes.

The attack has achieved its place in history, however, because of the heroics of the master bomber, Captain Edwin Swales DFC. Ted Swales, a South African Air Force pilot flying with 582 Squadron, had been the master bomber a few days earlier over Chemnitz. This raid had proved frustrating but not so the attack on Pforzheim, which he controlled to perfection.

In the course of his duties, however, and while orbiting the target, he was attacked and fatally hit in a series of German nightfighter attacks. (His probable victor was Oberfeldwebel Günther Bahr of 1/NJG6.) Despite severe damage to his aircraft, Swales managed to keep it aloft for some time until he had regained Allied airspace, whereupon he ordered his crew to bale out. Before the pilot could make it out himself, however, the aircraft crashed and Swales was killed. For saving the lives of his crew, and for his masterly control of the raid, Swales was awarded the Victoria Cross – the third and final VC earned by a member of Pathfinder Force (and the last to Bomber Command in the war).

Bennett later wrote: 'PRU cover of the target has subsequently proved that the attack was one of the most concentrated and successful of the war. He (Swales) showed heroism beyond praise in sacrificing his own life in order to ensure the safety of his crew.'

Swales's Lancaster was not the only PFF aircraft lost that night. The Light Night Striking Force was up in large numbers, with seventy Mosquitoes detailed to attack Berlin. They included the 608 Squadron aircraft of Flying Officer Robert Doherty DFC who failed to return. Doherty had flown not less than sixty-five operations.

Two further Mosquitoes fell to accidents before the month was out and two in combat, including another 608 Squadron crew missing over Berlin. Perhaps the most noteworthy loss was that of Squadron Leader Robert McLaren DFC of 1409 Met Flight – the only one that the 'weather men' suffered throughout the whole of 1945.

The logbook of Clive Dodson. Note the entry for February 23. He owes his life to his captain, Ted Swales.

MARCH 1945

In March 1945, according to the figures recorded in the 8 Group ORB, Pathfinders carried out a total of 4,285 sorties of which approximately half can be attributed to the LNSF. The total weight of

Record breaker. The tally of ops on this 1409 Squadron Mosquito (LR503) says it all.

A LONG WAY FROM HOME

Flight Lieutenant Gordon Blake.

Gordon Blake was nav two in the crew of one of the most effective but least known master bombers, Squadron Leader Norman 'Min' Mingard, flying some seven master bomber raids. Although born in Wallasey, Gordon went out to Africa with his parents when he was only three, joining the RAF at Eastleigh in Nairobi when he was eighteen. By the time he returned to the UK for service over the war-torn skies of Western Europe, he found adjusting to the British way of life somewhat awkward:

"When I arrived in Scotland at Gourock aged nineteen I discovered that I had in fact been commissioned before leaving Cape Town and so need not have spent all that time at the back end of the boat! I was lucky to have been crewed with Min who was one of the very best pilots. Indeed he is the reason I am alive today. I was the youngest in the crew, and admit that I found the whole thing a little daunting, and some of the English more than a little strange. Coming from Nairobi, however, I think that the rest of them thought I was the 'different' one.

"It was always good to keep in touch with other pals from Kenya but also difficult when you heard that yet another one of your school friends had been lost. I remember four of my friends being killed at different times and on various squadrons. It was difficult too when you made friends with others like the South African Ted Swales who then went missing. Being an officer had its advantage but it also had its downsides too. I didn't like that I could not take a friend of mine into the mess, for example, for a drink, because he was 'only' a sergeant, and we had to head off for a pub in St Neots instead.

GORDON BLAKE DFC
NAV TWO. 582 SQUADRON. FIFTY-SIX OPS.

heavy explosives that were dropped achieved a rather symmetrical 6,666 tons.

Perhaps not surprisingly the majority of aircraft that crashed, were shot down or were otherwise missing throughout the month were Mosquitoes: six in the first week. The only deaths, however, came from a 109 Squadron aircraft flown by Flight Lieutenant Alfred Payne. He and his navigator, Flight Lieutenant John Evans had been engaged on operations to Hallendorf on the night of March 5/6 and successfully attacked the aiming point. They then headed for Brussels-Melsbroek and crashed attempting to land. Both were killed.

The same squadron suffered the loss of another aircraft and crew the following night, when aircraft from 109 and 105 Squadrons were briefed to Oboe mark motor transport and troop concentrations near Wesel. Squadron Leader George Smith was just in the process of taking over the lead formation of six aircraft when he collided with one of their number and dived into the ground, taking both the pilot and navigator to their deaths.

Two Mosquitoes also perished from Bourn. Wing Commander Thomas Horton DSO, DFC & Bar RNZAF

Thomas Horton was an extremely popular pilot and flight commander who had flown daylights in Bostons.

landed with one engine stopped on his return, bounced heavily, and damaged his aircraft beyond repair. Squadron Leader Robert Burrell was just crossing the East Anglian coast when his aircraft was intercepted and shot down – by one of our own nightfighters. Happily for Burrell, both he and his navigator made it out just moments before their aircraft hit the ground. (Unhappily the same station lost another aircraft that month flown by Squadron Leader Leonard King, an old-Cranwellian, on his maiden operation with the squadron.)

The raids on Berlin accounted for a 128 Squadron aircraft shot down on March 7/8 – Squadron Leader John Armstrong, a thirty-one-year-old Canadian and his navigator were killed – and the death of Flight Lieutenant Alexander Waugh, an Australian from 692 Squadron on March 11/12. Two aircraft were lost on March 17/18, one each from 139 and 142 Squadrons, and a further aircraft from 162 Squadron the following night made an emergency landing at Woodbridge. Although the crew in this case got away with little more than a dent in their pride, death was never far away. Flying Officer Arthur Drake, navigator to Flying Officer John Rees of 163 Squadron, was killed when his skipper was forced to return early and crashed just short of the runway. From 692, the NCO crew of Warrant Officer Ian MacPhee and Flight Sergeant Albert Sullivan took off from Graveley in the early evening and never returned.

Worse was to follow and Berlin once again proved the graveyard for some of PFF's most experienced crews. On March 23/24, sixty-five Mosquitoes were sent to the German capital and two – both from 139 Squadron – failed to return. The two missing pilots – Flight Lieutenant Robert Day DFC and Flight Lieutenant Stanley Searles DFC had some 175 operations between them. Their respective navigators were also experienced men. On March 26/27, Flight Lieutenant Harold Tattersall DFC, who had been one of the select group chosen to take part in the New Year tunnels raid, collided with another Mosquito that had failed to clear the runway on landing but survived without injury. His aircraft, however, was written off.

Three more Mosquitoes went down over Berlin on March 27/28 on a disastrous night for the Pathfinders in which a further two aircraft were lost on other targets, making five in all. The dead included Flight Lieutenant Eric Vale MiD, an Australian with 692 Squadron who was believed to

Gordon Hudson whose luck ran out with the end of the war in sight.

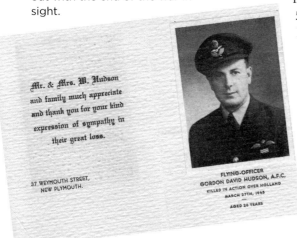

Mr. & Mrs. W. Hudson and family much appreciate and thank you for your kind expression of sympathy in their great loss.

37 WEYMOUTH STREET, NEW PLYMOUTH.

FLYING-OFFICER
GORDON DAVID HUDSON, A.F.C.
KILLED IN ACTION OVER HOLLAND
MARCH 27TH, 1945
—
AGED 26 YEARS

be on his seventieth operational sortie. They also included Flying Officer Gordon Hudson AFC of 571 Squadron who, along with his navigator Flying Officer Grant, was flying his eleventh successive sortie to the capital. Their burning aircraft was seen to come down in a cornfield.

The Mosquito pilots at Upwood had a busy night, their numbers divided between Berlin and Bremen and losing an aircraft at each. Most noteworthy was that of Flight Lieutenant Andre van Amsterdam, the appropriately-named Dutch pilot from the Royal Netherlands Navy. Amsterdam was flying with his navigator Squadron Leader Harry Forbes DFC – a second-tour Canadian who had previously flown with Johnny Fauquier at 405 Squadron – when their aircraft was suddenly hit without warning, the victim of a jet fighter attack. (Their vanquisher was Oberfeldwebel Karl-Heinz Becker, a lethal exponent of the Messerschmitt Me262.) Amsterdam attempted to bale out of the top hatch and was never seen again. Forbes had more luck in taking to his 'chute, and was captured. At the time of his death, Amsterdam was said to have completed more than 100 operations.

Of course it was not just over Berlin that the Mosquitoes suffered casualties: two were lost from the attack on Kassel on March 8/9 – one each from 163 and 608 Squadrons – and a further four aircraft, wrecked or written off between March 12-14, often returning from operations with serious battle damage.

But while March could be typified by the losses suffered by the wooden wonder leading Oboe attacks or on small-scale raids, it was also noteworthy for a number of main force operations that continued – or in some cases completed – the destruction of various major enemy centres.

Operation Thunderclap, for example, saw the continuation of the raids on cities to the east, with Chemnitz on the receiving end of bombs from more than 750 Lancasters and Halifaxes.

It was a rather unsatisfactory raid for Bomber Command, however, for although various important factories were destroyed (including the tank engine manufacturer, Siegmar) a large number of aircraft went missing, either in accidents caused by bad weather or to the German defences, who even at

Tony Harte-Lovelace and crew prior to joining PFF. The practice of adorning individual aircraft with 'nose art' was by now well established. This particular Halifax is a veteran of some 45 sorties.

Bernard Brooker and his pilot Archie Hardy (second and third from left) had an eventful tour. Brooker was later killed in a training accident.

THE CRUEL HAND OF FATE

The Pathfinder world was full of danger, and not only on operations. Training could be similarly hazardous, and there are several stories of men who survived the perils of forty or fifty operations over enemy territory, only to lose their lives in an innocuous accident. One such man was Flight Lieutenant Bernard Brooker DFC & Bar.

Brooker, a postmaster in civilian life, was at Dunkirk with the Territorial Army in 1940, transferring to the RAF in July 1941. After training as an air bomber in South Africa the following year, he returned to the UK, eventually joining 158 Squadron at Lissett in May 1943. As part of Sergeant Archie Hardy's crew he completed nine operations before volunteering for Pathfinders. He then completed an eventful tour with 35 Squadron, including the historic raids to Peenemünde and Nuremberg, earning the DFC in May 1944, as a warrant officer and a Bar in October. By this stage he had also gained expertise as a set operator, and qualified as a navigation leader.

Having flown more than forty operations, his experience was sought by Pathfinder navigation training unit (NTU), which was then sharing a station with 156 Squadron at RAF Warboys. On a day training flight on March 11, 1945 in a Lancaster piloted by Flight Lieutenant Arthur Diemer, the aircraft was seen to crash at high speed at Old Weston near Molesworth airfield. There were no survivors. He was buried five days later.

this late stage of the war, could still take a heavy toll.

Squadron Leader Fred Watson DFC of 35 Squadron was one of the casualties of the night, lost without trace. His crew included Warrant Officer Victor Roe who had been awarded an immediate DFM after only nineteen operations for shooting down a Bf110 despite being wounded in the hand. He added a Conspicuous Gallantry Medal having completed not less than eighty-five sorties – his fourth tour of operations. A 635 Squadron Lancaster flown by Flight Lieutenant Keith Beattie was also shot down, Beattie somehow survived but the rest of the crew were killed.

A most bizarre incident led to the loss of a 582 Squadron aircraft on its journey home. Making their descent over the English coast and flying in loose formation, there was suddenly a blinding flash followed by a huge explosion. The pilot, Flying Officer Johnnie Gould, could do nothing to prevent the aircraft from diving into the ground. Only the rear gunner had time to bale out, the rest were killed. A TI retained in the aircraft had fused and detonated in the bomb bay. Rather than being 'safe' as they should have been, they had somehow become 'live'. It was a tragic waste of a gallant crew.

Main force was split between three targets on March 7/8 – the largest element taking part in a devastating raid on Dessau, a new venue in the east. More than 500 bombers laid waste a large part of the town, and inflicted severe damage on all four Junkers aircraft factories, for the loss of eighteen of their number, including another 635 Squadron Lancaster flown by Flight Sergeant Thomas Kelly. Although the rear gunner survived, he was killed a few days later, ironically in an air raid.

Squadron Leader Danny Everett DFC & two Bars was killed that same night as master bomber for the attack on Hemmingstedt. Everett was somewhat of a legend at 35 Squadron, and indeed within the wider Pathfinder Force. He was an exceptional pilot and captain, shot down and killed, it is believed, on his ninety-ninth operation. He had been ordered not to fly, but the temptation was just too great.

Hamburg and Kassel were in the firing line the following night, although cloud prevented a successful attack on either. On March 11 Harris unleashed yet another of his 1,000-bomber raids on Essen – his last attack on the city of the war. Some have questioned whether it was truly necessary, but Harris persisted. What was left, and it was very little, was totally destroyed, and within days the Americans entered the city to find a scene of near-complete annihilation.

Another new record was set the following night when 1,108 aircraft took part in an attack on Dortmund. It was an almost perfect attack in every sense, with subsequent reports suggesting that the raid effectively stopped Dortmund's factories from making any further contribution to the war effort.

After these two 'set-piece' raids of major proportions, the rest of the month featured multiple raids on new and sometimes obscure targets: Wuppertal; Zweibrücken; Homberg; Hagen; Witten; Hanau; Rheine; Hildesheim; Dülmen; Dorsten; Wesel; and Münster.

On March 15/16, Pathfinders led a force from 1 Group to attack the Deurag refinery at Misburg. It achieved little, with the main weight of the raid being concentrated to the south, and only a small portion of bombs on the aiming point. A disappointing raid was made more disappointing still by the loss of two aircraft from the same squadron – 405 at Gransden Lodge. Flight Lieutenant Keith Parkhurst

Master bomber Bill Cleland (centre) and his crew including Jack Watson (far right). Cleland flew almost eighty ops in fifteen months without rest, receiving the DSO and DFC having commenced his fourth tour.

LUCKY DIP

"We were master bomber for a raid to Osnabrück on March 24 and clambered into our regular aircraft, D-Dog, which, to our best knowledge, was all ready for the off. When our skipper (Alex Thorne) and flight engineer ran through their checks, there seemed to be a problem with the fuel gauges. Harry, our flight engineer, made it clear he wasn't happy and so we parked up while someone went off and found a dipping rod. Sure enough, the tanks were dry. If we had attempted to take off, it would have ended in disaster.

"Fortunately a bowser turned up and within twenty minutes we were fully fuelled but in something of a dilemma. Alex asked me directly if we could make it in time; we were master bomber and could not be late under any circumstance. I drew a line from base to Osnabrück, did a quick calculation and said we could make it, but it would be suicide. It would mean flying over a heavy concentration of flak over the Dutch coast, we had no escort, and it was perfect conditions for enemy fighters. He said: 'are you coming then?' and since I didn't have anything better to do decided to go with them.

"As it was, the trip was surprisingly uneventful. We took plenty of flak as we approached the Dortmund-Ems canal, but were soon through it and over the target, controlling what turned out to be a very successful raid. When we returned from the operation Alex visited the airman responsible for the fuel oversight, who was on a charge in the station brig. Alex told him that all was well and that he was forgiven – we all make mistakes. That was the sort of man he was."

BORIS BRESSLOFF DFC
NAV TWO. 635 SQUADRON. FIFTY-THREE OPS.

and his seven-man crew were all killed; Flying Officer Leslie Laing MiD and three of his crew were also killed. Laing managed to leave the aircraft and take to his 'chute. Landing in a tree, he released his harness and fell thirty feet, breaking both legs. He was found dead at the scene. Sergeant Robert Morris, Flight Sergeant Francis Marsh and Flying Officer Donald Smith also all managed to make it out in one piece, but were killed immediately after.

Gransden lost a third crew three nights later when Flying Officer George Peaker and his crew failed to return from an otherwise successful raid on Witten. Mercifully this was the last crew to perish on operations from 405 Squadron as part of Pathfinder Force. They were not, however, the last crew to be lost that month, for on March 31 three crews failed to return from operations to Hamburg – two from 156 Squadron (Flying Officer Herbert Taylor DFC and Flight Lieutenant Anthony Pope DFC), and the third from Downham Market (Flying Officer Arthur Lewis). Only one man made it out alive. Taylor, who also went by the name of Benson, had only recently recovered from a wound sustained in a sortie to Nuremberg for which he won his DFC.

There were two other attacks during that month that are worthy of note. The first was on the Harpenerweg oil refinery near Dortmund, a raid led with impeccable finesse by the master bomber, Flight Lieutenant Stafford Harris DFC. But it was his 156 Squadron colleague, Flying Officer Gilbert Hampson who perhaps stole the limelight that night, or rather his flight engineer, Sergeant Dennis Bowers.

Hampson's aircraft was on its bombing run when it received a direct hit and was set on fire. Shrapnel wounded the flight engineer in the leg. The pilot ordered his crew to abandon aircraft, and two made it out before Hampson somehow regained control of the badly damaged bomber and told the rest of the crew to stay put. The set operator and rear gunner helped their injured colleague to the flight deck whereupon another direct hit severed his left leg at the knee. Despite the horrifying extent of his injuries, Bowers – a former medical orderly – used all of his knowledge

Stafford Harris (in cockpit) and his crew. Stafford's skills as a master bomber were much in demand in the latter stages of the war.

MASTER BOMBER – STAFFORD HARRIS

Born in Torquay in 1922 and educated at Kelly College in Tavistock, Stafford Harris joined the RAF in 1941. After flying training at Shawbury, his aptitude as a pilot meant he was singled out for a flying instructors' course. Stafford spent two years as an instructor before finally persuading his superiors to release him for operations. Converting to Lancasters, he was posted to 156 Squadron, flying his first operation on the day he arrived – September 11, 1944.

By his fourteenth trip, an operation to Essen, he had been elevated in Pathfinder circles to primary visual marker, one of the most important of all roles in PFF. On his fifteenth operation he had advanced a further step to deputy master bomber. He flew a further five operations as deputy to Walcheren (October 29), Goch (February 7), Hamburg (March 8), Dortmund (March 12) and Hannover (March 15), before, at last, being promoted to master bomber for the raid on Harpenerweg on March 24. His deputy for this raid was Flight Lieutenant Bill Cleland, and as long stop was another veteran master bomber, Squadron Leader Peter Clayton DSO, DFC.

Stafford flew one further trip as master bomber on April 18, leading the attack on Heligoland, a raid famous for turning the target area into a lunar landscape, with the bombing photographs to prove it.

Arguably his most satisfying operation, however, came as part of Operation Manna, dropping food to the starving people of Holland. It was Stafford who dropped a bouquet of flowers for Queen Wilhelmina and was later presented with a plaque by the queen herself in recognition of the RAF's role in keeping her people fed in their hour of need.

Rated at the end of the war as 'well above average', he was selected for the 35 Squadron goodwill tour of the US and on his return, was transferred to Transport Command. He flew more than 150 sorties from Wunstorf to Gatow during the Berlin Airlift, this time supplying the starving people of Germany. Qualifying as a test pilot with the Empire Test Pilot's School at Farnborough, he later became a test pilot with Vickers Armstrong.

Stafford believes he owes his survival on forty-nine Pathfinder operations to a particular tactic he adopted on every raid he flew. After completing his duties, he would fly onwards, in the opposite direction to base, and where the enemy would least expect to find him. He would then turn for home later, thus avoiding the flak and fighters. It meant inevitably he was almost always the last to make it back.

to supervise the dressing of his wound that doubtless saved his life.

By this time, Flight Lieutenant Bill Cleland DSO, DFC had witnessed his colleague's distress, and could see for himself a gaping hole in the Lancaster's fuselage. In an effort to divert the attention of the flak gunners below, Cleland flew alongside to draw their fire. Hampson eventually made it back to the emergency field at Manston where the aircraft was subsequently graded as

A CITY DIES IN FIFTEEN MINUTES

A graduate of Cranwell, a former fighter pilot and professional airman, Stafford Coulson was in the wrong part of the world when the war began, and it took him several years before he finally found the excitement he had been craving. Coulson flew his first Pathfinder operation in May 1944 with 35 Squadron, and during Christmas 1944 was posted to command 582 Squadron. He was still in charge at Little Staughton when called upon to act as master bomber for the attack on Paderborn:

Wing Commander Stafford Coulson. A master bomber whose crew would have followed him to the ends of the earth.

"The attack was scheduled to be a Musical Parramatta, but the Met Mosquito broadcast 10/10ths cloud. I checked with my deputy (Flight Lieutenant Paddy Finlay), and gave the basement (i.e. the cloud level) and indicated a blind attack (a Wanganui), repeating at regular intervals the words: 'This is a blind attack.'

"Wanganui was the least satisfactory of all Pathfinder marking methods, but in this instance accounted for one of my most successful attacks. Like Dresden it was a daylight raid, and we coolly wrote off a German town in less than a quarter of an hour. We razed the town to the ground and boy did it burn."

STAFFORD COULSON DSO, DFC
COMMANDING OFFICER. 582 SQUADRON. FORTY-SEVEN OPS.

ORDER OF BATTLE

MARCH 1945

Headquarters 8 Group – Huntingdon

Graveley	35 Squadron	Lancaster	Gransden	142 Squadron	Mosquito
	692 Squadron	Mosquito	Lodge	405 (RCAF) Squadron	Lancaster
Oakington	7 Squadron	Lancaster			
	571 Squadron	Mosquito	Upwood	156 Squadron	Lancaster
				139 Squadron	Mosquito
Wyton	128 Squadron	Mosquito			
	163 Squadron	Mosquito	Downham	635 Squadron	Lancaster
	1409 (Met) Flight	Mosquito	Market	608 Squadron	Mosquito
			Little	582 Squadron	Lancaster
Bourn	105 Squadron	Mosquito	Staughton	109 Squadron	Mosquito
	162 Squadron	Mosquito			
			Warboys	PFF NTU	Lancaster

Detached to 5 Group: 83, 97 and 627 Squadrons

beyond repair. Hampson and Bowers were awarded an immediate DFC and CGM respectively, and there were DFMs for two other members of the crew.

The second attack worthy of note in March took place on the 27th, when a force of fourteen Lancasters led by Wing Commander Stafford Coulson marked the ancient town of Paderborn with Wanganui for a main force of 254 aircraft that promptly destroyed the area in less than fifteen minutes. The marking was so accurate that the town was totally ruined, its narrow streets helping the fires to spread and contributing to its rapid destruction. It is generally considered to be the copybook example of a small-scale Pathfinder-led raid in the whole of the war.

APRIL/MAY 1945

The onset of spring represented the autumn of German resistance in Europe. Even with almost nothing left to bomb, Pathfinders still managed to notch up a further 3,482 sorties in April, bringing its grand total since August 15, 1942 to 50,593. The commander-in-chief received orders to discontinue area bombing and attack built-up areas only when directly requested to do so by the armies on the ground. Oil and communications remained a priority.

Leuna, Harburg and Lützkendorf – all major oil facilities – were attacked on April 4/5 with mixed results. The most successful raid was against Harburg, where the target was easily identified and severely damaged. Three aircraft were shot down including Flight Lieutenant Barry Wadham DFC of 7 Squadron. Wadham, with at least fifty-three operations to his name, was part of the marking force. His crew, who were all killed, included Flying Officer Haralambides DFC, his flight engineer. Haralambides was one of only a handful of Cypriots to fly with Bomber Command and one of the very few to lose their lives. A 635 Squadron Lancaster flown by Flight Lieutenant Philip Cawthorne DFC, RAAF was also shot down, four of the crew – including their skipper – were killed. These were the last wartime casualties this proud squadron would have to endure.

As well as oil, the shipyards and harbour installations at the major ports still in German hands – notably Bremen, Hamburg and Kiel – were also to be singled out for special attention in those last few weeks of the war. Hamburg was the first to be hit, or missed as it turned out, as cloud resulted in a rather poor raid with only minor damage inflicted on the target, the Blohm & Voss ship works.

One of the crews flying that night was led by Max Muller. A former policeman, he had been commended for bravery, helping people who had been buried in the blitz on Bristol much earlier in the war. Now a squadron leader, Muller was in charge of a 35 Squadron Lancaster in the vanguard of the attack. As he made a second run over the target, his aircraft received a direct hit, and immediately burst into flames enabling only the rear gunner (Flight Sergeant Charles Wilce DFM) to make it out in time. Actually, Wilce had been incredibly lucky: he had been unable to rotate his turret sufficiently to bale out, but as the aircraft spun out of control, the turret and the fuselage parted company and Wilce found himself in free air. There was one other survivor from the crash that resulted – Flight Lieutenant Patrick Ranalow – but the thirty-year-old succumbed to his injuries soon after.

A supremely-accurate raid on Kiel followed two nights later (April 9/10) when Pathfinder Force went ship-busting. Two aiming points within the main harbour area were easily identified in good visibility, and high-quality marking by the primary visual markers was sustained throughout the attack. What was left of the main German surface fleet was effectively destroyed: the pocket battleship *Admiral Scheer* was hit and capsized, and both the *Admiral Hipper* and *Emden* were badly damaged. The Deutsche Werke U-boat yard was also severely damaged, and on April 13/14, Bomber Command went back to finish the job, albeit with limited success.

Bremen – the third of the major ports to be raided that month – was allocated a much larger attacking force than either Hamburg or Kiel: 767 aircraft – most of them Lancasters – were led by

PFF Mosquitoes for an attack that was to overwhelm the German defences in preparation for an assault by British ground forces. Cloud, and the smoke and dust generated after the initial bombs had fallen, forced the master bomber to abandon the attack, sending more than 500 aircraft home with their bombs still onboard. Whether the raid was a success or not is difficult to assess, but suffice to say that the city surrendered just a few days later.

There were three other principal attacks in April worthy of note: a raid on Potsdam on April 14/15; the daylight attack on Heligoland on April 18; and another daylight on Wangerooge on April 25.

Potsdam was perhaps the most significant for in fact it represented the very last raid of the war by a major Bomber Command force on a German city. Only one aircraft was lost, and not surprisingly this was a PFF aircraft. Flying Officer Uryan Bowen-Morris was in the vicinity of the target area when an engine caught fire – apparently as a result of a nightfighter attack. Ordering his crew to bale out, six of them had gone by which time Bowen-Morris had recovered some semblance of control of the aircraft and made for Allied lines. Confident that he had reached Dutch air space, he at last took to his own 'chute and shortly afterwards the aircraft crashed. This was the last aircraft that 35 Squadron lost in the war, and the twenty-one-year-old flight engineer – Sergeant William Reynolds – who was killed in the incident and whose body was never found – was the final casualty.

The 'bad boys' at 156 Squadron at Upwood similarly suffered its last casualties of the war when the Lancaster of Flying Officer John Jamieson and his crew failed to return from an operation to the marshalling yards at Schwandorf. They had been with the squadron for only three weeks.

> **PLAYING WITH FIRE**
>
> *"We came across Bennett often. He would turn up on the squadron unannounced. One night I couldn't get the fire going in our billet and decided to use some petrol to help it along with disastrous consequences. I could have been court-martialed, but at the time we were in demand as a master bomber and so got off with it lightly."*
>
> STAFFORD HARRIS DFC
> MASTER BOMBER. 156 SQUADRON.
> FORTY-NINE OPS.

A forgettable raid on Leipzig that month proved memorable for one 405 Squadron pilot, Squadron Leader Campbell Mussels. After making his first run over the target, the aircraft was attacked by an enemy fighter and sustained serious damage; the rear turret and the starboard rudder were shot away, the port rudder smashed and both elevators badly damaged. Somehow Mussels kept control of the aircraft, and was obliged to rig the control column to maintain height. After crossing the English coast, he ordered his crew to abandon the aircraft and, with the exception of the mid upper gunner who was seriously wounded, they all departed safely. Mussels flew on to the nearest airfield with his wounded comrade, and despite his Heath Robinson automatic pilot, somehow managed to bring the heavy bomber safely into land, winning an immediate DSO for his efforts – one of the last immediate awards to PFF in the war.

But if there was one target and one raid that everyone in Pathfinder Force – and probably everyone in Bomber Command – wanted to take part in, it was the attack on the führer's 'house' at Berchtesgaden. The plan and timing of the attack was changed several times. In the end, the honour of leading the raid went to Wing Commander James Fordham who arrived to find the aiming point readily identifiable, and no doubt enjoyed controlling what was a textbook Pathfinder attack. The führer, sadly, was not at home for what proved to be the heavy squadrons' curtain call.

With peace in sight, there was one further cruel twist for the 'heavy' boys at Little Staughton. Flying Officer Robert Terpening DFC and his crew were on a training exercise on April 28 when they flew into a snow cloud, the aircraft iced up and they suddenly lost power on both port engines. The aircraft spun in, killing the pilot and his rear gunner, Pilot Officer John Watson DFM, and seriously injuring the rest of the crew. Terpening, an Australian, had been one of the pilots on the Cologne/Gremberg operation who had been shot down, and his faithful gunner had been awarded the DFM for fighting off repeated attacks from German fighters.

Two days later, in a dark and claustrophobic bunker a long way from the fresh mountain air of the appropriately-named Eagle's Nest, Adolf Hitler took his own life, and passed his commander's baton to Admiral Karl Dönitz. He would be führer for a little over a week.

Pathfinders and Bomber Command had carried out no offensive operations since April 26/27. While the heavies had been busy throughout the month, the Mosquito squadrons had similarly kept up their nightly assault on Germany, with 139 Squadron being particularly unfortunate in losing two very experienced crews in consecutive raids on Berlin. Flight Lieutenant Geoffrey Nicholls DFC and his navigator, Flight Lieutenant Jack Dawes DFC, perished without trace on the night of April 2/3; Squadron Leader Thomas Dow DFC and his navigator, Flight Lieutenant Jack Endersby were killed the following night. Both pilots had flown more than sixty operations.

On the night of April 4/5, while the heavies concentrated on destroying the last of Germany's oil production capabilities, the Light Night Strikers went to Berlin and Magdeburg. Two of their number were lost in the latter raid, one each from 142 and 571 Squadrons. The captain of the 142 Squadron Mosquito, Flight Lieutenant Kenneth Pudsey, had flown at least seventy-four operational sorties, and as well as having the DFM from his time with 115 Squadron had been twice mentioned in despatches.

The Mosquitoes at Oakington seemed to suffer a disproportionate number of casualties in those first two weeks of April. As well as the 571 aircraft lost on the Magdeburg trip, the squadron lost aircraft on April 9 (in an air test), the night of April 9/10 (a crew returning on one engine from Plauen), April 10/11 (shot down over Berlin – both pilot and navigator safe), and two on April 11/12 (both in accidents upon taking off). A further aircraft fell on April 13 when the pilot, Flight Lieutenant Maurice Cane DFM, misjudged a low-level pass, hit some trees and flick-rolled into the ground. Both Cane and his Australian navigator were killed.

A New Zealand pilot, Flight Lieutenant Geoffrey Dixon was in charge of a Mosquito XVI of 608 Squadron over Berlin and had just bombed the aiming point when his aircraft suffered

LITTLE FRIENDS

'We were master bomber on a daylight to Nuremberg and over the target we were hit by heavy flak and the skipper immediately put the control column hard forward. It took Alex and Harry, the pilot and flight engineer, all of their collective strength to pull the Lancaster out of the dive. Eventually we recovered to find the ailerons had been damaged and Alex trimmed the aircraft as best he could for level flight, at which point I looked out of the astrodome to see that we had been joined by two fighters. Fortunately they were P51 Mustangs, and I can clearly remember one of the pilots was black and smoking a huge Cuban cigar. He had to pull the cockpit canopy back to clear the smoke!

ERNIE PATTERSON DFM
WIRELESS OPERATOR. 635 SQUADRON.
FIFTY-ONE OPS.

an engine failure. Fortunately he had enough height and experience to make it to an airfield at Strassfeld, but as his wheels bit into the runway the undercarriage collapsed and the aircraft was wrecked. His Mosquito thus become the last Bomber Command aircraft to be written off during operations to Berlin.

After the heavy-bomber raid on Kiel on April 9/10, the LNSF mounted two large operations of its own on the target on April 21/22 and April 23/24, the former involving some 107 aircraft. The surprise was so total in the first of these raids that the sirens sounded after the first bombs had been dropped. Two Mosquitoes were shot down, however: Flight Lieutenant William Baker of 163 Squadron fell in the target area, probably the victim of flak since no nightfighter claims were made for a Mosquito that night; Squadron Leader Eric Few DFC, AFC of 608 Squadron was also missing. Neither squadron would lose any further aircraft or crews as a result of enemy action. Indeed although further Mosquitoes would be written off before the war was out, these were the last to be lost as a direct result of air operations, (notwithstanding a 109 Squadron aircraft that overshot and crashed attempting to land at Brussels-Melsbroek on its return from Schleissheim on April 24/25. The Kiwi pilot, Flight Lieutenant John McGreal DFC and his navigator, Pilot Officer Thomas Lynn DFC, DFM were both killed).

A very welcome change in the demands placed on PFF started on April 26 and would continue until after the first week of May. This was Operation Exodus, the repatriation of British prisoners of war. Each Lancaster could carry up to twenty-four men and Pathfinders of 8 Group played their part in transporting nearly 3,000 of the 75,000 men that would eventually be brought home before the war was over. Bennett flew the first trip himself.

Another distraction that caused equal satisfaction and which started three days later was Operation Manna – the dropping of vital food and subsistence to the starving people of Holland. In one of the more conciliatory acts of the war, the German commander in charge of the pocket in Western Holland still in Wehrmacht hands agreed a truce with local Allied commanders, allowing the Allied air forces to fly uninterrupted through a dedicated 'corridor', free from interference. Pathfinders still marked the relevant aiming points, and Bomber Command dropped some 6,672 tons of food during the operation. No crews taking part in Manna would ever forget the waving arms and smiling faces of the grateful people below, some of who were sick or dying and who would now be saved.

Intelligence reports suggested that the Germans were assembling ships at Kiel with a view to transporting troops and supplies to Norway, where they still retained a sizeable contingent. A final attack by 8 Group was therefore mounted on May 2/3, comprising 126 Mosquitoes in two raids, one hour apart, in which all but two carried out their bombing successfully and from which all of the aircraft and crews returned safely. Allied troops entered Kiel thirty-six hours later, and on May 7, General Eisenhower accepted the unconditional surrender of all German forces on all fronts, effective at 00.01 hours on May 9.

The final entry in the 8 Group Operations Record Book for the month of May and dated May 31 captures the true feeling of relief at the news:

'It is with pleasure, and a wonderful feeling of satisfaction that this month's resumé of our activities is written. For this month contains THE day of all days. The culmination of all of our efforts reached their never-doubted end (with apologies to the late Joe Goebbels) on the 7th, to be followed on the 8th by Victory in Europe Day.

'Our last and only 'operational' bombing night was on the night of 2/3 May when our Mosquitoes bombed Kiel and the airfields of Husum and Eggebek, the last bomb going down at 0054.9 hours on Eggebek Airfield.'

The Pathfinders' war was finally at an end.

Australian Bob Newbiggin (centre). His crew included Gwynne Price (left) who vividly recalls the Manna raids dropping food supplies to the starving Dutch.

MISSIONS OF MERCY

Gwynne Price trained as a flight engineer and at 1668 HCU crewed up with an Australian, Bob Newbiggin, who had been a champion swimmer and surfer. Posted to 195 Squadron at Wratting Common, after eleven operations the crew was singled out for Pathfinders and arrived at 35 Squadron in February 1945:

"On April 24 I was asked if I would make up a crew whose flight engineer had gone sick. My crew tried to talk me out of it but I insisted I should go. The flight was a mercy flight to a prisoner of war camp at Nieuwittenburg over six hours into Germany. HQ had been assured that no attacks would be made on this mercy mission. With our load of medical supplies we took off and proceeded to head for our destination at an altitude of 5,000ft. It was a nice, clear night and although there was an underlying fear that something might go wrong, the prison target was identified, the supplies dropped and the aircraft returned safely.

"Another mercy mission took place on April 30. This time we filled up the bomb bays with food desperately needed by the starving Dutch people. The selected 'target' for the much needed supplies was Valkenburgh on the Dutch coast. The Germans had stated they would not fire on the mercy crews. As we came in at about 100ft from the sea towards land, the cliff top was covered with people including many children, waving flags and cheering. It was a very emotional time for all of us."

GWYNNE PRICE AFM
FLIGHT ENGINEER. 35 SQUADRON. TWENTY-EIGHT OPS.

POSTSCRIPT

The process of dismantling Pathfinder Force started almost immediately, and Bennett himself handed over command to Air Vice-Marshal John Whitley on May 21. Bennett was alone among the group commanders not to receive a knighthood, and it is difficult to see any reason for the decision beyond a return to the petty rivalries and jealousies that existed in the higher echelons of the RAF and government at that time. What Bennett did have, however, was the unswerving loyalty of his men and the pride of wearing the small gold eagle below his medal ribbons – the eagle that marked out him and his men as being the *corps d'élite* of Bomber Command.

Bennett was not a man given to effusive praise. He did, however, send a victory message to his squadrons on VE Day that spelled out, in his words, the vital contribution that Pathfinder Force had made towards victory:

"I have led Bomber Command, the greatest striking force ever known. That we have been successful can be seen in the far-reaching effects which the bomber offensive has achieved. That is the greatest reward the Pathfinder Force ever hopes to receive; for those results have benefited all law-abiding peoples.

"Whilst you have been hard at work through these vital years, I have not interrupted you, as I would like to have done, with messages of praise and congratulation. You were too busy; but now that your great contribution to the world has been made, I want to thank you each man and woman personally and to congratulate you on your unrelenting spirit and energy and on the results you have achieved.

"Happiness to you all – always keep pressing on along the Path of Peace."

In exalted company. Donald Bennett (left) with the Father of the Royal Air Force Trenchard.

RETROSPECTIVE

Ray Wilcock was the nav one in a crew skippered by an Australian, Flight Lieutenant C.J. 'Dusty' Miller DFC. Having flown four trips with 514 Squadron at Waterbeach, they were 'volunteered' for Pathfinders and posted to the newly-formed 582 Squadron at Little Staughton via PFF NTU.

"I don't like to talk much about those days. I know what we did and I know what happened. We had a bit of trouble here and there, but nothing more or less than anyone else. We had a job to do and we did it pretty well. I am often asked whether, as navigator, I always managed to find the target. To be honest, I'm not sure. I am pretty certain I did. But one thing I do know: I always found my way home."

RAY WILCOCK,
NAV ONE. 582 SQUADRON. FORTY-FOUR OPS.

BADGE OF HONOUR

There is an interesting addition to the stories of the feud between Bennett and Cochrane, and the petty jealousies evidenced by Cochrane in particular, even after the war had been won.

"Just after the war, I was one of two service representatives to the court of the Guild of Air Pilots and Air Navigators (for whom I was later, and still am, a liveryman). A committee had been established to discuss RAF uniform, and various recommendations were made and agreed that included removing the coveted Pathfinder Eagle.

"Somewhat concerned about this, I later sought out Sir John Salmond and asked him if I might consult him on a service matter, even though we were both in civvies. When I told him, he immediately said: "Boom' (the nickname for Viscount Trenchard) will want to hear about this,' and led me over to meet the great man. (This is all remembering I am an acting flight lieutenant at the time talking to a marshal of the Royal Air Force!)

"When Trenchard learned that it was none other than Sir Ralph Cochrane who was chairman of the committee and had made the recommendation, he blurted out: 'Old so and so (I forget the precise term he used, but it wasn't very polite), I never could stand that man. Leave it with us.' I am not quite sure what happened after that, but suffice to say it was the only recommendation that was not ultimately taken up."

FRANK LEATHERDALE DFC
NAVIGATOR. 7 SQUADRON. FIFTY-NINE OPS.

Memorial Plaque to 'Pathfinder' Bennett that now resides in the Pathfinder Museum at RAF Wyton.

A MAN OF RUTHLESS EFFICIENCY

"Bennett was unquestionably an efficiency expert. He was not only a world-wide respected navigator but could orally and intelligently interview every category of aircrew aspirant for the PFF badge, including the flight engineers! He wasn't locked into the crew basis for operations and felt strongly that a crew should not be excused from operations if one of them was unavailable. He looked on the crew lists more as individuals than as crew members.

"He never set out to be the most popular commander; results were his aim and his target at any cost. The war had to be won, and an efficient bomber campaign was essential. Despite this somewhat cold efficiency, it was always noteworthy that in the mess of an evening when his lovely wife, Ly, joined him, there would be a group of adoring aircrew around their chairs. Bennett was a leader and one who led by example, doing himself whatever he asked of his men."

JACK WATTS DSO, DFC & BAR, CD
NAVIGATOR. 109 SQUADRON. 100+ OPS.

ACKNOWLEDGEMENTS AND SOURCES

As much of this book is as original as possible, drawing on hundreds of hours of interviews over several years with surviving veterans – many speaking for the first time – and combining these with official records and exclusive access to contemporary documents and exhibits at the Pathfinder Museum at RAF Wyton. I have also referred to Martin Middlebrook's superlative *Bomber Command War Diaries*, cross-referencing these with the 3 and 8 Group ORBs (AIR 25) as well as the ORBs of each individual Pathfinder squadron (AIR 27), and Bill Chorley's excellent series of Bomber Command losses. Two other books I found especially useful: Gordon's Musgrove's *Pathfinder Force – a history of 8 Group*; and Theo Boiten's *Nachtjagd War Diaries*.

THE VETERANS

It was always important to me that any book about the Pathfinders should be in their own words, as much as possible. To this end it has been a great privilege to meet and interview a good number of the *corps d'élite* over the last few years, some of whom have sadly since 'gone west'. I give my sincere thanks and pay tribute to them all:

Cliff Alabaster DSO & Bar, DFC & Bar
Gerry Sealy-Bell
Gordon Blake DFC
The late Boris Bressloff DFC
Don Briggs DFC
Roy Briggs
Ian Brownlie DFC
Percy Cannings DFM
George Cash DFC
The late Stafford Coulson DSO, DFC
The late Peter Cribb CBE, DSO & Bar, DFC & Bar
Allen Drinkwell DFM
Fred Edmondson DFM
Allan Edwards
Les Fletcher DFC & Bar
Doug Hadland
The late George Hall DFC & Bar
Stafford Harris DFC
Bill Heane DFC
Ian Hewitt DFC & Bar
Bill Higgs
Tony Hiscock DFC & Bar
Alf Huberman

Harold Kirby
Bob Lasham DFC & Bar
The late Roy Last
Frank Leatherdale DFC
The late Fred Maltas
John Mitchell LVO, DFC, AFC
Lawrence Nicholson DFM
Rupert Noye DFC
Ken Oatley
Reg Parissien
Joe Patient DFC
Ernie Patterson DFM
Bob Pearce
Fred Phillips DFC & Bar
Gwynne Price AFM
Doug Reed DFM
Ted Stocker DSO, DFC
'Tommy' Thomas
Arthur Tindell
The late Al Trotter DFC, DFM
John 'Jack' Watson DFM
Jack Watts DSO, DFC, CD
Norma Watts
Norman Westby DFC & Bar
Eric Wilkin DFC & Bar
Ray Wilcock
Bert Wilson DFM
Jim Wright

THE PATHFINDER MUSEUM ARCHIVE
The museum has a wealth of archive material left to it by veterans and families of veterans.

William Ball papers; Bernard Brooker papers; Ivor Broom papers; Gordon Carter papers; Alfred Colson papers; Ulrich Cross papers; Arthur Everest papers; Tony Farrell papers; Jerry Gosnell papers; Ronald Hands papers; John Jackson papers; Walter Layne papers; Pat O'Hara papers; Reg Reynolds papers; Bill Riley papers; Jim Rogers papers; Aubrey Strickland papers; Wilf Sutton papers; Roland Swartz papers; Alexander Wallace papers; Lionel Wheble papers.

PRIVATE ARCHIVES
The Mansel-Pleydell family archive
Jeff Chapman papers (including his logbook and private memoir *Desert Song*)
The logbook of Michael Finlay
The logbook of Tony Harte-Lovelace

SELECT BIBLIOGRAPHY

Anderson, Bill	*Pathfinder* (Jarrolds, 1946)
Ashton, Norman	*Only Birds and Fools* (Airlife, 2000)
Bending, Kevin	*Achieve your Aim* (Woodfield, 2005)
Bennett, Donald	*Pathfinder* (Frederick Muller, 1958)
Bowyer, Chaz	*Pathfinders at War* (Ian Allan, 1977)
Bowyer, Chaz	*Bomber Barons* (William Kimber, 1983)
Bramson, Alan	*Master Airman* (Airlife, 1985)
Celis, Peter	*One Who Almost Made it Back* (Grub Street, 2008)
Charlwood, Don	*No Moon Tonight* (Angus & Robertson, 1956)
Childs, Edgar	*Kismet – A Flight Engineer's Story* (Privately published)
Chorley, Bill	*RAF Bomber Command Loses, Volumes 1-6* (Midland Counties, 1999)
Cooper, Alan	*The Men Who Breached the Dams* (William Kimber, 1982)
Cooper, Alan	*In Action With the Enemy* (William Kimber, 1986)
Cooper, Alan	*Target Dresden* (Independent, 1995)
Cooper, Alan	*We Act With One Accord* (J& KH Publishing, 1988)
Coughlin, Tom	*The Dangerous Sky* (William Kimber, 1968)
Cribb, Julian	*Master Bomber* (Privately published)
Cumming, Michael	*Pathfinder Cranswick* (William Kimber, 2006)
Deane, Laurence	*A Pathfinder's War and Peace* (Merlin Books, 1993)
Docherty, Tom	*No 7 Squadron RAF in World War II* (Pen & Sword, 2007)
Evans, Tom Parry	*Squadron Leader Tommy Broom* (Pen and Sword, 2007)
Feast, Sean	*Heroic Endeavour* (Grub Street, 2006)
Feast, Sean	*A Pathfinder's War* (Grub Street, 2009)
Feast, Sean	*Master Bombers* (Grub Street, 2008)
Gould, Peter	*The Best Twelve Years* (Trafford Publishing, 2005)
Grierson, Bill	*We Band of Brothers* (J & KH Publishing, 1997)
Harris, Arthur	*Bomber Offensive* (Collins, 1946)
Hewitt, Clement	*Swifter than Eagles* (Privately published, 1987)
Johnson, Frank	*RAAF over Europe* (Eyre & Spottiswoode, 1946)
Johnson, Peter	*The Withered Garland* (New European Publications, 1995)
Lawrence, W.J.	*No 5 Bomber Group* (Faber and Faber, 1951)
Low, R.G.	*83 Squadron* (Privately published, 1992)
Mahaddie, Hamish	*The Story of a Pathfinder* (Ian Allan, 1982)
Maynard, John	*Bennett and the Pathfinders* (Weidenfeld Military, 1996)
Middlebrook, Martin	*The Nuremberg Raid* (Pen & Sword, 2009)
Middlebrook, Martin	*The Bomber Command War Diaries* (Midland, 2011)
Middlebrook, Martin	*The Berlin Raids* (Pen & Sword, 2010)
Middlebrook, Martin	*The Peenemünde Raid* (Phoenix, 2000)
Mitchell, Alan	*New Zealanders in the Air War* (Harrap, 1945)
Musgrove, Gordon	*Pathfinder Force* (Janes, 1976)

Northrop, Joe   *Joe: The Autobiography of a Trenchard Brat* (Square One
                         Publications, 1993)
Patient, Joe   *Pilot: A Tale of High Adventure* (Pen & Sword, 1997)
Price, Gwynn   *Bob's Crew* (Privately published)
Probert, Henry   *Bomber Harris* (Greenhill, 2001)
Rolfe, Mel   *Looking into Hell* (Rigel Publications, 2004)
Ryle, Peggy   *Missing in Action* (WH Allen, 1979)
Saunders, Hilary   *Royal Air Force 1939-1945, vols II and III* (HMSO, 1954)
Saward, Dudley   *Bomber Harris* (Ashford,Buchan & Enright, 1984)
Saward, Dudley   *The Bomber's Eye* (Cassell, 1959)
Searby, John   *The Everlasting Arms* (William Kimber, 1988)
Sniders, Edward   *Flying In, Walking Out* (Leo Cooper, 1999)
Spooner, Tony   *Clean Sweep – the Life of Air Marshal Sir Ivor Broom*
                         (Crécy, 1994)
Tavender, Ian   *The Distinguished Flying Medal* (J.B. Hayward, 1990)
Terraine, John   *The Right of the Line* (Wordsworth, 1998)
Trotter, Elmer   *Against the Odds* (Author House, 2009)
Wadsworth, Michael   *They Led the Way* (Highgate Publications, 1992)
Watts, Jack   *Four Amazing Years* (Privately published)
Watts, Jack   *Nickels and Nightingales* (General Store, 1995)
Webb, Alan   *At First Sight* (Christopher Webb, 2002)
Wells, Oliver   *Pitch Black to Plane Fare* (Valiant Wings)
Wright, Harry   *Pathfinder Squadron* (William Kimber, 1983)

PERSONAL THANKS

This book would not have happened had it not been for Johnny Clifford and Jim Blackwood of the Pathfinder Museum at RAF Wyton. Both gentlemen have been unstinting in their help on this and previous projects, and I owe them an enormous debt of gratitude. We said we would do this, gents, and we were good to our word.

This book would also not have come about had it not been for the good fortune of meeting John Davies some years ago and collaborating with him and his excellent Grub Street team on four previous adventures. May we continue to work together on many future projects.

Several other gentlemen I would like to single out for thanks: Dave Wallace for his extensive knowledge of 109 Squadron in which his father served with distinction completing seventy-three ops before the war ended. As Dave so rightfully says: 'ops count, and gongs don't always tell the full story'. Mike King in Cumbria has also always been a keen supporter and furnished me with many useful stories and photographs from a seemingly endless supply of contacts, as has Gary Rushbrooke. I thank them both.

From my own world of publishing, Bill Chorley has been most supportive, feeding the occasional story or update to his superb series of books (see bibliography) where they relate to Pathfinders, and Kevin Bending, Steve Darlow, Neil Morgan and Graham Pitchfork have all helped with information, introductions and filling in gaps were needed.

Of the veterans' families, and hoping that I don't leave anyone out, I would like to thank: Margaret Blake for information regarding her husband, Gordon; Julius Brookman for news of his great uncle, Alain Harvey; Peter Chapman for access to his father's memoirs; Nick Cleary for information on Daniel Cleary and Wilf Sutton (on his excellent website terrorfliegerwarlog. co.uk); Julian Cribb for photographs of his father, Peter; Ciara Finlay for information about her grandfather, Michael Finlay; Clive Harte-Lovelace for information regarding his father, Anthony; Michael Manton and Chris Manton for details of Michael's brother, Squadron Leader John Manton; John Mitchell for his memories of his friend, Kenny Lawson; Peter Nicholson for an introduction to his father, 'Nick'; Sean O'Donovan for details of his father, Gerald; Toby Mansel-Pleydell for information regarding the last flight of his father, David (and a particularly fine lunch); Leslie Zwingli for permission to quote from her father's memoir and for her unswerving commitment to commemorating the work of the bomber boys.

Of fellow enthusiasts, I would like to acknowledge: Robin Riley (156squadron.com); John Cameron; Jocelyn Leclercq for his detailed knowledge of the final hours of Jack Kerry; Bob Knox and Chris Wesley for sharing their research into the loss of James Foulsham; Mark Peacock for permission to quote from Oliver Wells' booklet *Pitch Black to Plane Fare*; Neil Smith and Peter Gulliver who have helped with every enquiry I have made concerning 51 Squadron (51history.org); and David Young, in Canada, for his constant interest and support that stems from my Lotus days.

Digby Oldridge deserves special mention for swapping the lunch he owes me for a photo-shoot, and producing some superb colour photography for the book (preye.co.uk).

Of my work colleagues, I would especially mention Alex 'Sandy' Simmons and his ability to translate my requests from the National Archive into tangible results, and Iona McIntyre, who has now put up with me for nearly a decade which must surely deserve a mention in despatch at least.

And of course I could never do any of this without the genius that is my wife Elaine and two boys Matt and James who are now both teenagers. It is perhaps sobering to think of them as being only a few years younger than many of the Pathfinders who lost their lives in the Second World War.

INDEX